NEGRO PLAYWRIGHTS
IN THE AMERICAN THEATRE
1925-1959

Negro Playwrights IN

THE AMERICAN THEATRE

1925 - 1959 🌷 *Doris E. Abramson*

COLUMBIA UNIVERSITY PRESS

New York and London

Doris E. Abramson is Assistant Professor of Speech and Drama
at the University of Massachusetts and is Drama Editor
of *The Massachusetts Review*.

ISBN 0-231-03248-X *clothbound*
        0-231-08593-1 *paperback*

Library of Congress Catalog Card Number: 69-19457

Printed in the United States of America

10 9 8 7 6 5 4

For Edwina Lewis' children

PREFACE

In 1926 THE Krigwa Players of Harlem declared that plays about Negro life "must be written by Negro authors who understand from birth and continual association just what it means to be a Negro today."[1] Years later, protesting against the distorted interpretations of Negro life by white playwrights, Langston Hughes declared that someday someone would write honestly about Negroes, and he predicted: "It'll be me myself!"[2] Over the years many writers, white as well as black, have reached the conclusion that Negroes themselves will give us the true picture of Negro reality. "No white man," an English critic stated recently, "however brave and well-intentioned, can ever sing the Negro song."[3]

With these opinions in mind, I have examined plays of American Negro authorship which were produced in the New York professional theatre between 1925, the date of Garland Anderson's *Appearances* (the first play by a Negro to be produced on Broadway), and 1959, the date of Lorraine Hansberry's celebrated Broadway play *A Raisin in the Sun* (the climax of a realistic emphasis in plays about Negro life). With her play we reach the end of a period during which, by and large, Negro dramatic art reflected the Negroes' desire for cultural assimilation. Black playwrights of the sixties, perhaps best represented by LeRoi Jones, were to take a different stance both artistically and socially. However, the revolution that breaks around us today is clearly foreshadowed in many of these earlier plays.

The term "professional theatre" is extended here to include Harlem and off-Broadway as well as Broadway theatres. All extant plays by Negroes that have been produced on Broadway during this period, as well as the most significant Harlem and off-Broadway plays, are studied. An effort has been made to find a representative group of plays from four significant decades in American Negro history, beginning with the Negro Renaissance of the twenties and concluding with the burgeoning Negro Revolution of the fifties. Twenty plays, the work of seventeen playwrights, are considered. Although other plays might have been usefully examined, only those published, available in collections, or lent by the authors themselves were included.

American Negro playwrights had, even prior to 1925, recognized the importance of putting on stage various aspects of Negro existence. In their plays, plot, setting, character, and dialogue have continued to be tied to Negro experience. Therefore, these plays are studied with the intention of fairly assessing them as reflections of the Negro's peculiar position and persistent problems in our society.

Very little has been written about Negro playwrights specifically. The several studies that have been made of the Negro in dramatic literature and theatre emphasize characters and performances in plays about Negro life. One of these is outstanding, a Yale Ph.D. dissertation by Fannin S. Belcher, Jr., entitled "The Place of the Negro in the Evolution of the American Theatre, 1767 to 1940." Other studies are informative, but Belcher's is a real contribution to theatre scholarship. Too many of the others—Frederick Bond's *The Negro and the Drama* (1940) is a case in point—rely too heavily on secondary sources and hearsay in an effort to define and even bolster the Negro image in art and life.

Books that give considerable attention to plays by Negroes are *Negro Poetry and Drama* by Sterling Brown (1937) and *The Negro in the American Theatre* by Edith J. R. Isaacs (1947). Brown wrote his book when he was directing editor of Negro materials for the Federal Writers' Project. An outstanding scholar, he brought to his work a knowledge of literary criticism that enabled him to put Negro literature into perspective. Mrs. Isaacs' well-documented and beautifully illustrated book has never been surpassed in the field of popular theatre history. She herself, in the introduction, pays tribute to James Weldon Johnson's *Black Manhattan* (1930): "James Weldon Johnson told the tale of the Negro's theatre progress up to the time he wrote as well as it could ever be told."[4] *Black Manhattan* deserves special mention here because all studies of Negro theatre history owe a debt to its chapters on the subject. This statement continues to hold true in the case of two books published in 1967, *Black Magic* by Langston Hughes and Milton Meltzer and *Black Drama* by Loften Mitchell. The pictures of the former and the on-the-scene recollections of the latter make them valuable reference books.

Chapter epigraphs, taken from poems by Langston Hughes, epitomize the periods under consideration. Two early plays by American Negroes—*The Escape* by William Wells Brown (1858) and *Caleb, the Degenerate* by Joseph S. Cotter (1903)—are analyzed in the introductory chapter even though they were tracts rather than theatre pieces, for they do serve to show how soon and how directly Negro authors made use of their experience when writing plays. In succeeding chapters, the plays, having been placed in the perspective of a period and its theatre, are considered in terms of place of production—Harlem, off-Broadway, and Broadway.

At the beginning of each chapter, the Negro's position in the political-economic-social scene in the United States is briefly described. Then, because a playwright is influenced by art as well as by life—or to put it another way, because a playwright writes for an audience as well as out of an experience—the theatre in which the plays were produced is considered. Finally, individual plays are analyzed for their reflection of Negro problems. Each analysis begins with a biographical comment on the playwright and ends with a critical appraisal of the play as literature and as a theatre piece. Conclusions at the end of each chapter provide further opportunity to show (1) relationships between periods and between plays, (2) developing dramaturgy, and (3) continuing concern on the part of Negro playwrights for current and persistent problems.

The demands of Negro and white theatre audiences must be kept in mind because both audiences influence the way in which Negro playwrights present their reality in the theatre. Most Negro playwrights seeking a commercial success in New York, especially on Broadway, have faced the fact that they must appeal to a predominantly white audience. In order to make their plays acceptable to that audience, the playwrights discover that they frequently have to distort the very truths they want to tell about Negro existence. It would seem, on the other hand, that they could "tell it like it is" to a Harlem audience. But there they are in the unenviable position of trying to present insights about Negro reality that may be rejected by those Negroes who wish either to be assimilated into white middle-class culture or to deny that culture totally. Simply stated, the Negro playwright's dilemma is that neither white nor black audiences can be counted on to support plays that attack or even question commonly accepted American mores.

I wish to express special gratitude to Mrs. Hallie Flanagan Davis, Miss Helen Channing Pollock, Dr. Sidney Kaplan, and the late Juanita Hall, who were able to direct me to material and persons important to this book. An interview with the late Langston Hughes helped to establish the authenticity of playwrights listed by Burns Mantle and others as Negroes and furnished names of plays and authors neglected in earlier studies. The chief source of unpublished scripts by Negro playwrights is the Schomburg Collection of Negro Literature and History, a branch of the New York Public Library. Ernest Kaiser, a librarian at that Collection, has given me invaluable assistance over the past several years. Thanks must also go to the curator, Mrs. Jean Blackwell Hutson. Other collections used were the Theatre Collection of the New York Public Library, the James Weldon Johnson Collection at the Yale University Library, the Harvard Theatre Collection, and the National Archives in Washington, D.C.

I was fortunate to have interviews and/or correspondence with the following playwrights: William Branch, Miss Alice Childress, Langston Hughes, Hall Johnson, Loften Mitchell, Louis Peterson, and Theodore Ward. Letters from Frederick O'Neal, Dr. Robert L. Hilliard, and Paul Green were helpful in establishing dates and relationships.

I am indebted to Dr. Magdalene Kramer, who had faith in me when I lacked it in myself; to Dr. Paul Kozelka and Dr. Frederick D. Kershner, Jr., who read and criticized the manuscript in its infancy; to Gene Benton, who typed and retyped the manuscript; to Miss Marion W. Copeland, Dr. Seymour Rudin, and Mrs. Betty Savereid, who were perceptive advisers and proofreaders; and to William Bernhardt, senior editor at Columbia University Press. I should also like to thank Miss Lee Collins of the Teachers College Library and Ransom Waterman of the University of Massachusetts Library for research assistance, the Danforth Foundation for grants that supported two years of research, and the University of Massachusetts Research Council for a faculty grant that covered expenses connected with the final preparation of the manuscript.

Acknowledgment is gratefully made to the following persons, agencies, and publishing houses for permission to quote material from copyrighted works: Harper & Row, Publishers, for *Native Son* by Richard Wright (Harper, 1940); Paul R. Reynolds, Inc., for the play *Native Son* by Richard Wright and Paul Green; Beacon Press, for *Notes of a Native Son* by James Baldwin (reprinted by permission of the Beacon Press; copyright © 1955 by James Baldwin); Alfred A. Knopf, Inc., for the poem "Dream Deferred" by Langston Hughes (from *The Panther and the Lash* by Langston Hughes; © copyright 1967 by Langston Hughes; reprinted by permission of Alfred A. Knopf, Inc.); Alfred A. Knopf, Inc., and Harold Ober Associates Inc., for *Selected Poems of Langston Hughes, The Weary Blues*, and *Fields of Wonder*, all by Langston Hughes; Theatre Arts Books, for *The Negro in the American Theatre* by Edith J. R. Isaacs; Fania Van Vechten, for *Nigger Heaven* by Carl Van Vechten; William Morrow & Co., Inc., for *The Crisis of the Negro Intellectual* by Harold Cruse (copyright © 1967 by Harold Cruse); Theodore Ward, for his play *Our Lan'*; Loften Mitchell and the Pioneer Drama Service, for *A Land Beyond the River* by Loften Mitchell (copyright 1963 by Loften Mitchell; published by the Pioneer Drama Service, Cody, Wyoming, who hold all performance rights and to whom all inquiries should be addressed); Louis Peterson and Ashley Famous Agency, Inc., for *Take a Giant Step* by Louis Peterson; The Free Press, for *Black Bourgeoisie* by E. Franklin Frazier; Random House, Inc., for *A Raisin in the Sun* by Lorraine Hansberry (© copyright as an unpublished play 1958 by Lorraine Hansberry; © copyright 1959 by Lorraine Hansberry; reprinted by permission of Random House, Inc.).

Amherst, Massachusetts
July, 1968

Doris E. Abramson

CONTENTS

NEGRO PLAYWRIGHTS
IN THE AMERICAN THEATRE
1925-1959

PROLOGUE

It has taken the Negro revolution of the 1960s to make the general public conscious of the Negro's position in American society. Although the issues have existed for over a century—providing during that time the themes of many novels, poems, and plays —they have only recently begun to appear daily in headlines and editorials. Just as it is no longer intellectually respectable to consider the Negro inferior or childlike, it is no longer so easy to invest him with invisibility.

The Negro as a theme has for some time been appreciated by both white and Negro artists. For example, an exhibition of paintings at the Bowdoin College Museum of Art a few years ago produced a catalogue entitled *The Portrayal of the Negro in American Painting*, and among the painters exhibited were such well-known white artists as John Singleton Copley, Thomas Eakins, and Jack Levine, along with lesser known Negro painters such as Joshua Johnston, Horace Pippin, and Jacob Lawrence. Sidney Kaplan observed in his Notes:

> Where, in these states, is there a living painter of stature who whispers the shibboleth of color? The names of Benton and Hirsch, of Soyer, Shahn and Wyeth are household words in our day and their images of the Negro are familiar in the land.[1]

The Negro's image has been projected by many white novelists and poets, too, among them Herman Melville, Walt Whitman, Mark Twain, Vachel Lindsay, William Faulkner, and Eudora Welty; and by such Negro writers as William Wells Brown, Charles Chesnutt, Langston Hughes, Gwendolyn Brooks, Robert Hayden, Ralph Ellison, and James Baldwin.[2]

An area of Negro literature that has not, until the present study, been examined to any great extent is drama by (or even about) Negroes. The selection of only twenty plays by seventeen Negro playwrights may seem to make this study somewhat rarified, but the fact is that the public nature of theatre, the proving ground of drama, has resulted in our having fewer plays than novels or paintings or poems. The theatre provides a special confrontation, one of an audience that is, for socioeconomic reasons, predominantly white with a world created by a Negro playwright out of his own experience. Baldwin has said that "a play is a confession in a more naked way than a novel."[3] It may well be that the living presence of Negro actors makes the significant difference between the experience of watching a play about Negroes and that of reading about them from the printed page. It is certain that it is not a simple matter for a man to expose his ideas and feelings from a stage to an audience that frequently wants either to ignore or to exploit him.

Plays by Negroes have been written, produced, and judged variously. It is possible by now to paraphrase what Robert Bone has said about Negro novels in terms of Negro plays. He wrote of the novels:

> There was a period in the history of the Negro novel when a simple literacy was to be marveled at. Now, a century after Brown's Clotel, historical relativity is no longer a valid attitude.

With the appearance of such novels as Cane, Native Son, and Invisible Man, the reading public has a right to expect no less than the best from the serious Negro artist.[4]

In a similar way we marvel at the crude effectiveness of William Wells Brown's *Escape*. A century later, given Louis Peterson's *Take a Giant Step* and Lorraine Hansberry's *A Raisin in the Sun*, we realize that American theatre critics and theatre audiences have a right to expect the best from serious Negro playwrights. It is therefore obvious that not all the plays considered here can be evaluated in exactly the same manner.

Elizabeth Drew observed that we may either focus on a playwright's use of "his artistic mediums—words and the theatre," or "simply rejoice in the sense of the lightening or enlargement or illumination of life which has visited our minds."[5] Not until recently has it been fair to look too closely at the techniques of Negro playwrights who have been barred from the theatre for which they wanted to write. It is, however, fair to ask of all these plays by Negro writers whether or not they illuminate Negro life for us. And one way to get at least a partial answer is to set these plays against the background of Negro thought, to look for what we know to be the main lines of that thought as they appear in the plays.

In their introduction to *Negro Protest Thought in the Twentieth Century*, the editors point out that throughout American history the Negro majority has favored cultural assimilation (the melting pot), and yet many Negroes—in favor of integration but alienated by white society—have supported "the maintenance of separate but cooperating strands of white and Negro culture, each enriching American culture in its own way (cultural pluralism)."[6] In real life and in the literature that purports to reflect that life, most American Negroes belong in one of these two categories. There is no doubt that the swing toward cultural pluralism in the 1960s is a reaction by Negroes for not being let into white society in earlier decades.

Simply stated, there are four ways that American Negroes have customarily sought to advance themselves, to improve their lot: (1) through the ballot box, (2) through education, (3) through migration and emigration, and (4) through economic nationalism. All four are reflected to varying degrees in the plays analyzed here, although few of these plays deal in total theme or emphasis with the four points. The plays seem to be mainly concerned with the individual Negro's problem of being assimilated into or revolting against the dominant white society. That society becomes a love/hate object for the heroes of all these plays—for ex-slave, worker, member of the black bourgeoisie, adolescent, actor, teacher, and preacher.

It seems fair to say that most Negro playwrights of the period discussed do not want to give up on America—Theodore Ward comes closest to it in his *Big White Fog*—but they do feel constrained to criticize and to attack the land of their birth when white society does not recognize Negro rights or listen to Negro opinion. In the sixties, we are haunted by these words written by Richard Wright in 1957:

> If the expression of the American Negro should take a sharp turn toward strictly racial themes, then you will know by that token that we are suffering our old and ancient agonies at the hands of our white American neighbors. If, however, our expression broadens, assumes the common themes and burdens of literary expression which are the heritage of all men, then by that token you will know that a humane attitude prevails in America toward us.[7]

I 🌾 BEGINNINGS

Birthing is hard

THE NEGRO AS A TYPE (soon to become a stereotype) was on the American stage by the time of the American Revolution. He was a character in plays of English authorship, the most popular of which was *The Padlock* by Isaac Bickerstaffe and Charles Dibdin, which was produced in New York in 1769. Mungo, a West Indian slave in that comic opera, was a low comic complete with dialect, profanity, and drunkenness. The role was created by Lewis Hallam the younger, and the great Negro tragedian Ira Aldridge occasionally played Mungo and Othello on the same night.[1]

Aldridge, it should be added, played these roles in Europe early in the nineteenth century. In the United States at that time and for many years to come, white actors blackened their faces with cork to play Negro roles or to sing and dance topical songs in dialect to banjo accompaniment. When, in 1823, Edwin Forrest played a Negro in a farce by "Sol" Smith, *The Tailor in Distress*, he sang and danced, "winning the compliment from a veritable black in his audience that he was 'nigger all ober!' "[2]

In early plays, then, the stage Negro was merely a buffoon who danced, joked, made uncouth remarks. He was usually docile, self-effacing, often amusing. His lines were written for him by a white author; he was placed where that author thought he belonged, in the background; and he was portrayed by white actors in blackface.

Sambo, in John Murdock's *The Triumph of Love* (1795), performed comic antics and used a Negro dialect that became very popular on the American stage, surviving even into our own period. A sample of one of Sambo's monologues also demonstrates his use of the third person, a stock characteristic of stage Negro servants. Viewing himself in the mirror, Sambo says:

> *Sambo, what a gal call a pretty fellow. Dis wool of mine will curlee up so, can't get him straight—dat all de fashion among gemmen. Sambo tinks himself handsome. He berry 'complished, too: he sing well; he dance well; he play fiddle well; can tink so, so, pretty well. He tink—he berry often tink why he slave to white man; why black folks sold like cow or horse. He tink de great somebody above no order tings so.*[3]

Murdock's play is the earliest extant native American play with this kind of "darky" character in it. There must have been many of them, the beginning of a stage tradition.

A recent commentator has this to say about the language of the Negro stage type, whether minstrels or characters in plays:

> *In the beginning was the darkie, chirping "Yassuh" and "Nosuh" and "Ahse gwine down to de sprink house 'n' ead me some waddemelon."* . . . *There must have been a reason for him— comic relief, no doubt—and a basis in fact for his speech and actions. Perhaps the old slaves did dance and skip and, in trying to combine their various tribal tongues with the graciously developing mouth-full-of-grits English of the White Southerner, did say "gwine" and did pronounce some g's and k's. Not all did, of course; but then, not all Irishmen say "Wurra, wurra" and "Soints presarve us," although one would have a hard time proving it if he were to use American plays and novels as historical sources.*[4]

There is little doubt that early Negro stage types were inspired in part by the antics of the slaves on Southern plantations. There is an anonymous watercolor in the Abby Aldrich Rockefeller Folk Art Collection called "The Old Plantation" in which Negroes are shown dancing, singing, playing a banjo and a drum. One man— wearing a handsome jacket and knee breeches, but with a kerchief on his head and no shoes on his feet—wields a walking stick as he dances. The Negroes are performing before their rough cabins; dimly visible in the distance is the master's elegant house. It is a crude painting, a revealing one in that it is dated c. 1790 and shows the "happy plantation slaves" at their revels. They are, presumably, the forerunners of later minstrels.

Since the plantation performers were presenting what might be called a caricature of themselves primarily to please their masters, and since the "blackface" white performers in turn parodied the caricature, the next development—Negro minstrelsy, the Negroes' imitation of their "blackface" forerunners—was especially artful. Not until after the Civil War, a quarter of a century after the beginnings of minstrel shows, did Negroes appear in such troupes as Callender's Consolidated Spectacular Colored Minstrels, Johnson's Plantation Minstrel Company, and the Georgia Minstrels. Whatever their color, these Negro performers blackened their faces with cork and thickened their lips. They were performing a ritual, one that has been a long time dying. Edith J. R. Isaacs has called minstrel shows "our first authentic American theatre form."[5] Their extreme popularity lasted into the 1890s, and their influence has been felt in musicals and in serious drama for over a century.

White writers, and not only the ones who wrote lines for Mr. Tambo and Mr. Bones, continued to find a place for Negro characters in plays in the nineteenth century. Negroes were there for comic relief and/or for purposes of social commentary. Slavery was the subject of many plays by white playwrights. Theatre historians seem to agree that the best written of them was Dion Boucicault's *The Octoroon* (1859), and the most influential as a social document was George Aiken's adaptation of Harriet Beecher Stowe's *Uncle Tom's Cabin* (1852).

EARLIEST PLAYS BY NEGROES

Two early unproduced plays by Negro authors claim our attention not only as forerunners of later work but also as examples of crude art which obviously reflects the artists' concerns. Never again, after these early plays, were Negro authors' personal experiences to be so directly translated from life to art. William Wells Brown had been a slave, and he wrote about slavery. Joseph S. Cotter was a teacher, a disciple of Booker T. Washington, and he wrote about industrial training for Negroes.

Brown's *The Escape* (1858) and Cotter's *Caleb, the Degenerate* (1903) were really tracts, meant for the library or the platform. That is not to say that the theatre of their periods left these authors unaffected. Even primitive artists are somewhat bound by the limitations of their times. Brown and Cotter were affected by theatre to the extent that they were allowed to witness it. Even here, then, the theatre of his day was part of the reality a Negro playwright put into his art. William Wells Brown's play was in the tradition of the protest poems of James Whitfield and the polemics of Frederick Douglass. By the turn of the century Joseph Cotter's message was directed more against the attitude of his own people than against white society. These two strains were to continue even when plays were produced in New York; apparently there will always be plays urging protest against, and those favoring acceptance of, the status quo.

The Escape; or, A Leap for Freedom

William Wells Brown was born a slave; later, after his escape from bondage, he became a professional lecturer. He was also the author of novels, plays, travel accounts, and a history of the Negro's contribution to the Civil War. In all these literary forms he was a pioneer as a Negro writer. Between roughly 1830 and

1865, Negro leaders worked closely with Northern abolitionists. Brown, along with Frederick Douglass, lectured for New York and Massachusetts antislavery societies. The lectures were occasions for the reading of his dramas. These plays were probably never performed on stage, only on platforms.

A review in William Lloyd Garrison's abolitionist paper, *The Liberator*, praised an antislavery play by William Wells Brown that was probably *Experience; or, How to Give a Northern Man a Backbone* (1856):

> On Tuesday evening, Mr. Brown read his Drama, written by himself. The scene is played in a Boston parsonage, the pastor is a Northern man with Southern partialities. The author takes him South on a pleasure tour, and by a strange turn of events, the pastor is sold into slavery, and undergoes the frightful "breaking-in" process applied by planters to refractory slaves. He is kept there long enough to convince him that his views of slavery were taken from a wrong standpoint, and he is brought back by his friends with opinions thoroughly changed on the subject. The Drama closes by introducing to the pastor a fugitive slave seeking aid to escape to Canada. There are many vivid, graphic and thrilling passages in the course of the reading, and they are brought out by Mr. Brown with telling power.[6]

The Escape; or, A Leap for Freedom has been characterized as "a hodge-podge with some humor and satire and much melodrama."[7] It would be difficult to defend the play against the charges. Two things should be said in its favor, though: it is no more a melodramatic hodge-podge than most plays by white playwrights of the period; and, however crude the container, it carries an honest message of importance. In his preface the author stated that many incidents in the play came from his experience of eighteen years "at the South"; the characters were based on real persons then residing in Canada. There is something admirable in the concluding sentence of the preface: "The play, no doubt, abounds in defects, but as I was born in slavery, and never had a day's schooling in my life, I owe the public no apologies for errors."[8]

The Escape, a drama in five acts, is set in the Mississippi valley, a clearing in the forest, a Quaker home in a free state, and finally at the Canadian border. Clearly it is autobiographical. Just as clearly it is nineteenth-century melodrama. Boucicault, with all his education in the theatre of England and France, would have been pleased with the plot and could have written some of the dialogue.

The chief antagonists are a white couple, Dr. and Mrs. Gaines, who mouth Christian sentiments while threatening to whip their slaves. When a clergyman, Reverend John Pinchen, visits Mrs. Gaines, he recounts a dream he has had of Paradise and of old friends he visited there. The slave Hannah asks him, "Massa Pinchen, did you see my ole man Ben up dar in hebben?" The ensuing dialogue may be rather blatant in its humor; it is, nevertheless, telling:

MR. P.: *No, Hannah, I didn't go amongst the niggers.*
MRS. G.: *No, of course Brother Pinchen didn't go among the Blacks, what are you asking questions for? Never mind, my lady, I'll whip you well when I am done here. I'll skin you from head to foot. (Aside) Do go on with your heavenly discourse, Brother Pinchen; it does my very soul good, this is indeed a precious moment for me. I do love to hear of Christ and Him crucified.*

Hero and heroine of the piece are Glen and Melinda, two young slaves. Their dialogue is not the "darky" dialect used by the other slaves. Presumably they have had a chance for some education. We know that their creator, William Wells Brown, was chosen to be the playmate of his master's son and thereby gained some advantages early in life. Slaves who were chosen to work in the household rather than in the fields had a chance to acquire literacy and perhaps to learn a craft. Often their light skins moved slaves from field to parlor. Since Melinda is described by Dr.

Gaines as a "yellow wench," lightness no doubt helped her to gain refinement of speech as well as of sentiment.

Two of their speeches from Act I, scene 3, reveal the special quality of Glen and Melinda in contrast to the other slaves. There is, in keeping with the trend of Negro drama to reflect the problems of the time, a comment made upon marriage among slaves and the Negro woman's special position in a slavocracy.

GLEN: *How slowly the time passes away. I've been waiting here two hours, and Melinda has not yet come. What keeps her, I cannot tell. I waited long and late for her last night, and when she approached, I sprang to my feet, caught her in my arms, pressed her to my heart, and kissed away the tears from her moistened cheeks. She placed her trembling hand in mine, and said, "Glen, I am yours; I will never be the wife of another." I clasped her to my bosom, and called God to witness that I would ever regard her as my wife. Old Uncle Joseph joined us in Holy Wedlock by moonlight; that was the only marriage ceremony, I look upon the vow as ever binding on me, for I am sure that a just God will sanction our union in Heaven. Still, this man, who claims Melinda as his property, is unwilling for me to marry the woman of my choice, because he wants her for himself. But he shall not have her. What he will say when he finds that we are married, I cannot tell; but I am determined to protect my wife or die.*

. . .

MELINDA: *It is often said that the darkest hour of the night precedes the dawn. It is ever thus with the vicissitudes of human suffering. After the soul has reached the lowest depths of despair, and can no deeper plunge amid its rolling, foetid shades, then the reactionary forces of man's nature begin to operate, resolution takes the place of despondency, energy succeeds instead of apathy and an upward tendency is felt and exhibited. Men then hope against power, and smile in defiance of despair.*

By the end of the scene they have determined to escape to Canada. Flight can be the only answer to this intolerable situation.

Marriage among slaves, except by the kind of pledge exchanged by Glen and Melinda, was unknown. William Wells Brown's mother gave birth to seven children, no two of them having the same father. Frederick Douglass saw his own mother only a few times during his lifetime, for they were separated during his infancy; nor did he know who his father was. (Psychologists Kardiner and Ovesey have observed that, since a slave was no more to his master than a horse, something to be exploited for his "utility value," all cultural practices which might harm that value had to be suppressed. Slaves were allowed sexual activity, even entertainment after working hours, but *not* family organization. "Neither paternity nor permanent marriage could be recognized, for this would interfere with the free mobility of the slave for sale purposes.")[9]

Melinda's position in the household of Dr. Gaines is the special one that could be attained by sexual attractiveness. It is common knowledge that the white plantation owners took attractive Negro women as concubines. It is also true that the white master or his son often discriminated in favor of the Negro mistress' offspring, even to the point of freeing some of them. This sort of situation has provided many a novelist and playwright with a plot. In *The Escape*, Mrs. Gaines tries to sell Melinda because her husband is overly fond of the slave.

Another of the Gaines's slaves, Cato, speaks the so-called "darky" dialect already observed in Sambo's speech from Murdock's *The Triumph of Love*. Cato has been trusted by Dr. Gaines to "doctor" other slaves.

CATO: *I allers knowed I was a doctor, an' now de ole boss has put me at it. I muss change my coat. Ef any niggers comes in, I wants to look suspectable. Dis jacket don't suit a doctor; I'll change it.* (Exit Cato—immediately returning in a long coat.) *Ah! now I looks like a doctor. Now I can bleed, pull teef, or cut*

*off a leg. Oh! well, well, ef I ain't put de pills stuff an' the
intment stuff togedder, by golly, dat ole cuss will be mad when
he finds it out, won't he? . . . Ah! yonder comes Mr. Campbell's
Pete an' Ned; dems de ones massa said was coming. I'll see ef I
looks right (goes to the looking glass and views himself.) I em
some punkins, ain't I?*

His comic speeches are the stuff of minstrelsy and, like Topsy in
Uncle Tom's Cabin, he even has songs to sing. (One song, a
long list of wrongs done to Negro slaves on Southern plantations,
must have been very popular with abolitionist audiences.) Cato,
like so many other "happy slaves," has a longing to go to Canada.

The Escape is a message play from beginning to end. Sometimes the action stops for a soliloquy, sometimes for a song. The
following soliloquy by Glen is particularly moving—again with
echoes of Murdock's Sambo, here in sentiment rather than in
dialect—especially when one remembers that William Wells
Brown declaimed it from abolitionist platforms:

*Oh, God! thou who gavest me life, and implanted in my bosom
the love of liberty, and gave me a heart to love, Oh, pity the
poor outraged slave! . . . Oh, speak, and put a stop to this per-
secution! What is death compared to slavery? Oh, heavy curse,
to have thoughts, reason, taste, judgment, conscience and pas-
sions like another man, and not have equal liberty to use them!
Why was I born with a wish to be free, and still be a slave?
Why should I call another man master?*

A Quaker, who helps the escaping slaves, sings "The Underground
Wagon" to the tune of "Wait for the Wagon."

> *Oh, where is the invention
>   Of this growing age,
> Claiming the attention,
>   Of statesman, priest, or sage,
> In the many railways
>   Through the nation found,*

> *Equal to the Yankees'*
> *Railway underground?*

CHORUS: *No one hears the whistle,*
> *Or rolling of the cars,*
> *While Negroes ride to freedom*
> *Beyond the stripes and stars.*

Glen and Melinda, as well as the good Cato who knew how to please while despising his master, escape to Canada with the help of Northern abolitionists. When Mr. White, a citizen of Massachusetts, tells the men in a Mississippi bar that he thanks God that he is from a free state and thinks slavery the worst act a man can commit, he is accused of talking treason. The answers Mr. White receives from a barkeeper when he claims that the Constitution gives him the right to speak his sentiments is one sometimes heard even today—from Congressmen as well as barkeepers: "We don't care for Constitutions nor nothin' else. We made the Constitution, and we'll break it."

This crude yet effective play ends with a rousing fight in which Mr. White of Massachusetts fends off the Mississippi villains—with his umbrella! Glen, Melinda, and Cato, leaping into the boat just as it pulls away from the shore, are shouting loudly for freedom as the curtain falls or, more exactly, as the reading ends.

Opinions of the press in Philadelphia and in various New York towns are quoted at the end of the published version of the play. A critic from the Philadelphia *Morning Times* was of the opinion that "the Drama is instructive, as well as very laughable."[10] One can agree with him on both points and add that the play is a remarkable statement of the evils of slavery by a man who learned in bondage how to please and lived to be a free man who could instruct other free men.

Caleb, the Degenerate

Booker T. Washington mapped out a course for his people to follow when he gave a speech at the Cotton States' Exposition in

Atlanta, Georgia, in 1895. In this speech he urged his fellow Negroes to cultivate friendly relations with white men. He recommended that Negroes devote themselves to agriculture, mechanics, domestic service, and the professions. He placed more value on acquiring industrial skill than on attaining a seat in Congress. He assured members of the white race that they could rely on eight million Negroes, "whose habits you know, whose fidelity and love you have tested in days when to have proved treacherous meant the ruin of your firesides." His people, he reminded the whites, had tilled the fields and cleared the forests "without strikes and labor wars." The audience cheered when Booker T. Washington said, "In all things that are purely social we can be as separate as the fingers, yet one as the hand in all things essential to mutual progress."[11]

Joseph S. Cotter's play, *Caleb, the Degenerate*, with the amazing subtitle *A Study of the Types, Customs, and Needs of the American Negro*, is one Negro's way of expressing appreciation of Booker T. Washington's point of view. It is a slight, pretentious play, written in blank verse. The author—at the time of publication principal of the Colored Ward School in Louisville, Kentucky—could read, we are told in the Preface, before he was four years old but had little opportunity for schooling. At twenty-two he went to a night school for colored pupils. It is significant that the Preface was written by Thomas G. Watkins, financial editor of the *Courier-Journal*. The benevolent white man was pleased to praise the wholly self-taught Negro who advocated that Negroes mind the teachings of Booker T. Washington.

Joseph Cotter states the purpose of his play in the Author's Preface:

The aim is to give a dramatic picture of the Negro as he is today. The brain and soul of the Negro are rising rapidly. On the other hand, there is more depravity among a certain class of Negro than ever before. This is not due to anything innate. It is the result of unwise, depraved leadership and conditions growing

*out of it. . . . The Negro needs very little politics, much indus-
trial training, and a dogged settleness [sic] as far as going to
Africa is concerned. To this should be added clean, intelligent
fireside leadership.*[12]

There is no doubt that Cotter listened attentively to Booker T.
Washington's "Atlanta Compromise."

Caleb, the Degenerate, which is in four acts, is filled with un-
believable characters spouting incredible lines. There is no moment
when they touch reality, even to the extent of characters in *The
Escape* or in early melodramas by white authors writing about
Negro characters. There is no minstrel type here, no Cato or
Topsy. The characters, forced to speak in blank verse that tries
to soar no matter how the vocabulary would pull it down, are
merely vessels for ideas. Here Caleb, who is described in the cast
of characters as a pupil of a "depraved leader," is speaking to an
undertaker who wishes to know if he wants to buy a coffin for his
deceased father.

> *A thirty-dollar coffin! I say no!*
> *Five dollars for a robe? No, death-worm, no!*
> *Four carriages? No, undertaker, no!*
> *Think you a son must curb his appetite*
> *Because a pauper father breathes no more?*
> *The living must have money! I'm alive!*
> *Cold dignity is all the dead require.*

None of the characters in the play seem to exist as men but
rather to represent types. Caleb and his leader, Rahab, represent
wicked types, the degenerate Negroes. Goodness is personified by
Olivia and her father, the Bishop. Olivia, in the course of the
play, establishes an industrial school for the children of Negroes
her father has described as "a people, friendless, ignorant,/ living
from hand to mouth, from jail to grave." Olivia and the Bishop
rise to such an emotional pitch in their enthusiasm for industrial

training that they give it credit for "health, wealth, morals, literature, civilization." Somehow one senses that even Booker T.
Washington would not have made such extravagant claims.

Two minority views expressed by depraved characters are
that Negroes should vote and that they might consider going back
to Africa. The playwright did not consider either viewpoint worth
much attention. The Bishop refers to his people as "primitive
people" and seems to conclude that suffrage is beyond them at the
moment. He recognizes, however, that they are Americans—"And
this our land shall be our paradise"—not Africans.

The degenerate Caleb is found dead of his profligacy in the
woods on the grounds of Olivia's industrial school. His death is
represented as being horrible because he followed the wicked
Rahab who professed to lead, not to love, his race. Had Caleb
listened to Olivia and the Bishop, he might have reaped the ben-
efits of the school, which Olivia says was built with gifts from
millionaires. He might at least have been able to go to war with
Dude, who at the very end of the play announces:

> I go to war. Some say the Negro shirks
> The tasks of peace. Who says he will not fight?
> I go to war.

Joseph Cotter set out to write a moral tract that would show
the dangers of depravity and the values of industrial training over
mere book learning—"Go, cage life's life before you pause to
read." He put into the play good and bad characters, drew his
message, killed off the wicked, rewarded the virtuous, and even,
in conclusion, waved the American flag.

Though never performed, *Caleb, the Degenerate* was published
and probably read by a number of civic and religious leaders of
the period. The copy of the play at the Schomburg Collection
was once owned by the Unitarian minister Edward Everett Hale,
who became chaplain to the United States Senate in 1903. Joseph
Cotter's message on the flyleaf to the Reverend Mr. Hale was:

"If you can say a good word for 'Caleb,' please do so." Anyone who believed in the Atlanta Compromise probably had a good word to say for *what* the play said. It is difficult to believe that anyone had a kind word for *how* it was said.

Having noted the autobiographical elements in *The Escape* and *Caleb, the Degenerate*, we are still left with the portion of the plays that must be attributed to the authors' knowledge, or lack of knowledge, of either dramatic writing or theatre of the period.

When he was in England on a lecture tour, delivering over a thousand abolitionist lectures between 1849 and 1854, William Wells Brown may very well have seen plays by Dion Boucicault and other melodramatists. Boucicault's plays were being presented in many London theatres at the time, and nothing would have prevented a black man from attending the theatre in London. Many of the stage effects suggested in Brown's plays were similar to those employed in Boucicault's.

Though reviews of Brown's play readings praised his message and fervor rather than his skill as a playwright, it remains that *The Escape* is a well-made play by standards of the period. The play has variety of characterization, careful exposition, a well-designed if obvious plot, and spine-chilling scenes of seduction and revenge. The last-minute escape in the boat is not the only stage effect familiar to readers and viewers of contemporary English and American plays. A striking example of melodrama occurs in Act III, scene 5. Dr. Gaines, having imprisoned the lovely slave, Melinda, tries to force his attentions on her. She protests that the doctor would be committing a double crime: outraging a woman and forcing her to be false to her husband. The doctor is enraged at the idea of her being married. He goes off to find Glen "and roast him at the stake." On the heels of the doctor's departure, Mrs. Gaines arrives with a proposition that could be anticipated by any audience familiar with nineteenth-century melodrama.

MRS. G.: *I know that your master loves you, and I intend to put a stop to it. Here, drink the contents of this vial—drink it!*

MELINDA: *Oh, you will not take my life—you will not!*

MRS. G.: *Drink the poison this moment!*

MELINDA: *I cannot drink it!*

MRS. G.: *I tell you to drink this poison at once . . . or I will thrust this knife to your heart! The poison or the dagger this instant!*

William Wells Brown turned the drama of his own experience into the melodrama acceptable in the theatre of his day. That his plays were not produced may have been due to his being a Negro. On the other hand, as a militant reformer he may have chosen the platform over the stage. The combination of his overwhelming antislavery bias and what he learned of dramaturgy from playwrights of his time makes *The Escape; or, A Leap for Freedom* an interesting document from both the social and the theatrical point of view.

The theatre of Joseph Cotter's time was made up of minstrelsy, melodrama, and the beginnings of musical comedy. (Bob Cole's *A Trip to Coon Town*, in the 1898-99 season, is thought to have been the first Negro musical comedy with a story line and something more than skits.) It is unlikely, however, that Cotter visited the theatre. His play, for all that it denounces book learning, reflects only that and not experience in the live theatre of his day. He had probably read Shakespeare and the nineteenth-century English poets, hence the use of blank verse.

When we look for the wellsprings of *Caleb, the Degenerate*, it is not in the theatre but in the fiction of the day that we find them. Between 1890 and 1914, American fiction was extremely race conscious. White writers like Thomas Dixon, Thomas Nelson Page, and Robert Hilliard wrote novels of hate in which they pictured the Negro as half animal, half child, a threat to the United States. Many Negro writers and some white ones answered their propaganda by glorifying the Negro and exposing those who exploited him. Of these writers of counterpropaganda, Hugh Gloster observed:

> In their counterpropaganda Negro fictionists usually portrayed educated and well-mannered colored characters . . . who often engage in long discussions of racial and political issues and are almost invariably presented as teachers, clergymen, physicians, lawyers, politicians, or journalists. A favorite practice is the depiction of these individuals attending lectures, literary societies, political councils, and institutions of higher education.[13]

Gloster goes on to say that Negro writers were determined in their fiction to call their audiences' attention to the various repressions experienced by Negroes and to write of their time from a Negro's point of view. If Joseph Cotter's play seems to keep step with the counterpropaganda, it is well to be reminded that he was not with the majority of Negro writers when he took Washington's side in the Booker T. Washington-W. E. B. DuBois debate. According to Gloster, this controversy received a great deal of discussion, and the majority of the writers indicated, either through implication or direct statement, a preference for the militant DuBois rather than for the pragmatic and conciliatory school of race leadership espoused by Washington. Cotter's play did share one thing with most of the turn-of-the-century polemical fiction: melodrama.

As interesting as *The Escape* and *Caleb, the Degenerate* are, it is certain that their publication was not due to their being successful in anything but a very limited sense. Untried in the theatre, they were published during a period when it seemed important for liberals—abolitionists, philanthropists of a certain persuasion, and others—to encourage Negro talent and thereby foster Negro social advancement. However, these two early playwrights, one a more professional writer than the other, also exhibited several tendencies which characterize the work of later Negro playwrights as well: their knowledge of and concern for Negro problems determined the subject matter of their plays; their lack of

experience in and knowledge of the theatre of the period limited
the effectiveness of their dramaturgy; their predominantly white
audience forced them at times to portray the Negro as the whites
wanted to see him rather than as the playwright knew him. Even
as plays by Negroes moved onto the stage in the twentieth century, the playwrights were faced with these same limitations in
terms of lack of theatre experience and the dilemma of adapting
to a white audience. There was no Negro audience of any consequence until the 1920s, and it was a segregated one in most
Broadway theatres until the early forties.

II THE TWENTIES

Black renaissance

World war i had more to do with the cultural emancipation of the American Negro than did any other event between 1900 and 1920. When the influx of European immigrants was halted and thousands of nationals from the belligerent countries were recalled to their homelands, American industry was forced to turn to Negro laborers. The underpaid Southern Negro was tempted northward by industrialists who were enjoying a wartime boom. It is estimated that half a million Negroes migrated to the North during the World War I years. Most of them stayed on after the war, and many of them sent for their relatives. Although they were crowded into congested areas, caught up in labor conflicts and race riots, they did make economic and social gains. They still felt the sting of discrimination, but they had left Jim Crow behind.

Dude, at the end of *Caleb, the Degenerate,* went off to war proudly. It is true that in World War I, as in all the wars involving United States troops, Negro soldiers fought as willingly and bravely as their white counterparts. We should remember, however, the "Silent Protest Parade" organized by Harlem Negroes for July 28, 1917. On that date the famous Fifteenth Regiment, a Negro regiment, sailed for France. These Negroes had already suffered humiliation and seen fellow soldiers beaten and killed because Northern Negroes were trained in the South without prior knowledge of mores relating to color. Those who participated in the parade in New York marched silently down Fifth Avenue, to the sound of muffled drums. Negro boy scouts distributed circulars, one paragraph of which read:

> We march because we are thoroughly opposed to Jim-Crow Cars, Segregation, Discrimination, Disfranchisement, LYNCHING, and the host of evils that are forced on us. It is time that the Spirit of Christ should be manifested in the making and executing of laws.[1]

W. E. B. DuBois urged Negroes to get behind the war effort, because American democracy, unlike German imperialism, at least held promise for the Negro. It is greatly to DuBois' credit that he lost no time in bringing Negroes back to problems at home at the close of the war. In an editorial in the NAACP magazine, *The Crisis*, he addressed "Returning Soldiers":

> Under similar circumstances we would fight again. But by the God of Heaven, we are cowards and jackasses if now that the war is over, we do not marshal every ounce of our brain and brawn to fight a sterner, longer, more unbending battle against the forces of hell in our own land.[2]

Negro soldiers came home to a life they had vaguely hoped would be better, and for many of them it was far worse than segregated soldiering had been. Lynchings were on the increase in the South, and there were bloody race riots in the North. White workers in the North fought to get their jobs back in the postwar depression. In the South there were the old lines of suspicion and fear. The Ku Klux Klan, summing up "the whole body of the fears and hates of the time . . . brought them into focus with the tradition of the past . . . the ancient Southern pattern of high romantic histrionics, violence, and mass coercion of the scapegoat and the heretic."³

While DuBois and other intellectual leaders began to speak of a "New Negro movement," and such young Negro socialists as Chandler Owen and A. Philip Randolph preached labor solidarity, a Jamaican named Marcus Garvey, a full-blooded Negro, appealed to the masses of American Negroes by exalting their very blackness and turning their humiliation into pride. Charlatan and racist he may have been, but, in the confusion of those postwar years, his schemes stimulated the imagination and hope of countless Negroes. His Universal Negro Improvement Association, the first mass movement of American Negroes, collapsed when its leader was deported for using the mails to defraud in connection with the sale of stocks for the Black Star steamship line on which he had proposed taking his people home to Africa. That was the end of Marcus Garvey, who died in London in poverty in 1940, but it was not the end of this kind of black nationalist response on the part of the Negro masses. Garvey woke them to their unrest and their deep dissatisfaction with America.

Literary historian Benjamin Brawley has even credited Marcus Garvey with an "influence . . . beyond all estimate" on the school of Negro writers referred to as "The New Realists."⁴ He meant, presumably, that Negroes felt free, in the twenties, to begin to write about things as they saw them in Negro society, because they did not need to be ashamed of their Negroness. Whatever the reason for it, Negro writers did indeed begin to write about Negro life more openly than they had formerly.

Postwar prosperity, liberal white sympathy, black nationalism, black intellectuality, all conspired to create the Negro Renaissance. The New Negro, as Alain Locke named him, was to be a human being, not something to be "kept down" or "in his place," patronized or harassed, defended or condemned.

The day of "aunties," "uncles" and "mammies" is . . . gone.

*Uncle Tom and Sambo have passed on, and even the "Colonel"
and "George" play barnstorm roles from which they escape with
relief when the public spotlight is off. The popular melodrama
has about played itself out, and it is time to scrap the fictions,
garret the bogeys and settle down to a realistic facing of facts.*[5]

The watchword was "reality," a reaction against sentimentalism
and social mimicry as they had been forced on American Negroes
for generations. Through their lives and their art New Negroes
were determined to be noticed by the society in which they moved,
noticed for themselves, not for what the sociologist, philanthropist,
or race leader had called them.

THEATRE OF THE PERIOD

Montgomery Gregory, organizer and director of the Howard
Players between 1919 and 1924, wrote this challenge to the New
Negro in the theatre:

*Our ideal is a national Negro Theater where the Negro play-
wright, musician, actor, dancer, and artist in concert shall fashion
a drama that will merit the respect and admiration of America.
Such an institution must come from the Negro himself, as he
alone can truly express the soul of his people. The race must
surrender that childish self-consciousness that refuses to face the
facts of its own life in the arts. . . . The only avenue of genuine
achievement in American drama for the Negro lies in the development of the rich veins of folk-tradition of the past and in
the portrayal of the authentic life of the Negro masses of to-day.
The older leadership still clings to the false gods of servile reflection of the more or less unfamiliar life of an alien race. The
"New Negro" . . . places his faith in the potentialities of his
own people.*[6]

It was not a simple thing in the twenties, or for some time to
come, for Negro playwrights writing for the New York theatre to

fulfill an obligation to write honestly about their race. In Harlem in 1923 the ubiquitous W. E. B. DuBois founded the Krigwa Players, a little theatre group that made an effort to present Negro reality. "It was always a somber reality," according to Loften Mitchell, "unwelcome to playgoers during the false prosperity of the pre-depression days." The Lafayette Theatre in Harlem, with its policy of strict commercialism, offered Negro audiences vaudeville, which was "more representative of the life of the community than the more earnest 'slice-of-life' plays."[7] One is tempted to say that vaudeville humor was "more essential to" rather than "representative of" the community, but whatever the case, the theatre succeeded.

It was *Shuffle Along*, the Negro revue that opened at the 63d Street Theatre in 1921, which ushered in the Negro Renaissance that Carl Van Vechten extolled in his novel *Nigger Heaven* (1926), and that Langston Hughes celebrated in youthful memoirs and poems. *Shuffle Along* represented the kind of theatre that Negro performers, musicians, and writers had moved to from minstrelsy with great success. Originally written and produced by Negroes for a Negro audience, it was to become, along with jazz and the blues, what white audiences expected of Negroes. *Shuffle Along* and other Negro revues and musicals matched the mood of the flaming twenties, when the Negro was in vogue.

On Broadway in the twenties most successful plays about Negro life were by white playwrights. It was almost as if they had listened to Montgomery Gregory when he asked for plays in the folk tradition about the past as well as plays about the Negro's current reality. To cite just two examples, there was Paul Green, who won a Pulitzer Prize in 1924 for a Negro folk drama, *In Abraham's Bosom*, and, the year before, Eugene O'Neill, who attempted to write about serious problems of contemporary Negro life in *All God's Chillun Got Wings*.

Commenting on the success of white playwrights writing about Negroes, Langston Hughes once said to a group of Negro writers:

*Sometimes I think whites are more appreciative of our unique-
ness than we are ourselves. The white "black" artists dealing in
Negro material have certainly been financially more successful
than any of us real Negroes have ever been.*[8]

It should be added that these white playwrights, by their treatment of Negro themes and their attempts to destroy an earlier
minstrel stereotype, did help make it possible for the Negro to
come before the public in serious drama. They paved the way,
usually inadvertently, for the "real Negroes."

Though white playwrights wrote well on Negro themes, audiences and critics alike were pleased when two plays by Negro
playwrights did manage to reach Broadway—Garland Anderson's
Appearances in 1925 and Wallace Thurman's *Harlem* in 1929.
Appearances had the distinction of being the first play by a Negro
to be produced on a Broadway stage. Unfortunately, it was so
didactic, so filled with Anderson's personal belief in "New
Thought" and healing by faith, that it provided only glances at
the Negro problems of his or any other day. Not until *Harlem*
was there a play on Broadway, written by a Negro playwright
(with a white collaborator), that had about it the ring of truth.
Though it was laced with minstrelsy, melodrama, erotic dances,
and stereotypical characterizations, *Harlem* was an attempt to
show Negro life with a degree of realism hitherto not attempted,
let alone attained. Perhaps even more important to future Negro
playwrights, these two plays were well received by Broadway audiences and by the majority of the critics. Both plays enjoyed
respectable runs, and *Appearances* was revived during the 1929–30
season.

Appearances

Unlike Joseph Cotter, who, with an immediacy only occasionally
experienced in the theatre, reflected Booker T. Washington's
philosophy even as it was being formulated, Garland Anderson

did not directly reflect his own period in *Appearances*. He chose not to question the Negro's position in American society, but rather to use it to his advantage. He settled for a compromise that could even overlook racial prejudice:

> *I don't resent the prejudice that white men have against the Negro. Not anymore, that is. Before I studied these matters, the white man's antipathy to the Negro got under my skin. Now, I don't think that anybody should be forced to accept a race. They should judge the individual, not the race!*[9]

There is no doubt that *Appearances* is a highly autobiographical play. Its hero is a bellhop named Carl, who believes that he can do anything if he has faith. Garland Anderson was a bellhop who attended psychology lectures, studied the Bible, wrote this metaphysical play, and in 1935 became a minister in the Seattle Center of Constructive Thinking. A judge in the play says of Carl, "He reasons this way. That if he, with color, lack of education, lack of money and all against him, can work his dream out in real life, it will prove that other people with greater advantages can naturally do other things." Anderson expressed his personal faith in these terms:

> *Now here is a practical illustration of what I mean by believing. My reason told me that I could not write a play. I had only four years of school, knew nothing of dramatic technique. I didn't worry my head about it. I firmly believed I could do it. I did.*[10]

It is only fair to add here that Anderson backed up his faith with "good works" worthy of a Madison Avenue agent. He sent the script to Al Jolson ("he read it and financed my trip to New York"), invited Governor Al Smith of New York to attend a reading of the play, and sent invitations to an audience of prospective backers selected from the New York Social Register. "That name Al Smith on the invitations brought them in," he told an interviewer.[11]

The side of his nature that Anderson showed to the public, especially to newsmen, was humble and submissive. When asked how he happened to write the play, he replied:

> At the time it occurred to me to do so the thought of service was in my mind. Service to me is the rent I pay for the space I occupy on earth. I felt that unless I could be of some service to my fellow man, there was no excuse for my occupying space here.[12]

In the play when someone suggests to Carl that one day he may be famous, his humble answer echoes Garland Anderson's: "Famous; my dream hasn't anything in it about being famous, all I ask it to realise it for the help it may bring others."

Certainly we can recognize in his humility a variety of Negro reality. To label Carl a stereotype is not to deny his reality. Realism for Negroes must include the artful roles they play for their white bosses—Carl for the hotel manager, Garland Anderson for a predominantly white audience in the theatre. The temptation —for psychological, sociological, even literary reasons—has been to think that Uncle Tom is the whole reality. The mask of humility has become attached to faces white men have never seen and some Negroes have forgotten exist.

Carl and Rufus, a stereotype "darky" porter, are both caught up in a whirlwind of false evidence. They are accused of a crime for which they could be lynched (the accusation would be enough in some states): the attempted rape of a white woman. Elsie Benton has several witnesses to testify that Carl attacked her and then called Rufus to help him. Carl, who waives his rights to an attorney, tells his own story: the woman asked him for ten dollars, said she was just out of jail, that she would risk going back, and that she would claim he had assaulted her if he refused her the money. Truth, says Carl, is his only witness. As others say he was trying to assault the woman, he protests that she held onto his coat when he tried to move away.

Carl's dialogue is platitudinous and seemingly foolish in view of his position in society. Rufus' is what we have come to expect from this stage type, but there is a social comment buried in the Amos 'n Andy dialogue. When Rufus takes the stand, the Judge asks where he lives, and Rufus says he's living "at the jail right now." He gets everything wrong, forgets what he is saying, and goes into unnecessarily elaborate details in telling his side of the story. Then he tells about what happened to him in the South:

> I was workin' for a lady back home and she 'cused me of stealin' a ring, so they takes and locks me in the smoke house till the Constable can come. So I digs myself out and gets away an' into a swamp an' hides myself. In the middle of the night the baying of the dogs wakes me up and I knows they got the scent by the way they bays, and I starts travellin', but 'taint no use, so I climbs up a big old stump and soon the dogs is all around me, then the white folks come and they want to string me up, but the Constable wouldn't let them; and they drags me back to the house, when he gets the lady she finds her ring where she lost it, and tell the folks I didn't steal it at all.

The story has an element of pathos, though it is dissipated by the unexplained actions of a kind-hearted constable and a forgiving white lady. Audiences may very well have been moved by the story. They probably were in 1925 when DoDo Green, *the only Negro actor among those in leading roles,* created the part of Rufus. To take the edge off the seriousness of the speech, the playwright gave Rufus a "laugh line" in answer to the Judge's next question: "Did they arrest her?" Rufus answers that she gave him two dollars and his job back. "First time I ever had two dollars in my whole life."

The same kind of social comment, here even more buried in "gags," is also presented in the discussion of the ice cream Rufus was on his way to buy when the supposed crime took place. Rufus tells the Judge that he had to go across town to find a drugstore that would serve a colored man. When the District Attorney says that it is against the law to refuse to serve a colored person, Rufus answers, "I never said they refuse to serve you, sir . . . they will serve you, sir, but they put some flavor on that ice-cream that just spoils it for eatin', sir." What follows is the climax of the scene:

WILSON: *That's preposterous.*
RUFUS: *Is that so, sir? I never hears what they calls it before. It sure tastes worse than it sounds.*

The Judge dismisses Rufus. Now it is Carl's turn, and the District Attorney appeals to the members of the jury as husbands and fathers to protect their homes and the honor of their wives, daughters, and sweethearts from the black man. Carl speaks in his own defense, stating that truth is more powerful than prison bars and that he feels nothing but sympathy for this lady who so falsely accuses him.

It is not, however, the truth of his story that exonerates Carl. Instead, it turns out that Mrs. Benton is a woman who has deserted husband and children and been arrested for blackmail. Not only is her character blackened; it is also proved that she is not a white woman but a "Negress" who is light enough to pass for white. Author Anderson must have decided that this solution would satisfy that element of the audience which might worry about a white woman being portrayed as an immoral character in a play about a highly moral Negro.

The day in court is saved for Carl, if we are to believe him, by faith. If, however, we listen to questions prompted by natural doubt of circumstantial evidence, the weakness of the denouement is evident. Carl's acquittal is, after all, accidental. It makes one wonder about his miracle-working faith; though perhaps we are to think that God works in mysterious ways even to the point of turning accidents into minor miracles.

A reviewer for the *Wall Street Journal* made an interesting observation about *Appearances:*

Appearances was careful to tread on no dangerous ground in racial relations but it gave a suggestion of the terrifying thought which must be pretty constantly present in the minds of colored people who know that in their case accusation is almost equivalent to conviction with the unthinking crowd. No effort was made by the author to emphasize this point, but he evidently had it in mind.[13]

Like this reviewer, one can only assume that Garland Anderson had in mind the injustices suffered by his people and yet was "careful to tread on no dangerous ground" for fear of losing an audience in the theatre of his day.

Harlem

The period that Garland Anderson could ignore was of great importance to Wallace Thurman who, with the assistance of William Jourdan Rapp, wrote the play *Harlem* (1929). Wallace Thurman was a talented writer and editor, part of the socio-literary movement known as the Negro Renaissance; an educated man, a Negro who wanted both to succeed commercially and to write authentically of his period and his people. He may have chosen to do the impossible, but the twenties dealt in impossibilities.

His friend and literary adviser, Carl Van Vechten, wrote of Wallace Thurman's letters that they "are the letters of a most neurotic young man, already suffering from the disease which carried him off two or three years later, but they are remarkable letters indeed."[14] Thurman died of tuberculosis at the age of thirty-two in a charity hospital. Before that time, however, he had written novels and plays that, for all their commercial bias, were amazingly truthful pictures of Negroes and their environment.

Wallace Thurman was born in Salt Lake City, Utah. His skin defined him as a Negro, though he had an Indian grandmother who married a Jewish peddler. He finished high school, had two years as a medical student at the University of Utah, and after a nervous breakdown continued his studies for two more years at the University of Southern California. In 1925 Thurman made what he later described as a "hectic hegira to Harlem."

> *Three years in Harlem have seen me become a New Negro (for no reason at all and without my consent), a poet (having had 2 poems published by generous editors), an editor (with a penchant for financially unsound publications), an erotic (see articles on Negro life and literature in The Bookman, New Republic, Independent, World Tomorrow, etc.), an actor (I was denizen of Cat Fish Row in Porgy), a husband (having been married all of six months), a novelist (viz: The Blacker the Berry. Macauley's, Feb. 1, 1929: $2.50), a playwright (being co-author of Black Belt). Now—what more could one do?*[15]

Black Belt was eventually entitled *Harlem: A Melodrama of Negro Life in Harlem*. The collaborator was William Jourdan Rapp, whose autobiographical notes at the James Weldon Johnson Collection indicate that he was born in New York City, that he lived among Irish and German immigrants and later saw the relationship between their struggle and that of the Harlem Negroes. He was a graduate of Cornell University, a bacteriologist employed by the Department of Health. The story, the details, the dialogue of *Harlem* were all Wallace Thurman's. William Rapp shaped the play, and both men made penciled revisions.

Carl Van Vechten, in his notorious and very influential novel *Nigger Heaven*, defined Harlem by putting these words into his Negro hero's mouth:

> *Nigger Heaven! That's what Harlem is. We sit in our places in the gallery of this New York theatre and watch the white world sitting down below in the good seats in the orchestra. Occasionally they turn their faces up towards us, their hard, cruel faces, to laugh or sneer, but they never beckon. It never seems to occur to them that Nigger Heaven is crowded, that there isn't another seat, that something has to be done. It doesn't*

*seem to occur to them either . . . that we sit above them, that
we can swoop down from the Nigger Heaven and take their
seats. No they have no fear of that! Harlem! The Mecca of the
New Negro! My God!*[16]

On the other hand, a Negro writer, Rudolph Fisher, recorded this
impression of Harlem as seen for the first time by King Solomon
Gillis, a Negro from North Carolina:

*Gillis set down his tan-cardboard extension-case and wiped his
black, shining brow. Then slowly, spreadingly, he grinned at
what he saw: Negroes at every turn; up and down Lenox
Avenue, up and down One Hundred and Thirty-fifth Street; big,
lanky Negroes, short, squat Negroes; black ones, brown ones,
yellow ones; men standing idle on the curb, women, bundle-
laden, trudging reluctantly homeward, children rattle-trapping
about the sidewalks; here and there a white face drifting along,
but Negroes predominantly, overwhelmingly everywhere. There
was assuredly no doubt of his whereabouts. This was Negro
Harlem.*[17]

In a sense, these two quotations help to identify Wallace Thur-
man's attitude toward the place that gave a name to his play.
He moved in circles that thought of Harlem as Nigger Heaven.
Carl Van Vechten was his friend and mentor. It was clear to
Thurman that to be successful he should address himself to the
white audience that was titillated by the subject matter of Van
Vechten's novel. Another side of this Negro writer, however,
wanted to tell the story of a Southern family in Harlem as honestly as Rudolph Fisher told the story of King Solomon Gillis.
(One of the working titles for *Harlem* was "City of Refuge" and
may have been discarded because Fisher's story was widely read
by 1929.)

The first and only issue of *Fire!!*, a magazine "devoted to
younger Negro artists," was edited by Wallace Thurman. In it
was a two-page story entitled "Cordelia the Crude, a Harlem
Sketch," Thurman's first treatment of the story that was to be-

come *Harlem*. This description of the Cordelia of the story will serve as a good introduction to the play:

> *Cordelia, sixteen years old, matronly mature, was an undisci-plined, half literate product of rustic South Carolina, and had come to Harlem very much against her will with her parents and her six brothers and sisters. Against her will because she had not been at all anxious to leave the lackadaisical life of the little corn pone settlement where she had been born, to go trooping in the unknown vastness of New York. . . . Physically, if not mentally, Cordelia was a potential prostitute, meaning that although she had not yet realized the moral import of her wanton promiscuity nor become mercenary, she had, neverthe-less, become quite blasé and bountiful in the matter of bestow-ing sexual favors upon persuasive and likely young men.*[18]

The first act of *Harlem* is set in a five-room railroad flat in Harlem. There are a mother, father, at least two sons, two daugh-ters, and three boarders living in the five rooms. Times are bad. To pay the rent the family gives rent parties, a common phenome-non in Harlem during poor times. The idea probably came from the South, where Negroes used to give "chitterling switches" to raise money for an individual or a cause. The sponsors of rent parties usually provided food and drink, entertainment in the form of a "hot" piano, and dancing. Twenty-five cents per person was the customary admission fee. After a week of washing clothes and doing other chores downtown, Ma Williams has to come home to preparation for a party. She is a religious woman who does not like the dancing and drinking, but she recognizes the necessity to supplement the little income they have.

Pa Williams is a transplanted Southern Negro who sees many disadvantages in the North. Down home he knew his neighbors, but Harlem is inhospitable. He taunts his son Jasper:

> *You had to drag us up North here. You writes, "Come on up." Dey ain't no prejudice here, plenty jobs and the colored folks got plenty money, homes and cars. Come on to Harlem. . . . All*

> *de good jobs is held by dese West Indian fellows. Now I ain't*
> *got no prejudice 'gainst 'em. . . . We're all black together, but I*
> *ain't see why dey'll take up al de jobs and work for less money*
> *den we Americans. . . . You know what's wrong wid Harlem?*
> *Dey's too many niggers!*

The father's dialogue in *Harlem* is a reminder that prejudice is often the result of competition for social and economic security. The West Indian was the foreigner the American Negro looked down on because, like the European immigrants who competed with white workers, the West Indians competed with their Negro brothers for jobs.

Jasper still thinks that Harlem is the greatest place in the world for Negroes, a place where they can be men.

JASPER: *You can ride in the subway and go anywhere your money*
an' sense can carry you.
FATHER: *Yeah, an' you can slave in some dingy hell hole like dis.*
Dey ain't nothin' for a nigger nowhere. We's de doomed chil-
dren of Ham.

Scenes like this one led critic Burns Mantle to observe that the message "appears to be a plea that the Southern black should be urged to stay where his soul is comparatively safe rather than brought north, where he finds the jobs scarce, the gin terrible and immorality at least rampant."[19] Mantle felt the message was buried in "surface showiness," as indeed it must have been by the time the rent party started at the end of Act I.

There is no real action until the rent party, but from then on there is plenty of it—all melodramatic. Gangsters attend the party and provide the excitement of fighting for the teen-age daughter Cordelia's affections as well as the violence that erupts over a gangland dispute about "numbers."

Roy Crow, described as a "slick sheik" or ladies' man, has an easy time winning Cordelia away from the devoted, maligned West Indian boarder, Basil. Roy is in partnership with Kid

Vamp, a big-time gambler. They run a gambling house for "ofays" or white people. Their numbers racket, however, is for, or perhaps better described as against, their own people. Roy boasts that he and the Kid "are about the biggest niggers in Harlem. He's got more runners bringing him numbers every day than any banker up in this neck of the woods."

When one of Roy's runners comes to the rent party claiming that he has been robbed, Roy has a chance to show off his prowess in front of Cordelia by accusing the frightened runner of lying and then giving him another chance to make his collections. Cordelia chooses Roy for her partner, and the act ends in the wild dance sequence for which *Harlem* was particularly famous.

There is nothing gained by a close analysis of the plot of *Harlem*. A sketch of the action will be enough to indicate what, if any, specifically Negro problems are introduced in the last acts. Act II takes place in Roy Crow's apartment two hours after the scene at the Williamses'. Briefly told, Kid Vamp shoots Roy, who has become a rival in the gambling business. Cordelia is persuaded to leave, but Basil arrives on the scene to take her home and, innocent bystander that he is, is knocked out by Kid and left with Roy's corpse.

Act III returns to the party that is still going on at the Williamses' apartment. Ma Williams is ordering out the dancers, praying for her wayward daughter all the while. When the police arrive with Basil, Cordelia turns against him and would leave with Kid except that her brother and his friends try to stop them, thereby provoking Kid to draw a gun. At this point Rafferty's men—the white gangsters who are said always to lurk behind the Negro gangsters in Harlem—arrive; Kid is doomed and Basil saved.

Cordelia leaves the apartment alone, proclaiming that she intends to make "de whole world look up at me." The play ends with her mother's prayer: "Lawd! Lawd! Tell me! Tell me! Dis ain't de City of Refuge?" The final stage direction is "Loud jazz" as the curtain falls.

Most of the reviewers in the white press praised *Harlem* as a play representing Negroes honestly though melodramatically. In the Negro press critics were divided; some felt the sordid had been overemphasized, but others found the atmosphere and background genuine. The *New Yorker* critic was among the many who found the play desirable because it was not boring. What he had to say about the characters and the construction was not very flattering.

> The mother of the family . . . is one of those holy negresses who are such a trial on or off the stage, and she goes about moaning over the goings-on, and the ruin Harlem has wrought on her family. I doubt, however, whether Harlem is wholly responsible for her daughter Cordelia . . . one of those completely and exultantly bad girls. . . . The play is artless in such minor details as exits and entrances, the dialogue is occasionally very labored, and now and then the plot stands still.[20]

Negro critic Theophilus Lewis praised *Harlem* because "it emphasizes 'I will' character instead of the gypsy type of Negro . . . a wholesome swing toward dramatic normalcy."[21] He saw the characters as everyday people who were exaggerated for the purpose of melodrama, "a sound theatrical purpose." He found the play to be well constructed with only a few minor flaws. Mostly he seemed delighted that Harlem types were recognizable. Critics of *Harlem* were quick to credit Thurman with an honesty about Negro life that stemmed from his being a Negro. In more than one instance *Harlem* was contrasted with *Lulu Belle,* an earlier play (1926) about Harlem by two white playwrights, Charles MacArthur and Edward Sheldon. Edith Isaacs paraphrased several critics of the twenties when she wrote at a later date:

> There was no romance rose-lighting the realism of Harlem as there had been in Lulu Belle. It showed a simple Southern mother, terrified and helpless as she sees her family caught in the eddies of life in a Harlem railroad flat, with its by-products of rent parties, of the "sweetback," of the "hot-stuff man," of lotteries and vice. Thurman knew his streets and his houses,

the people he dealt with, their temptations, and the emotions
that directed their actions. Violent and undisciplined as the
play was, it left a sense of almost photographic reality.[22]

There is something disturbing about Garland Anderson and his
play *Appearances.* In a period noted for advances by white playwrights writing on Negro themes, this Negro playwright limits
himself to writing a sermon not unlike Brown's or Cotter's but
in the form of a courtroom melodrama. It should be remembered,
however, that in the twenties Negroes were barred from attend-
ance at most professional theatres, and that aspiring Negro playwrights had no real chance to serve an apprenticeship in any
American theatre. Also, Garland Anderson, unlike Wallace Thurman, was for the most part a self-educated man. Whatever value
we may place on the play, it is remarkable that *Appearances* ever
became a Broadway production.

Most critics and historians, black and white alike, choose to
ignore Garland Anderson, for he can be fitted comfortably into
no theatrical or social movement in the twenties. In one of the
few substantial discussions of *Appearances,* James Weldon Johnson wrote that the play was "a dramatization . . . of the doctrine
that simply by willing our subconscious force into action we can
accomplish the seemingly impossible. The load of such a message
is generally more than any play can carry; and *Appearances* was
pretty heavily weighted." He observed further that the message
of "cheerful uplift" was acceptable to Broadway audiences only
because it was presented "with such direct, almost childlike simplicity."[23]

It is not quite fair, however, to dismiss *Appearances* merely as a
statement of naïve faith and a catering to white superiority.
Garland Anderson knew how to please the public with speeches
that would have been at home in a minstrel show, but his ironical
comments were as close to the surface at times as those in Negro
spirituals and the blues. Negroes in the South have sung these
words for years:

Yo' head 't ain no apple fo' danglin' from a tree
Yo' body no carcass for barbecuin' on a spree.[24]

City-bred Rufus, when the District Attorney asks him why he ran if he was innocent, replies, "Because you're innocent ain't goin' ter do yer no good if your hangin' from a telegram pole."

Garland Anderson did sacrifice plot and characterization to preserve stereotyped responses to situations and persons. We must give him credit for getting his play onto a Broadway stage, even while we recognize that to do so he was willing to capitalize on the white audience's conditioned response to the childlike Negro. Apparently he felt that he could only hint at the faces behind the masks of his characters. Whether he could not or did not dare do more than hint is a question to be answered only by speculation. It is likely that he was as brave as he dared to be.

Wallace Thurman was the first Negro playwright who deliberately set out to write for Broadway about Negro life as only a Negro can know it. How well he succeeded depends really on how much is expected of him at this point in his career, writing in what was a new medium for him, with the assistance of a white friend, and for an audience that liked *Appearances* well enough in 1925 to have it revived during the same season in which *Harlem* opened.

Wallace Thurman was the man of his time that Garland Anderson was not. Reviewing Thurman's novel *The Blacker the Berry*, a Negro critic took him and other writers of the period to task for their pessimism:

> They leave a bad taste in the mind, if not in the mouth. The authors pass over the thousands of Negroes who are living bravely, if not happily, and select the sickliest characters they can find. Thus their books are peopled with cowards, toads, degenerates and plain fools, with hardly a manly or womanly fibre in them.[25]

All this dwelling on the worst features of Negro life, the critic observed, is not good either for the Negro's ego or for his literature.

Garland Anderson's characters live "bravely, if not happily," but Cordelia is among the "degenerates and plain fools." Thurman himself, in an article in *New Republic*, defended his honest portrayal of Negro life and at the same time showed that he understood the reluctance of Negroes to face the ugly side of their lives in art.

> *This is just the part of their life which experience has taught them should be kept in the background if they would exist comfortably in these United States. It makes no difference if this element of their life is of incontestable value to the sincere artist. It is also available and of incontestable value to the insincere artists and prejudiced white critics.*[26]

Wallace Thurman risked being damned by members of his own race for showing the sordid side of their lives.

What was new about *Harlem* was the author's attempt to let sensational melodrama grow out of the *real problems* of Harlem: overcrowded apartment living, prejudices among men of color, the numbers racket, transplanted and unemployed Southern Negroes. George Jean Nathan wrote of *Harlem* that "with all its holes, it gets under the skin of the characters and their lives and it has all the actuality of an untouched-up photograph, . . . a dozen and one vivid hints of niggerdom at its realest."[27] Brooks Atkinson, who also wrote that "with *Harlem* we begin to see modern, urban negro life through the eyes of a negro, and what must be its true colors—from black to brown to high 'yaller,' "[28] gave credit to Negro Wallace Thurman for the ring of authenticity.

There was one strongly dissenting voice among the critics of *Harlem*. R. Dana Skinner recorded his fear that the Negro was being exploited as an actor and as "a subject for sensational dramatic writing." He was concerned that the Negro's contribution to American society was being cruelly limited, that audiences were being deprived of the fruits of Negro genius, and that the Negro was being shown on stage merely as a vaudeville curiosity.

Of *Harlem,* which he felt should never have been produced, he wrote:

> None raised a voice to protest against the particular way in which this melodrama exploits the worse features of the Negro and depends for its effect solely on the explosions of lust and sensuality. The chief desire of the authors seems to be to show as the law permits—gambling, drunkness, sordid dancing, shooting and the amours of Cordelia. . . . Anyone given to prejudice or haphazard judgments would come away from this play with the impression that Harlem is a den of black filth where animal passions run riot and where the few Negroes with higher ideals are hopelessly snowed under by black flakes from a sodden sky.[29]

Wallace Thurman was one of the New Negroes who, suffering the indignities of being a Negro in America, wanted to record Negro life honestly, but who usually settled for capitalizing on its exotic-erotic elements in order to succeed. Ironically, he probably never experienced either the financial or the social success of which he dreamed. As a Negro he met discrimination everywhere. He wrote to William Rapp that he had tried five times to buy center seats for *Harlem.* Each time he was put at the side with other Negroes. Nor was he often welcome in Negro society. He complained to his friend:

> I am fighting hard to refrain from regarding myself as a martyr and an outcast. I wish you could take my place in Negro society for about a week. Even on the train I was beset by a Pullman porter for my dastardly propaganda against the race. And here at home a delegation of church members (at my grandmother's request) flocked in on me and prayed over me for almost an hour, beseeching the Almighty to turn my talents into the path of righteousness.[30]

In another letter he outlined his plans for a play about Norah Holt Ray, who was the original for Lasca in Carl Van Vechten's *Nigger Heaven:*

*She has figured in innumerable divorce and alienation of affec-
tion suits, all with prominent and wealthy Negro men, and she
has a whole slew of white suitors. While in New York she
resides at the Ritz or Plaza and makes all the first nights with
Carl Van Vechten!! . . . I have in mind a woman who seems
utterly ruthless once she gets going, but who is shown at the end
to be entirely the slave of the most worthless person with whom
she has ever come in contact. . . . The morons would eat it up
especially in movies, if given a deal of darky dancing, nigger
comedy, and coon shouting.*[31]

One may guess that Wallace Thurman was "entirely the slave"
of white values of the twenties, those that emphasized getting
rich quick and living for the moment. But neither *post facto*
psychosocial analysis of this complex young man nor a value
judgment of his attitude toward his people is intended here.
George Jean Nathan may have praised him for the wrong reasons.
On the other hand, R. Dana Skinner probably blamed him unjustly. Wallace Thurman exhausted himself trying to please the
public while at the same time trying to write with a New Negro
honesty. He was far from the last Negro playwright to be caught
on the horns of the dilemma which had, consistently since the
time of Brown and Cotter, limited the honesty with which the
dramatist could portray his race and its problems and still retain
an audience.

III ❦ THE THIRTIES

The job we never had

EVEN DURING the prosperous twenties Negro workers had been less secure than their white counterparts. During the Depression, however, the Negro's marginal economic position was catastrophically demonstrated:

> In 1931, sixty per cent of the Negro workers in Detroit were unemployed, as compared with thirty-two per cent of the white workers. Unemployment among both races was understandably higher in the industrialized North than in the more agricultural South, but in the North, in 1937, Negro unemployment stood at thirty-nine per cent and white unemployment at eighteen per cent. In 1935, more than half of the Negroes in Northern cities were on relief as compared with one-third in Southern cities.[1]

It was Langston Hughes who commented that Negroes in the thirties lost the jobs they never had. "It's hard to stumble when you got no place to fall" is the way the Blues put it. And Richard Wright expressed the problem in a dialogue between two Negro postal clerks in *Lawd Today*, his novel about the Depression in Chicago:

> "Slaughter was saying that the white clerks around here's done got up some kind of organization to run us and the Jews out."
> "Well, the white folks didn't want this job when times was good."
> "No white man wanted to work nights and breathe all this dust."
> "And now 'cause the Depression's on, they want to kick us out."
> "Look like the white folks don't want us to have nothing!"[2]

Ironically, while most Negroes felt the impact of the Depression more harshly than did most white people, some Negroes, the playwrights among them, made gains they might never have made otherwise. Negro playwrights found in the Federal Theatre a laboratory, a way to gain experience in the professional theatre that had previously been closed to them.

Now that some time has passed, we can begin to judge the Federal Theatre fairly. Unfortunately, it was judged in its own time by legislators who feared the Communist Party so much that they failed to recognize a valuable experiment that for a few years gave America a national theatre. This WPA project that put actors, directors, technicians, and writers to work and brought theatre to the culturally neglected hinterlands existed from August, 1935, to June, 1939, when it was abolished by an act of Congress.[3]

Hallie Flanagan, director of the Federal Theatre, and her staff realized that theatre is a broad term, that it can include everything from vaudeville to opera. Across the country the Federal Theatre sponsored dance programs, classical plays, musical revues, marionette shows, drama—presented both traditionally and experimentally, though experimental productions were favored as being more economical. While the technical innovation called the Living Newspaper, with its documentary influence, is especially memorable, it is important to note that a great variety of theatrical activity went on under the aegis of the Federal Theatre.

"No part of the Federal Theatre brought more ample returns to the project itself," Edith Isaacs wrote, "than did the Negro units and, conversely, no American theatre project (except perhaps the Lafayette Theatre during its long history) has meant more to Negro players and other theatre artists than the Federal Theatre did."[4] According to Hallie Flanagan, "The people at the first meeting in Rose McClendon's house when we were setting up the Negro theatre . . . felt strongly that they wanted help, at least to start, and had the good sense to ask for John Houseman and Orson Welles."[5] Unavoidably, though, the Federal Theatre did as much as Broadway to perpetuate the minstrel-melodrama syndrome, because, again, there was a need to create an audience and a need for the nation to be cheered.

In its attempt to serve a total theatre, the Federal Theatre ran into the old problems of entertainment versus instruction and of escape versus slice-of-life drama. These were not new problems for the Negro theatre. Sterling Brown once observed that to many Negroes the theatre means "escape from drudgery and insult by laughter."[6] He noted further that they did not wish to see serious plays about their own lives. It seems an inescapable fact of human nature: out of fear we want to run from what we ought to confront in order to dispel the fear.

Morgan Himelstein, in his recent study of left-wing theatre in the thirties, contends that the American stage, contrary to what we have been accustomed to reading, was not dominated by social drama.[7] The theatre of the thirties was at best only partially a theatre of revolt or even of social significance. Plays about Negro life, whether by white or Negro playwrights, continued to be attempts at honest representation but often ended, as had their predecessors, in commercial compromise. In 1937 Sterling Brown could remark:

Broadway, for all its growing liberal attitudes, is still entranced with the exotic primitive, the comic stooge and the tragic mulatto. The anecdote of the manager who, having read a serious social drama about Negro life, insisted upon the insertion of "hot spots," of a song and dance, is still too pertinent.[8]

Negro and white playwrights were in agreement: Negro life had not been honestly portrayed on the stage except in rare instances and never in a sustained fashion. The need to provide entertainment and to make money kept breaking in on social significance. George Sklar, who, with Paul Peters, wrote a "serious social drama about Negro life" called *Stevedore* (1934), was a white playwright who worried about the neglect of Negro themes on the American stage:

Sensationalism is profitable and sensationalism has been provided. . . . Never have we had a realistic picture of the Negro. Certainly not in Green Pastures, *where the characters are quaint, romantic, picture post card caricatures.*[9]

Frank Wilson, Negro actor and playwright, concurred with this opinion and added that "the greatest thing we have to combat is the effort of the producer to make us act and do things that fit into his idea of what the public wants or what is 'Box Office.' "[10] It is significant, for instance, that the New York Negro unit of the Federal Theatre in Harlem is remembered particularly for a sensational production in 1936 of a Haitian *Macbeth*, complete with voodoo chants and dances. Another favorite was a jazz-inspired *Swing Mikado* in 1938, which moved from the Federal Theatre onto the commercial stage.

Still, the Federal Theatre must be credited with trying to develop Negro playwrights who could write honestly about Negro life. In 1936 the managing directors of the Negro Theatre Project 806 in New York City decided to invite one hundred Negro writers to attend "a three or four month symposium and lectures that would improve their style and form of writing plays."[11] Fifty writers enrolled the first month and attended lectures on such subjects as script forms, research techniques, technical requirements, the need for a strong social message, copyright laws, and Negro theatre possibilities generally. John Houseman told them that the hope of Negro authors was a permanent theatre. Francis Bosworth, Director of the Play Bureau of the Federal Theatre, started them on a project that led to their writing a play collectively:

> [He] discussed the needs of the middleclass comedy as a medium for themes and he spoke of what he called "The Chekhov Technique of Collective Playwriting" which inspired and instructed the classes in an approach toward writing a play collectively.[12]

The class presented themes for this collective project, and the one chosen was "If the Townsend Plan." After a month of research and criticism, the class wrote a first act. How much this approach to playwriting helped the individual playwrights is difficult to judge. Large numbers dropped out during the second and third months, and by the end of the fourth month there were twenty-five active members. During this period members had written and submitted to all Federal Theatre production sources about eighteeen full-length plays and five short ones. Three were produced, two of them by the Federal Theatre and one by the commercial or Broadway theatre. (There is no record of which plays these were.)

The plays to be analyzed here for their reflection of Negro problems all rose out of such efforts and, with the exception of one, were all produced on Broadway. *Run, Little Chillun* (1933) by Hall Johnson, *Brother Mose* (1934) by Frank Wilson, and *Conjur Man Dies* (1936) by Rudolph Fisher were produced both by Federal Theatre units and by Broadway companies. Langston Hughes's *Mulatto* (1935) was a Broadway "hit," while his *Don't You Want to Be Free?* (1938) is the best example we have of an agitprop play produced in a little theatre in Harlem.

FEDERAL THEATRE PLAYS
Run, Little Chillun

The title of Hall Johnson's play is from a spiritual:

Run, little chillun, run!
Fo' de devil's done loose in de lan'.

The play is a Negro folk drama with incidental music composed and arranged by the author. It opened on Broadway on March 1, 1933, in the depths of the Depression, and ran for four months.

The reviews of this popular play fell into two categories: cautious appreciation of the play with outright delight in the singing, and unreserved praise for the whole enterprise. Hilda Lawson may have been right in her opinion that the script was less than a work of art, something that "can be regarded tolerantly only as the libretto for a Negro opera."[13] To judge any script without benefit of production is difficult. It is exceedingly difficult when the script so definitely calls for music.

The contest in the play is between two faiths, pagan and Baptist. It is acted out in primitive orgies by the New Day Pilgrims and in the revival services of the Hope Baptist Church. The clash between a kind of voodooism and a revival meeting gives the play both structure and dramatic climate.

Hall Johnson, the son of a minister of the African Methodist Episcopal church in Georgia, knew that there was a conflict between the primitive African side of the Negro and an acquired Christian mode of worship. More important, he knew that religion, whatever form the worship, was and always has been central in the lives of American Negroes. Through the years Negroes have used religious institutions to shout and sing out against injustice and to ask for release from the troubles of this world.

Basically, *Run, Little Chillun* is an attempt to show the sustaining power of Negro folk religion. What Hall Johnson put on the stage was a simple story about saving the soul of the minister's son, Jim Jones, who is threatening to leave the Baptists and go across the river to "de Pilgrims." Bolstering the story were songs, but the story itself has interest and real suspense. By the end of the first act of this two-act play, Jim is determined to go with Sulamai to visit the Pilgrims "jes' this once." He is a sinner, a man committing adultery with Sulamai, but he tells his wife Ella that he does not feel wicked. "I feel like a man that wants a man's life." The Hope Baptist Church wants him to feel guilty. Sulamai wants him to go across the river (an early title for the play was "Across the River"[14]). He agrees to visit the nature worshipers. It cannot do him any harm, he reasons, and he is both curious about and jealous of Brother Moses, the leader who has so impressed Sulamai.

The second scene of Act I is the meeting of the Pilgrims of the New Day, an outdoor scene in moonlight, with soft chants, drums, solo dances, and ejaculatory speeches in "unknown tongues." The stage directions are very explicit:

> The general impression should be of something approaching voodoo—not too directly African, but with a strong African flavor. . . . Any feature may be introduced which serves to make the whole scene more striking without any chance of controversy or any possibility of offense to any existing religious group. There should be . . . references (in the chants) to Sun, Moon, Water, etc. . . . The whole betokens and partly expresses a religious attitude of joy and freedom toward life, in sharp contrast to the well-known spiritual joy of suffering which characterizes the more orthodox religious services of Negroes.

The founder of this cult is Elder Tongola, an exalted Being who rarely speaks, a member of a perfect race that used to dwell on this earth before being replaced by lower races. He has returned from a higher plane with a message of joy rather than of suffering for black mankind. Through Brother Moses he proclaims:

> The very chains that once bound your feet so securely have also taught them how to dance the rhythm which sets the Universe

in motion; and out of the deep-throated cries of your most
bitter anguish you have created the song that makes articulate
the soul. The black man's god has never been a God of blood
and malice. He has never meant that His children should suffer
in His name.

This stirring evocation of the magic that turns past suffering into
present and abiding joy is followed by an orgiastic dance in honor
of the full moon. At its conclusion, which must in performance
have reached a very high pitch, Brother Moses confesses a carnal
interest in Sulamai. She chooses to leave with Jim, who has been
stirred though not converted by the Pilgrims.

The first scene of the second act is very much more earthbound
than the preceding scene. Sulamai announces to Jim that she is
pregnant, but she declines his invitation to run away with him,
preferring to stay and show the town "how good I is!" There
are subtle psychologies at work here. Sulamai is proud in her
shame. Jim is stung, after all his denials of guilt feelings, by her
lack of remorse. He goes back to his wife and his church saying,
"If I jes' mus' be disturbed an' upset I'll at least be among
familiar things." Brother Moses invites Sulamai to go away with
him. Her retort is a rather farfetched observation obviously made
for the sake of a laugh:

> Glory be! Ain't I gittin' good? All de boys want to stoop down
> from Heaven an' pick me up de same night. Want to take me
> away on de same train, too. Gospel Train is right!

The plot progresses when Brother Moses agrees to meet her at
the Baptist church at "twelve bells, big boy."

The final scene of the play must have been very exciting to
see and especially exciting to hear. A member of the original cast
recalls that, although the "Voodoo scene was spectacular and we
ended up in a mad frenzy," her favorite scene was the last one
in the "old fashioned regular church in Southern style. . . . You
really felt everything you were doing and I was moved to tears
until I became used to it."[15] Hall Johnson could scarcely miss

stirring an audience with spirituals, eloquent prayers, shouted sermons, confessing sinners—all the trappings of a Southern revival meeting.

Converts step forward, and the struggle to bring Jim back into the church begins. Elder Jones tells the parable of the ninety and nine sheep, plus the one that was lost and then found with great rejoicing. Jim will be welcomed back into the Baptist fold if he truly repents.

When Sulamai enters the church she is at first attacked by —"Oh-o-o-oh, you big-breasted daughters of Babylon"—then shown charity by Elder Jones. It is the latter act that wins Jim, and he rushes forward exclaiming, "Pray for me! Pray for me, so I can find peace."

The climax of the play occurs when the congregation is singing "Return, Oh, Holy Dove, Return Sweet Messenger of Rest." Sulamai walks to Jim, embraces him briefly, then runs toward the door. What happens next and finally is all suggested in these elliptical stage directions:

> But three-fourths of the aisle, and a terrific flash of lightning, together with a roar, she falls as one would fall in such an event. She is in a comparatively empty place, as all the congregation has pressed up around Jim in the pulpit. . . . With the last flash of lightning, Brother Moses' face may be seen at the window. With reminiscent strain of "New Day Pilgrims" music offstage. Who is revenged, Jehovah, or Elder Tongola?

It is intriguing that this question is in the stage directions. Whether or not it was conveyed to the audience by the play's action is not clear, though awareness is more likely to have occurred with Negro audiences at Federal Theatre productions than with the predominantly white Broadway audiences. What is clear is that an impression was made by the music, the pageantry, and maybe in part by the story of Run, Little Chillun.

Of all the commentaries on this play, the one that had something more than simply praise for the music and the authenticity of setting was Kenneth Burke's in the *Saturday Review of Literature*. Burke took *Run, Little Chillun* very seriously. It had been easy, he wrote, for Americans to open their hearts to *Green Pastures*, because it carried them "into a region of gentleness, this in contrast with the harsh demand of our day." Hall Johnson's play was not so well received as *Green Pastures* because it was written by a Negro and brought out "the power side of the Negro."

> One white playwright, Eugene O'Neill in Emperor Jones, did partially stress this power emphasis, as distinct from the child-symbol Negro of the minstrel show tradition. But only as a kind of powerful persistence in error. In "Run, Little Chillun," one sees a Negro genius, an attractive positive ability, exemplified with a conviction, a liquidness, a sense of esthetic blossoming, and a gift of spontaneous organization.[16]

Burke went so far as to suggest that *Run, Little Chillun* offered an insight into a way of life. Audiences were seeing on the stage the power that has made it possible for American Negroes to survive in a society that has continually kept them down. No reading of the script would have led Burke to this conclusion, but it is easy to imagine how the production, with the Hall Johnson choir singing Negro spirituals, did so.

In the midst of a Depression that was wearing everyone down, Kenneth Burke insisted that the buoyancy of the Negro spirituals was something more than an expression of childlike, exuberant faith. He noted an artistry that had pattern as well as power and a will to survive expressed with a faith that the period did not seem to warrant. In a sense, Burke reviewed the spirituals, not the play. The play, he seemed to feel, was an excuse for the music, and the music was dramatic.

The play and the music both, however, are about Negro folk religion and its sustaining power. This religion was "born in slavery, weaned in segregation and reared in discrimination . . . chosen to bear roles of both protest and relief."[17] Hall Johnson knew enough to set the important action of *Run, Little Chillun* in a church, and not just so that his choir could sing, but because the church is where the Negro community makes most of its decisions.

Hall Johnson is a better musician than he is a playwright, although he is to be congratulated for a use of language in this play that is both colloquial and, at times, poetic. He fashioned a play that served his music well. In his late seventies Johnson spoke of his play affectionately, adding, "It's about what's behind the spirituals, you know."[18] Johnson may well have been reiterating Kenneth Burke's estimate that Negro art exemplifies the dominating force in Negro life—the will to survive in an adverse environment.

Brother Mose

Another Negro playwright who was trained in the Federal Theatre was Frank Wilson, the author of *Brother Mose* (1934). Wilson was a well-known actor both on Broadway and in Harlem. A list of his accomplishments will serve to indicate how his two careers, as playwright and actor, overlapped. He was born in Manhattan in 1886 and sang in vaudeville quartets in his early years. In 1914 he started writing one-act plays for the Lincoln and Lafayette theatres in Harlem. The titles of some of these early plays—*Race Pride, Colored Americans, Confidence*—point to a concern with the problems of his race. After studying at the American Academy of Dramatic Arts in New York, he played Jim Harris in Eugene O'Neill's *All God's Chillun Got Wings* in 1924 and Lem in the even more famous *Emperor Jones* in the following year. In 1926 he opened in Paul Green's play *In Abraham's Bosom*; that same year his own play *Sugar Cane* won a prize and was published in *Opportunity* magazine; and in 1927 he created the title role in Dorothy and DuBose Heyward's *Porgy*. In fact, counting the times he played the role in London, he appeared as Porgy 850 times. In 1928 Mayor James J. Walker spoke at the opening of Frank Wilson's first full-length play, *Meek*

Mose. During the thirties Wilson appeared in *Sweet Chariot*, *Singin' the Blues*, *Bloodstream*, *We the People*, *They Shall Not Die*, *Roll Sweet Chariot*, and a stage revival as well as the film version of *Green Pastures*. In 1934 *Meek Mose* was revived under Federal Theatre auspices, and in 1936 his *Walk Together Chillun* was a Federal Theatre production. All through the forties he was on Broadway. His last appearance was as Frank in *Take a Giant Step* in 1953.

Although it was as *Meek Mose* that Frank Wilson's play was initially produced on Broadway, it was revived in 1934 as *Brother Mose*, described by the Federal Theatre as a three-act "social drama about the struggles of a Negro group against adverse living conditions in a small Southern community."[19] This description might lead one to believe that it was a play of social significance. It was not. Its hero, Brother Mose, a religious leader who tries to get Negroes to live in accordance with the tenets of his faith, is related to the hero of Garland Anderson's *Appearances* or even to Mrs. Stowe's Uncle Tom.

Interestingly enough, although the Federal Theatre called *Brother Mose* a social drama, the title page of the prompt copy used by the Federal Theatre Project has on it the subtitle *A Comedy of Negro Life with Music and Spirituals*. At the front of this typescript appears the statement: "A Negro play, showing the efficacy of prayer and optimism." This is the version produced by the Negro units of the Federal Theatre and, presumably, the one used for the 1934 Broadway production.

Even though the characters in *Brother Mose* are specifically described in terms of lighter and darker complexions and the texture of their hair, there seems to be no distorted use of this kind of characterization. In other words, there is no suggestion that either light or dark is superior. The playwright seems simply to want a representative group of Negroes, light and dark, young and old, plain and fancy. There are twenty characters, plus a crowd, and only one white character, a police officer. Whether or not the playwright addressed himself to any problems of the thirties in the script of his play, he solved the problem of unemployment for Negro actors by providing them with roles.

Conflicting viewpoints in *Brother Mose* are held by Mose Jenkin, who preaches that the meek are blessed, and Enos Greene, who will not bow to the inevitable, namely white authority. When the Negroes of Mexia, Texas, are asked to leave the land on which they live because there are plans for a factory to be built there, these two men become the leaders of factions supporting and opposing the white men's decision. A meeting is called to discuss whether or not they should move from their homes to the swamp tract known as "the Gut" which has been offered to them. Negroes are not alone among American minority groups who enjoy meetings, but they seem especially to delight in the fuss over protocol, disgressions, all the attendant socializing. On stage, of course, meetings are also interspersed with songs, as they may be in real life.

Brother Mose states his intention to move to the Gut because Mr. Harmon, the white man who owns the land they are on, has offered them this new location when he sells the old. Brother Mose's wife agrees that "Mr. Harmon's our best friend." They know him and trust him; they do not know "dese corporation white folks" with whom they would have to deal if they stayed.

The description of Brother Mose when he first enters reads: "His coat on his arm and his hat in hand. He is an old fashioned Negro . . . with gray hair and closely cropped beard, kindly eyes, pleasant smile, soft spoken, and deeply religious." Who could doubt that he is among the meek of the earth? His followers, believing in him and in the power of his religion, go with him to the Gut. Enos Greene's faction disbelieves in both and remains to confront the white men.

When Mose's faithful wife very hesitantly asks her husband who, outside the Bible, has inherited the earth by being meek, Mose answers, "De Jews. . . . Who's any mo meek and humble den de Jews; dey never fight, and dey got ebery thing?" His logic escapes Josephine, who says that "de Jews ain't no relation to us," and who wonders why Negroes do not have money, since they are meek and humble, too. "We got ebery thing but patience," her husband answers.

Songs and dances frequently interrupt the action of the play. In the first scene of the second act, some of Enos Greene's followers gather around for a good time. One has a guitar; another, a jew's harp. A song follows. The stage directions then indicate a dance called a Boston, more choruses of the song, a rendition of "Shortenin' Bread," more singing and clowning. Certainly this is a minstrel turn in the midst of what has been described as social drama.

In contrast, the following scene takes place in the Gut, where Brother Mose's followers are beginning to mutter against him after a month in the swamp land. An intelligent young man named Nathan, who is among other things the love interest for Mose's daughter, Penolia, questions Brother Mose's decision to trust a white man:

NATHAN: *Mr. Mose, doan you depen on dis white man. Dese folks are evil, I tell you.*

MOSE: *I knows dat, but dese white folks ginus a certain 'mount of money and built dese shacks. We took it, now what else is dere for us ter do?*

NATHAN: *Mr. Jenkin, yo sho is a quiet livin man.*

MOSE: *I live according ter de Bible.* (solemnly) *I follows God's Commandments. I wuz raised ter do dat fum a baby, an I never inten to do anything else. His word says, "Love your enemies. Do good ter dem dat hat' yo. Bless dem dat curse yo," and "Pray fo dem dat dispitefully use you." An "Unto him dat smittith you on one cheek, turn de odder."*

Act III brings justification of Brother Mose's faith: oil is discovered on the Gut. His followers' mutterings turn to hymns of praise. Mr. Harmon advances one thousand dollars, and everyone rejoices at the prospect of newly acquired riches. One woman says of white folks after Mr. Harmon's kindness, "Yes, Lord, we

cain't do wid em or widout em." To add to this joyous, melodramatic moment, Enos Greene is arrested for selling dope. He is
as wicked as we suspected him to be from the moment he
opposed Brother Mose.

The last few speeches of the play allow us to hear the new
generation speaking through Nathan, but the overriding voice is
that of Brother Mose, who has proved "the efficacy of prayer and
optimism":

MOSE: *Children, you know the first thing I'm gwine to do is clean
up this Gut and make it a decent place for people to live, and
the next thing ahm goin ter build one of the finest churches in
Texas, right here.*

NATHAN: *Mr. Mose, course I ain't tryin to tell you how to spend
yo money, but don't yo think it would be a good idea to build
some business places here so me and my children would have
some place to work?*

MOSE: *Wait a minute, children, the good book says, "Blessed are
the meek, for they shall inherit the," what?*

ALL: *(in unison) The Earth!*

(offstage—song—"Good News")

Though the critics were kind in 1928 and in 1934, Brooks
Atkinson recorded reactions to *Meek Mose* that, unfortunately,
seem to hold true for the later *Brother Mose* too:

*With all the good-will in the world toward a Negro theatre as a
necessity both of the drama and of contemporary life, it is difficult to record Meek Mose as anything better than a childishly
naive endeavor, full of sepia tint John Golden and depicting
life only in slightly shop worn terms of the theatre. . . . The
Negro, in writing about himself, sees himself not as he is, or
even approximately, as he is, but in the vivid reds, blues, and
greens of the comic strip, becomes, in brief, a caricature and
such a caricature as even few whites make him out to be.[20]*

Frank Wilson was certainly perpetuating stereotypes. His experience in the theatre may have taught him the necessity of

doing so, but as Fannin Belcher observed, "Had the playwright been more interested in interpreting Negro life than in making a show, there might have been less of the minstrel aroma in dialogue and characters."[21]

Another play by Frank Wilson, *Walk Together Chillun*, was the first production of the Negro unit of the Federal Theatre in New York City. It opened at the Lafayette Theatre, February 2, 1936. There is no script extant, and the Federal Theatre listing describes it simply as a three-act social drama with "structural weakness. Southern vs. Northern Negro."[22] It seems to have been about Southern Negroes brought North to compete with Negroes already there. Because of their willingness to work for lower wages, the Southerners are at first boycotted by their own people. Sectional differences are forgotten after a time because the Negroes have to band together in the face of white hostility. Without a script in hand, it is impossible to know whether or not this play had any more social significance than *Brother Mose*. Judging by Brooks Atkinson's review of *Walk Together Chillun*, it may have been more substantial than the earlier play.

> He [Frank Wilson] is no street minstrel, strumming his lyre for Harlem tap-dancers. He is a crusader, and the laughs and roars his lines draw from the audience show that he knows where the sore points lie. Following the familiar pattern for Negro plays, he includes one scene in a church where the mass revelry is solid with animal magnetism.[23]

The critic went on to observe that such a scene is a good way to provide employment for large numbers of actors, not the least of the accomplishments of either the Federal Theatre or Frank Wilson's plays. Since Wilson's audiences at the Lafayette Theatre were mainly Negro, one assumes he was saying something to them simply by writing plays for and about them.

Conjur Man Dies

The author of *Conjur Man Dies*, a play presented by the Negro unit of the Federal Theatre in Harlem during the 1935–36 season, was Rudolph Fisher. He was a friend of both Wallace Thurman and Langston Hughes. The latter once described him as "the wittiest of these New Negroes of Harlem, whose tongue was flavored with the sharpest and saltiest humor."[24] His short stories and novels exhibited animated wit and humor abundantly, but his play failed to be anything more than an evening's light entertainment, with some suspense of the "whodunit" variety.

Rudolph Fisher was born in Washington, D.C., in 1897, the son of a minister. Brought up in Providence, Rhode Island, where he graduated from high school with honors, he entered Brown University in 1915 and majored in biology and English, the double major leading to his double career as doctor and writer. He was elected to Phi Beta Kappa and Sigma Xi. When he received his A.B. degree in 1919, he was Class Day Orator. He earned an M.A. at Brown in 1920 and a medical degree with highest honors at Howard University in 1924. For a while he did research at Columbia University, and in 1927 he began his practice in Harlem.[25]

Rudolph Fisher was still in medical school when he wrote the short story, "The City of Refuge," a title Wallace Thurman once borrowed for the play that became *Harlem*. His stories were published in many of the leading magazines—*Atlantic Monthly*, *American Mercury*, *McClure's*, *Crisis*, *Redbook*—and one, "Miss Cynthie," was included in *The Best Short Stories of 1934*.

At the time of the publication of *The Conjure-Man Dies: A Mystery Tale of Dark Harlem* (1932), Rudolph Fisher was the only Negro to have published a detective story. When asked if Harlem and Negro life there provided a rich field for detective stories, he answered, "Oh, yes. Darkness and mystery go together, don't they? The children of the night . . . are children of mystery."[26] A critic for *Time* magazine put it another way: "Negroes are suitable for mystery stories because they are hard to see in the dark and because white folk, not knowing much about them, believe them primitively prone to violence."[27]

The novel *The Conjure-Man Dies* became the play *Conjur Man*

Dies,[28] but by the time it was on stage at the Lafayette Theatre (it opened March 11, 1936), Rudolph Fisher had been dead for over a year. He died December 26, 1934, just a week after the death of Wallace Thurman; both men were in their thirties. One cannot help thinking that *Conjur Man Dies* needed cutting and rewriting during the rehearsal period, and that no one but the author could have done these things to make it a better play.

Although *Conjur Man Dies* was very popular with Federal Theatre audiences and was toured by traveling WPA outdoor players as part of New York's recreation program,[29] the script is far from satisfactory. The structure of the play is clumsy, a three-act play in fifteen scenes (five, four, and six), with none of the rich language and subtle characterization for which Dr. Fisher's short stories are famous.

One reviewer of *The Conjure-Man Dies* set the scene and introduced the characters in this fashion:

> *Frimbo, the conjure-man, was a queer one. He lived next to an undertaker and died, apparently, from having a handkerchief stuffed down his throat. It would have been impossible for a normal person to find out who killed him, but not for Dr. Archer, a colored physician almost as erudite as Frimbo himself.*[30]

The erudite Dr. Archer, at the opening of the play (as well as the novel, for they share a parallel development), is called in to examine what turns out to be Frimbo's corpse. He receives the call from Bubber and Jinx, two low comics who speak a kind of Amos 'n Andy patois.

ARCHER: *You gentlemen will pardon my undue curiosity, I hope, but which of you, if either, stands responsible for the—er—expenses of medical attention in this case?*
BUBBER: eMan—who goin pay you?
ARCHER: (smiling) *That makes it rather a bald question.*
BUBBER: *Bald? Well hyer's one with hair on it, doc. Who's gettin' the medical attention?*

The doctor speaks a little too properly. The comics never speak except to get a laugh.

With the help of a detective named Dart, Dr. Archer discovers that Frimbo's full name was N'Gana Frimbo; that this "conjure-man, caster of spells, prophet-wonder" had an M.A. in philosophy from Harvard; and that he was originally from West Africa. The suspects are all those who were in the conjur man's waiting room at the time of his death: Jinx; Easeley Jones, a "darky" railroad porter; Aramintha Snead, a gossip; and Martha Crouch, the undertaker's wife from next door. What they have in common is superstition. These are urban Negroes, the same ones who play the "numbers" in Thurman and Rapp's *Harlem*, not the rural types who are attracted to voodoo worship in Hall Johnson's *Run, Little Chillun*.

The investigations of Dr. Archer and Mr. Dart lead to the reappearance of Frimbo and the discovery that it was really his assistant who had been killed. Frimbo has been trying to destroy the body as part of a West African tribal custom. The disclosure forces the murderer to attempt to kill Frimbo again. This time he succeeds. Our heroes are on hand to arrest the murderer, who turns out to be the undertaker disguised as Easeley Jones. He has committed both murders because he was jealous of Frimbo's attentions to his wife Martha.

N'Gana Frimbo, for all his bizarre qualities, is the most interesting and believable character in the play. He is on the stage, unfortunately, only a short time. His explanation, when he returns from "death," as to why he did not really die is intriguing. He describes the original "murder":

> He struck from behind, in the dark. At the moment my mind was elsewhere—contemplating the future of that man, Jenkins. Physically I was murdered. Mentally I could not be, because mentally I was elsewhere.

This man, with his Harvard degree, who had been a king in Africa, who dealt in dark chambers and disguises, is not a new phenomenon in our society. His existence suggests the only Negro problem in the play—and one that is not a strictly Negro concern —a tendency to superstition.

Rudolph Fisher's *Conjur Man Dies* only touched on the whole problem of superstition and its role in the lives of Negroes. Brooks Atkinson, who entitled his review of the play "Harlem Mumbo Jumbo," had this to say about the production and the audience's reaction to it:

> To a paleface, fresh from Broadway, the play seems like a ver-bose and amateur charade, none too clearly written and soggily acted. But the Lafayette was bulging with family parties last evening who roared at the obese comedian, and howled over the West Indian accent of a smart Harlem landlady. With con-siderable and judicious cutting and after a few ruthless rehearsals, Conjur Man Dies will doubtless improve and become a routine mystery show.[31]

It apparently became just that, "a routine mystery show," and Harlem audiences could safely laugh, however unconsciously, at their own foibles.

Turpentine, The Trial of Dr. Beck, Liberty Deferred

There are no scripts available, at the moment, for two Federal Theatre plays by Negro authors: *Turpentine* by J. Augustus Smith and Peter Morell, which opened on Broadway on June 27, 1936; and *The Trial of Dr. Beck* by Hughes Allison, which first played in Newark, New Jersey, and moved to Broadway, where it opened on August 9, 1937.[32] Each exemplified a type of Negro drama with which American theatre audiences were becoming familiar. *Turpentine* was a social drama that in pro-duction became a folk play with choral arrangements, this time by Leonard de Paur. *The Trial of Dr. Beck* was a murder-mystery drama with sociological complications. Whether these plays in script form were dramaturgically an improvement over *Brother Mose* or *Appearances* we cannot know because all we have as a basis for comparison with the earlier plays are reviews of and comments on the productions.

The authors of *Turpentine* set out to protest conditions in the naval stores industry of Florida. According to Hallie Flanagan: "While the writing lacked fluency, the production possessed breathtaking fervor." It is impossible to know how much of that fervor was generated by the problems dramatized and how much by songs and stage effects. Some Congressmen took exception to what they called radical ideas in *Turpentine*, but then it is not surprising that they disapproved of a play that attempted to expose "the tyranny and injustice of the southern labor-camp system."[33]

The Trial of Dr. Beck was New Jersey's first big Federal Theatre success, the kind of success that led to Broadway. As Mrs. Flanagan recorded it: "J. J. Shubert wrote me that *The Trial of Dr. Beck* was the best play he had seen anywhere in Federal Theatre; and it was partly at his suggestion that we moved it to New York where it ran for four weeks."[34] In the play, Dr. Beck, mulatto, is on trial for the murder of his wealthy, dark-skinned wife. He is a natural suspect because he has developed a theory that Negro men should marry light-skinned women in order, eventually, to eliminate the Negro race. One portion of a review of *The Trial of Dr. Beck* will indicate to what extent this play belongs among those by and about Negroes.

> The doctor, a sort of *Sepia Carrel*, with definite race and eugenic theories, is quite a hero in a humanitarian way and author Allison manages to introduce through his character quite a bit of propaganda for his people. . . . The court, incidentally, is a white court, but that does not tempt Mr. Allison to indulge himself in howls of race prejudice. His trial might just as well have been of all white characters although his particularizing on the habits and mores of a race in process of change and adjustment add spice to the stock courtroom melodrama characters.[35]

Instead of this far fetched, seemingly innocuous play in support of the gradual elimination of the Negro race, why was there no Living Newspaper about Negro life in America? After all, the largest minority group in the United States in the thirties consisted of fifteen million Negroes, and this minority suffered oppressions of a dramatic nature: lynching, Jim Crow laws, segregation. The fact is that a Living Newspaper about Negro life in America was written by two Negro playwrights, John Silvera and Abram Hill. It was entitled *Liberty Deferred* and was publicized but never produced. Another—"one that would expose the common practice of lynching Negroes and also the plight of the sharecroppers"[36]—was outlined by white playwright Elmer Rice but rejected by the Federal Theatre.

In a brief prepared by the Negro Arts Committee of the Federal Arts Council, a number of citizens—including ministers, labor leaders, both Negro and white artists, librarians, theatre committees—criticized the Federal Theatre for not producing *Liberty Deferred*, in fact for not doing more for Negro playwrights in general. Too few plays about Negroes, according to this committee, were outside the Broadway pattern: "The novelty of 'swinging' the classics does not cover the field. New Negro plays will be needed, and the Negro playwright is the logical one to write them."[37] Plays by Negroes had been acclaimed worthwhile for production, they went on, but then were lost in red tape.

Part of a review by Dan Burley, drama critic for the *Amsterdam News*, was quoted in the brief:

> The Negro according to Liberty Deferred is, has, and may be expected to be a victim of oppression because of his place on the economic ladder.—Done in the best living-newspaper manner, Liberty Deferred presents its history through the eyes of its authors.—I believe the authors have assembled a singularly thought-provoking piece of propaganda and a valuable contribution to Negro literature.[38]

The committee contended that authors Silvera and Hill had been waiting for six months for action to be taken on their play by the New York City Federal Theatre Planning Board. "And this play but illustrates the fate of numerous worthy Negro plays by Negro playwrights."[39]

These were serious charges, and they were answered by Emmet

Lavery, director of the National Service Bureau. In his letter to the committee he stated that he had originally had great hopes for this Living Newspaper about Negroes, but when he read the completed script he "felt definitely that it did not bear out the high hopes I had for it."[40] His letter concluded with a statement of concern for the development of Negro drama and the hope that he had for a Negro trilogy being written by Hughes Allison. The trilogy has never appeared; *Liberty Deferred* has only recently turned up at the Lincoln Center Theatre Collection.

We can understand the frustration of those preparing the brief even as we respect the artistic integrity of Lavery. Had the Federal Theatre been simply the radical platform that Congressional committees accused it of being and not what Eric Bentley has called "a triumphant piece of private enterprise in the public domain,"[41] a play by Negro playwrights that crudely proclaimed the Negro's problems could have been staged in New York. It would not have been, however, a Living Newspaper of the quality expected from the producers of *Triple-A Plowed Under* and *One-Third of a Nation*.

Unfortunately, the Federal Theatre did not last long enough for Negro playwrights to perfect the rather special art form known as a Living Newspaper. Anyone who supposes that this style of presentation was simple should read John Gassner's description of it:

> The "Living Newspaper" style can be described as an amalgam of motion-picture, epic theatre, commedia dell' arte, and American minstrel show techniques kept within the framework of a question asked, usually by a puzzled little man who represents the public, and answers supplied by a series of presentational devices consisting of scenes, demonstrations, slides, lectures, and arguments. Symbolism was not excluded from this technique. . . . Pageantry was also not foreign to the medium. . . . Naturalism could also be assimilated into the medium, when this was deemed theatrically feasible.[42]

Writing a Living Newspaper demanded a theatrical sophistication that was probably beyond John Silvera and Abram Hill. It would have been beyond most of the Negro playwrights, with the possible exception of Langston Hughes, at this stage in their development.

LANGSTON HUGHES
Mulatto

Langston Hughes has been called a New Negro, an old-fashioned Negro, a radical, a conservative. He was famous as a poet, a playwright, a short-story writer, a novelist, a popularizer and creator of Negro legends. An indefatigable professional writer, Hughes was writing and being published in the twenties; at the time of his death on May 22, 1967, he had two books, one a book of poems, the other a pictorial history of the Negro in American entertainment, at the publishers. He had produced several volumes of poetry, two autobiographies, novels, a history of the NAACP, and a volume of plays. He had an international reputation, his plays having been translated into several languages. (*Mulatto* alone has been translated into Italian, Spanish, French, Portuguese, and Japanese.) He was the editor of anthologies for both children and adults. He wrote opera librettos and scripts for television. All this he managed to accomplish while writing a daily newspaper column and founding little theatres in New York, Chicago, and Los Angeles.

When five of his plays, with copyright notations ranging from 1931 to 1962, were published in 1963, the editor called Langston Hughes "America's outstanding Negro man of letters." He went on to say of Hughes's subject matter, the Negro in America:

The position of the Negro in the United States is one of the facts that any Negro must face if he is to write at all. No one has more faith in the strength and dignity of his people than does Hughes, but only a few of his works can be called militant or didactic. *Some few readers might wish that he were more belligerent, but he is an artist, not a propagandist.*[43]

The last statement seems, at first glance, to contradict what the author said of himself in a radio symposium in 1961: "I am, of course, as everyone knows, primarily a—I guess you might even say a propaganda writer; my main material is the race problem."[44] But is it really a contradiction in terms—artist and propagandist? It seems an unnecessary separation. Art that has at its center a social problem, in this case all the social problems related to race, has almost an obligation to be propaganda. Unless one reserves the term "propagandist" to describe someone who is part of a movement organized to spread information, Langston Hughes may, without casting doubt on his artistic merit, be called a propagandist. As an individual he seemed intent upon letting his readers, and in the theatre his audience, in on what it is like to be a Negro in America.

Langston Hughes was born in Joplin, Missouri, in 1902, and grew up in Lawrence, Kansas, Cleveland, Ohio, and Toluca, Mexico. In *The Big Sea* he wrote of adventures in these cities and in his favorite "city," Harlem. He wrote also about traveling as a seaman to Europe and Africa (where he was not black enough to be considered a Negro), and about living through the "Black Renaissance" as he called it. When he was a student at Lincoln University, he spent weekends in Harlem, but then he was alive not only to the literature but also to the hectic life of the era. He had friends among the white literati and among the "niggerati," as Wallace Thurman bitterly characterized himself and other Harlem writers. He also had a Park Avenue patroness. All these people and places influenced him as a writer and provided him with money, material, and a point of view.

As a child he had gone with his mother to see all the shows that came to Topeka: such plays as *Buster Brown, Under Two Flags,* and *Uncle Tom's Cabin.*[45] When he went to Columbia University, where he stayed for only one year, he missed classes and exams but not Florence Mills in *Shuffle Along.*[46] In the twenties, which were his twenties too, he went to parties given by Carl Van Vechten and to Harlem shows and revues. These experiences, along with his good eye for the dramatic situation whenever and wherever it occurred, helped to foster the playwright in Langston Hughes.

Edith Isaacs once observed that "Negro poets, although not many of them are writing plays as yet, seem to turn spontaneously toward the dramatic, in form or content, in situation, or character, or mood."[47] When she wrote of envying the "many play-kernels that are buried in short poems," she might have been thinking of Langston Hughes's "Cross":

My old man's a white old man
And my old mother's black.
If ever I cursed my white old man
I take my curses back.

If ever I cursed my black old mother
And wished she were in hell,
I'm sorry for that evil wish
And now I wish her well.

My old man died in a fine big house.
My ma died in a shack.
I wonder where I'm gonna die,
Being neither white nor black?[48]

The subject of this early poem, miscegenation, was to be the subject of several short stories and at least one other poem as well as the kernel for Hughes's play *Mulatto,* which opened on Broadway, October 24, 1935, and had the longest run of any play by a Negro until Lorraine Hansberry's *A Raisin in the Sun* broke the record in 1959.

In 1935 he was addressing himself as a poet to "Comrade Lenin of Russia,"[49] but it was a more commercially-minded Hughes who brought the subject of miscegenation to Broadway.

Audiences proved to be as intrigued by it as the readers of nineteenth-century novels on the subject had been. Langston Hughes himself acknowledged that "the problem of mixed blood in America is . . . a minor problem, but a very dramatic one."[50] Writers before and after him, recognizing the dramatic value of the problem, have played upon both the fears and the fascination engendered in American society by this subject.

Especially in fiction, but also in drama, white writers of the nineteenth century had written about "the tragic mulatto."

> In the fiction of Thomas Nelson Page and Thomas Dixon the mixed-blood is portrayed as the embodiment of the worst qualities of both races and hence as a menace to the dominant group. . . . On the contrary, other writers in varying degrees were sometimes sympathetic toward the Negro-white hybrid because of his possession of Caucasian blood, which they often considered as a factor that automatically made this character the superior of the darker Negro and therefore a more pitiable individual. Hence, the mulatto, thwarted in social progress because of Negro blood, became one of the popular characters of American fiction.[51]

To be sure, there were Negro writers, such as William Wells Brown and, later, W. E. B. DuBois, who counteracted this kind of propaganda, but they did not have a very wide audience among even educated Americans.

In the twentieth century, poets, novelists, and playwrights continued to concern themselves with miscegenation. Edward Sheldon's play "The Nigger," first produced in 1909, was about the governor of a Southern state who discovers that his mother was a Negro. Perhaps the most famous, even infamous, of these plays was Eugene O'Neill's All God's Chillun Got Wings, a disturbing, distorted, but psychologically profound play about a mixed marriage. Paul Robeson starred in the 1924 production, which provoked bitter discussions in the press. James Weldon Johnson has quoted an editorial in a Hearst publication:

They should not put on plays which are, or threaten to become, enemies of the public peace; they should not dramatize dynamite. . . . We refer to the play in which a white woman marries a black man and at the end of the play, after going crazy, stoops and kisses the Negro's hand.[52]

The subject of *Mulatto*, then, was not a new one in literature or on the stage. What was new was that a Negro was writing about miscegenation for predominantly white audiences. Langston Hughes was not writing for the Negro unit of the Federal Theatre; *Mulatto* was not to be produced at the Lafayette Theatre. He set himself the task of writing a tragedy about miscegenation in the Deep South of his own time (between World War I and World War II) for audiences accustomed, on the one hand, to *Green Pastures* and, on the other, to Frank Wilson's *Walk Together Chillun*. Langston Hughes did not write anything like *Green Pastures*, which on one occasion he had called "a naïve dialect play about a quaint funny heaven full of niggers,"[53] nor even a play interspersed with spirituals and minstrel material. He wrote a successful tragedy that had elements of melodrama, and he dealt, to a surprising degree of honesty, with an old problem in a contemporary setting.

Mulatto is a well-constructed play in two acts. The setting is the same in each act, and the action proceeds during an early fall afternoon and evening. The setting immediately suggests a naturalism akin to that of Ibsen's. If it were possible to imagine the Norwegian describing "the Big House on a plantation in Georgia," he might well have done so in these details:

Rear center of the room, a vestibule with double doors leading to the porch; at each side of the doors, a large window with lace curtains and green shades; at left a broad flight of stairs leading to the second floor; near the stairs, downstage, a doorway leading to the dining room and kitchen; opposite, at right of stage, a door to the library. The room is furnished in the long outdated horsehair and walnut style of the nineties; a crystal chan-

delier, a large old-fashioned rug, a marble-topped table, uphol-
stered chairs. At the right is a small cabinet. It is a very clean,
but somewhat shabby and rather depressing room. . . . The
windows are raised. The afternoon sunlight streams in.

Just as there is nothing in this description that is not used, ulti-
mately, in the action of the play, so there is no action that is not
pertinent to exposing the problems peculiar to miscegenation in
American society.

Mulatto has obvious exposition at the beginning, with speeches
designed to tell a great deal in a short space of time. It has a kind
of retrospection by means of which past actions are revealed in
present ones, something similar to Ibsen's analytic exposition.
Early in the play, for example, Cora, the brown woman who has
been Colonel Norwood's housekeeper-mistress for some thirty
years, tries to justify the actions of their son: "He don't mean
nothing—just smart and young and kinder careless, Colonel Tom,
like ma mother said you used to be when you was eighteen."

This is not an answer calculated to please Colonel Tom, who
has been complaining about the boy's impudence, but it lets him
know that she does not forget whose children she has borne, and
it lets us know that she is in a privileged, if sometimes uncomfortable, position in this household. In a very short time we learn
from the Colonel's outbursts that he has fathered mulatto children by Cora Lewis; that the oldest son, William, stays in his
place among the plantation laborers; that one girl is away, working up North; that another, Sallie, is about to go back to school;
and that Robert, the one who most resembles the Colonel in
looks and fiery temperament, is home from college and home to
stay. Robert, or Bert as he is usually called, is the immediate
focus of attention and cause for conflict in the play. Incidentally,
it is only by indirection that we know that these children are the
Colonel's. He always refers to them simply as Cora's, except for
one slip that is nearly buried in a long speech:

Just because Bert's your son, and I've been damn fool enough
to send him off to school for five or six years, he thinks he has

a right to privileges, acting as if he owned this place since he's been back here this summer. . . . There's no nigger-child of mine, yours, ours—no darkie—going to disobey me. . . . Schools for darkies! Huh! If you take that boy of yours for an example, they do 'em more harm than good. He's learned nothing in college but impudence, and he'll stay here on this place and work for me awhile before he gets back to any more schools.

The Colonel's contention is that he sent "Cora's kids" to school because he could not bear to see them stay as dumb as the other "darkies." Of course, as soon as Bert begins to act like something other than a dumb "darkie," he is stepping out of line. There is no doubt that each race has its role and its place. When the old Negro retainer, Sam, asks if he may move Sallie's trunk down the front stairs, because it will not fit down the back, Colonel Norwood replies:

No other way? (Sam shakes his head) Then pack it on through to the back, quick. Don't let me catch you carrying any of Sallie's baggage out of the front door here. You-all'll be wanting to go in and out the front way next. (Turning away, complaining to himself) Darkies have been getting mighty fresh in this part of the country since the war. The damn Germans should've . . . (To Sam) Don't take that trunk out that front door.

This speech not only helps to characterize the Colonel and place the scene in terms of time, but it also gives Sam a chance to tell the Colonel that Bert has been using the front door, an act which gains symbolic importance as the plot develops. The first act curtain, for instance, will fall on Bert walking defiantly out that door. But before that occurs, there are two scenes that further develop the characterization of the Colonel, of Bert, and of Cora. These scenes also move the action of the play ahead with an inexorable air of tragedy.

In a scene between Colonel Norwood and his friend Fred Higgins, the latter reports that Cora's boy, "that young black fool," is speeding in Colonel Norwood's Ford and acting as if he were as good as a white man. Even worse, Bert has been boasting "to the wall-eyed coons" of his parentage, that his name is Norwood, that his money is as good as a white man's any day. If Colonel Norwood is a stereotype of the Georgia plantation owner, Fred Higgins is even more a stereotype of the fat, elderly county politician. He huffs and puffs as he is helped in and out of a chair by his Negro chauffeur, Mose. He drinks too much, speaks crudely, and divulges a great deal of information as well as vulgar comment upon it. His remarks about how a Negro should act in the South are particularly striking:

> A darkie's got to keep in his place down here. Ruinous to other niggers hearing that talk, too. All this postwar propaganda on the radio about freedom and democracy—why the niggers think it's meant for them! And that Eleanor Roosevelt, she ought to been muzzled. She's driving our niggers crazy—your boy included. Crazy! Talking about civil rights. Ain't been no race trouble in our county for three years—since the Deekin's lynching—but I'm telling you, Norwood, you better see that that buck of yours goes away from here. I'm speaking on the quiet, but I can see ahead.

Colonel Norwood is furious, not only with Bert, significantly, but at the white man's dependence upon the Negro. "Everything turns on niggers, niggers, niggers!" he exclaims. It is obvious, of course, that Colonel Norwood has been dependent on Cora for some years for many favors. Higgins disapproves not of the favors but of what living with only Negroes can do to a man:

> Nothing but blacks in the house—a man gets soft like niggers are inside. (Puffing at cigar) And living with a colored woman! Of course, I know we all have 'em—I didn't know you could make use of a white girl till I was past twenty. Thought too much o' white women for that—but I've given many a yellow gal a baby in my time. (Long puff at cigar) But for a man's own house you need a wife, not a black woman.

Colonel Norwood agrees with him but observes that it is too late for him to marry again. Their short scene contains one statement after another in support of white supremacy.

In a scene that serves as a transition to Cora's scene with Bert, and that adds to the suspense growing all through the act, she reminisces with her son William about the time that Bert called the Colonel "papa." He was then seven years old, and the Colonel beat him unmercifully. Bert is home now only to please Cora, who is fast changing her mind about the visit. She is frightened for her boy. "Somethin' gonna happen to my boy," she tells William. "I had a bad dream last night. . . . I seed a path o' living blood across this house, I tell you, in my sleep."

When Cora is alone with Bert—who enters through the front door, announcing that "*Mister* Norwood's here!"—she tries to reason with him, to remind him of the ways of the South. He stubbornly defies those ways and announces his intention to have his rights, to be a Norwood and not a "field-hand nigger." Cora answers him quietly from the depths of her experience:

> I knows, honey, you reads in de books and de papers, and you knows a lot more'n I do. But, chile, you's in Georgy. . . . This ain't up North—and even up yonder where we hears it's so fine, yo' sister has to pass for white to get along good.

She tells about moving up to the Big House when the Colonel's wife died, of how good he was to let her keep her children with her in the house when they were little, and of how he sent them to school:

> Ain't no white man in this county done that with his cullud chilluns before, far as I can know. But you—Robert, be awful, awful careful! When de Colonel comes back, in a few minutes, he wants to talk to you. Talk right to him, boy. Talk like you was colored, 'cause you ain't white.

Bert's angry answer, "And I'm not black either," hits at the center of the play's theme.

The climax of the first act occurs when Colonel Norwood enters the front door just as Bert is preparing to leave by it. The Colonel raises his cane to strike the boy. Cora screams. The boy looks insolently into his father's eyes, and the Colonel, unable to strike him, orders the boy to leave the house. As Bert walks proudly out the front door, the Colonel takes a pistol from the cabinet and starts to follow him. Cora intervenes with the moving, if melodramatic, line: "He's our son, Tom. Remember he's our son."

In spite of lengthy speeches, the action moves ahead rapidly in the two scenes in the second act of *Mulatto*. At sunset, after supper, the Colonel and Bert confront each other. After a long speech in which Colonel Norwood tells Bert about all the advantages he has given Cora's children and how kind he is to all his "darkies," he concludes with the comment that he is going to give this impudent boy a chance to explain himself. He adds that he wants Bert to "talk right." When Bert asks what he means by that, the Colonel answers in a way that sets off the violence that has been stirring just under the surface of the scene.

NORWOOD: *I mean talk like a nigger should to a white man.*
ROBERT: *Oh! But I'm not a nigger, Colonel Tom. I'm your son.*
NORWOOD: *(Testily) You're Cora's boy.*
ROBERT: *Women don't have children by themselves.*
NORWOOD: *Nigger women don't know the fathers. You're a bastard.*

(One remembers the refrain from an early poem by Langston Hughes:

A nigger night,
A nigger joy,
A little yellow
Bastard boy.)[54]

This particular "boy" will not accept his bastardy. He flings accusations and challenges at the Colonel, who answers him in kind. After heated words on both sides, the Colonel draws his pistol to prevent Bert from leaving by the front door, but Bert twists the gun from his father's hand. There is a struggle, and the younger man strangles the older one. Cora enters the room and finds Colonel Norwood dead. When we read that Bert drops his father's body at his mother's feet "in a path of flame from the setting sun," we remember her dream of the house bathed in blood.

There is only one course for Bert to take. He must run away to avoid being lynched by the white men who are on their way to visit Colonel Norwood. He sets out for the swamp, promising Cora to return to the house if he finds he cannot make it that far: "Let them take me out of my father's house—if they can. *(Puts the gun under his shirt)* They're not going to string me up to some roadside tree for the crackers to laugh at."

The white men, on discovering Colonel Norwood's body, form a posse to get Bert. Cora is left alone with the corpse. In a long, emotional speech she moves from tenderness to outright hatred of the Colonel:

He's your boy. His eyes is gray—like your eyes. He's tall like you's tall. He's proud like you's proud. And he's runnin'—runnin' from po' white trash that ain't worth de little finger o' nobody what's got your blood in 'em, Tom. (Demandingly) Why don't you get up from there and stop 'em, Colonel Tom? What's that you say? He ain't your chile? He's ma bastard chile? Ma yellow bastard chile? (Proudly) Yes, he's mine. . . . He's ma chile. . . . Don't you come to my bed no mo'. I calls you to help me now, and you just lays there. I calls you for to wake up, and you just lays there. Whenever you called me in de night, I woke up. When you called for me to love, I always reached out ma arms fo' you. I borned you five chilluns and now one of 'em is out yonder in de dark runnin' from yo' people. Our youngest boy out yonder in de dark runnin'. (Accusingly) He's runnin' from you, too. . . . You are out yonder in de dark, runnin' our chile, with de hounds and de gun in yo' hand. . . . Damn you,

> *Colonel Norwood!* (Backing slowly up the stairs, staring at the rigid body below her) *Damn you, Thomas Norwood! God damn you!*

This is less than half of the speech that brings the curtain down on the scene. Cora is released by madness to cry out what she has suppressed over the years.

Cora's fantasy persists in the last scene. Her madness mounts, and after she has said goodbye to William, she reports to Colonel Tom:

> *Colonel Tom! Look! Bertha and Sallie and William and Bert, all your chilluns, runnin' from you, and you layin' on de floor there, dead!* (Pointing) *Out yonder with the mob, dead. And when you come home, upstairs in my bed on top of my body, dead.*

This outburst is followed by a long speech of reminiscing, repetitious but charged with lively images. The sounds of the approaching mob are growing stronger and stronger. By the end of the speech Cora knows that Bert is coming home.

He bursts into the room, exchanging shots with the loud mob outside. Voices can be heard shouting, "Nigger! Nigger! Nigger! Get the nigger!" Cora bolts the door after Bert and sends him upstairs to hide in a hole in the floor under her bed. He has one bullet left, which they both agree he must use for himself. They bid each other good night almost formally, glad to reach this ending with dignity.

Cora is on the stairs when the white mob bursts into the living room with guns, knives, rope, clubs, flashlights. She turns on the stairs and tells them to be quiet. Her boy is going to sleep. Before they can get past her, a single shot rings out. "My boy . . . is gone . . . to sleep!" are Cora's last words. Her last action, however, comes just as the curtain falls. It is not an action so much as a lack of one. Talbot, the overseer, furious at having been cheated of a chance to lynch the boy, "walks up to Cora and slaps her once across the face. She does not move. It is as though no human hand can touch her again."

Cora Lewis wins. Her kind of dignity gives the play a special dimension. Webster Smalley put it this way.

> The patient love and rich dignity of Cora and Bert's final recognition of the totality of his tragic situation raise Mulatto above the level of a mere problem play. One forgives Hughes the sometimes obvious exposition of the opening scenes (as one does the early O'Neill in Beyond the Horizon) for the tragedy and power of the play's final scenes.[55]

It may very well be that Broadway audiences in 1935 were moved by the production more than they were by the script and the ideas expressed in it. Rose McClendon played the part of Cora, and this great Negro actress brought power and dignity to the role, the last one she played before her untimely death the following year. There was, however, along with the intensity provided by the script and the actors, a touch of sensationalism added by a producer with an eye on the box office. Sallie, in the Broadway production, was made to miss her train back to school so that she could later be raped by the wicked overseer. This bit of melodramatic action was added without the consent of the author.[56] Whatever the reasons for its success, Mulatto ran for nearly a year on Broadway and then toured the country—with the exception of the South, which included even Philadelphia— for eight months.

Don't You Want to Be Free?

Don't You Want to Be Free? was not, strictly speaking, an agitprop play, although its purpose was agitation and propaganda. Early agitprop plays in this country were crude in characterization and plot, full of labor clichés, hard-hitting, direct, and, it should be added, Marxist. A play directly influenced by this kind of theatre is Clifford Odets' Waiting for Lefty (1935). The main difference between it and the early, purer forms of agitprop was one of literary value. John Gassner has defined the classic form of what he terms "agitprop" as a "short play, usually a skit of no literary value but of immediate theatrical incandescence."[57] The authors of *Waiting for Lefty* and *Don't You Want to Be Free?* both strove for the immediacy of agitprop theatricalism but, at the same time, wrote something more than skits, something of value on a page.

According to Langston Hughes, *Don't You Want to Be Free?* had "the longest run of any dramatic show in Harlem so far, 135 performances, weekends over a period of almost two years."[58] In 1937 Hughes founded the Harlem Suitcase Theatre, which was sponsored originally by labor groups. Whatever other plays and lampooning skits were performed there in the next couple of years, *Don't You Want to Be Free?* was on the stage every weekend during 1938 and 1939. A description of the theatre helps us to picture the production:

> The Suitcase Theatre is located in a second-story loft in Harlem, where its two small stages are devoid of curtains and backdrops. The actors frequently bring needed properties from their own homes for performances. Two hundred persons, who pay thirty-five cents each, are a capacity audience. Approximately three quarters of those attending are Negroes; and one quarter white.[59]

An examination of the play itself shows that it employs many theatrical devices associated with both the Living Newspaper and agitprop plays. Characters are not individualized. They are listed as "A Young Man, A Mulatto Girl, A Boy, A Wife, A Girl, A Husband . . . An Overseer, A Chorus." No scenery and few props are called for. Only actors and an audience are needed. The Young Man who addresses the audience at the opening establishes immediately an agitprop atmosphere and educates the audience to the kind of theatre they are to expect:

> Listen, folks! I'm one of the members of this group, and I want to tell you about our theatre. This is it right here! We haven't

got any scenery, or painted curtains, because we haven't got any money to buy them. But we've got faith in ourselves. And in you. So we're going to put on a show. Maybe you'll like it because it's about you, and about us. . . . It's about me yesterday, and about me tomorrow. I'm colored! I guess you can see that. Well, this show is about what it means to be colored in America.

From then on the script becomes poems interlaced with set speeches—sometimes a monologue, sometimes a dialogue—with music and dancing. To tell what it is like "to be colored in America" Hughes made use of his poems and of music he had always known. For example, a Young Man recites a poem about the beauty of the African now caged in the white man's "circus of civilization." The poem is followed by this speech in praise of revolt:

We were never wholly quiet! Some of us always carried on our fight and kept alive the seeds of revolt. Nat Turner was one. Denmark Vesey was another who tried to lead the slaves to freedom. Harriet Tubman was another who sought roads to escape. Sojourner Truth another. Some they beat to death. Some they killed. But some of us always kept on, even though the way looked dark.

A mournful yet sustaining spiritual serves as a coda when an Old Woman sings at the end of the speech, "Oh, nobody knows the trouble I've seen!/ Nobody knows but Jesus." The poet-playwright has made a powerful statement about the Negro's position in America.

Many Negro problems are treated in this poetic, dramatic fashion. Here are the lines Langston Hughes gives a Mulatto Girl who is shown beside the hanging body of her lynched lover:

Way down South in Dixie
(Break the heart of me!)
They hung my dark young lover
To a cross road's tree.

Way down South in Dixie,
(Bruised body high in air)
I asked the white Lord Jesus
What was the use of prayer.

Way down South in Dixie
(Break the heart of me)
Love is a naked shadow
On a gnarled and naked tree.

She is answered by an Overseer, who in turn is answered by a Man
who gives the message to which the poem-scene has been building:

OVERSEER: *Pull at the rope! O!*
        Pull it high!
        Let the white folks live
        And the black man die.

MAN: *Yes, pull it, then,*
        With a bloody cry!
        Let the black boy swing
        But the white folks die.

There is no doubt that "immediate theatrical incandescence" is
inherent in this scene, but so is the literary value that was found
lacking in earlier, avowedly Marxist agitprop productions.

The treatment in the play of a specific, contemporary Negro
problem, the Harlem race riots of March 19, 1935, must have
invited the kind of audience response that true agitprop plays
required.

NEWSBOYS: *Riots in Harlem! Negroes running riot! Riot! Read all
about it! . . .* MARCH 19th RIOT IN HARLEM! RIOT IN HARLEM!
Read all about it. HARLEM IS TIRED! *Harlem's tired!*
MEMBER OF AUDIENCE: *Riots won't solve anything, will they,
brother?*
YOUNG MAN: *No, riots won't solve anything.*
MEMBER OF AUDIENCE: *Then what must we do?*

YOUNG MAN: *Organize . . . with the others who suffer like me and you.*

Like Clifford Odets, Hughes had a firm if not very doctrinaire notion that the answer lay in organizing.

At the end of the play the audience is invited to link hands with the characters in the play (one wonders about the Overseer) "until the players and the audience are one," all singing:

Oh, who wants to come and join hands with me?
Who wants to make one great unity?
Who wants to say, no more black or white?
Then let's get together, folks,
And fight, fight, fight!

Hilda Lawson, who apparently saw *Don't You Want to Be Free?* when it was presented at the Nora Bayes Theatre on June 10, 1938, felt that Langston Hughes "overstates the facts of Negro existence in support of his thesis that the overseer of slave days still confronts the Negro in every phase of his present life."[60] Neither the frustrations of everyday Negro existence nor the need for organization seem overstated in view of recent history. Miss Lawson accused the playwright of laziness, of stringing together poems already published in *The Dream Keeper* and *Weary Blues.* It would seem fairer to credit Langston Hughes with a use of his poems that raised agitprop to a rare level of literary value.

Plays written by Negroes in the thirties reflect the authors' desire to write about "what it is like to be colored in America"; but that desire was coupled with the very human need to succeed, and so the plays often contain compromises in terms of melodrama, music, and the buffoonery of Negro stereotypes. Langston Hughes stands out as the only Negro playwright of this decade who managed to write literate plays that satisfied both Broadway and Harlem audiences. He did not write for the Federal Theatre, and there is more than a little disappointment with that project expressed in his poem "Notes on Commercial Theatre":

You've taken my blues and gone—
You sing 'em on Broadway
And you sing 'em in Hollywood Bowl,
And you mixed 'em up with symphonies
And you fixed 'em
So they don't sound like me.
Yep, you done taken my blues and gone.

You also took my spirituals and gone.
You put me in Macbeth and Carmen Jones
And all kinds of Swing Mikados
And in everything but what's about me—
But someday somebody'll
Stand up and talk about me,
And write about me—
Black and beautiful—
And sing about me,
And put on plays about me!
I reckon it'll be
Me myself!

Yes, it'll be me.[61]

The poem oversimplifies the problem. Even if it will be Negroes who will write honest plays about themselves, their being Negroes will not automatically make them write effectively about their lives. Negro playwrights needed to learn how to write about their experience, but the Federal Theatre did not exist long enough to give them as much training as they needed. Only time and an apprenticeship in the theatre, freedom to experiment with styles and to watch plays in rehearsal and production, only involvement in the theatre process will enable Negro playwrights to turn their life experiences into effective plays. It is significant that Langston Hughes's *Mulatto* was "tried out" at Hedgerow Theatre before it ever reached Broadway, and Hughes, a professional writer, was on hand to watch rehearsals.[62]

Among the Federal Theatre records there is a prescription for a dramatic epic that may someday be written about the Negro in American civilization:

> It will involve African folk-ways and American vestiges thereof, gang-labor and slave discipline, abolition chaos and latter-day repression, concubinage, mulattos and "passing for white," rural isolation and urban congestion, dialect and manners, caste and caste within caste, songs and prayers, sermon and schisms, the nonchalance and bewilderment, the very human hopes and fear, the protest and acquiescences of a somewhat peculiar people through cataclysmic changes in a very complex land.[63]

It is interesting to notice how many of the elements listed here were subjects for the plays of the thirties. Hall Johnson wrote about American vestiges of African folkways and made use of songs, prayers, and sermons. Smith and Morell's *Turpentine* dealt with gang-labor, *Mulatto* with concubinage, and *The Trial of Dr. Beck* with "passing." *Brother Mose* had songs, prayers, sermons, schisms, and castes. *Conjur Man Dies* was concerned with "the very human hopes and fears" of urban Negroes. Scarcely a problem named here was missing from *Don't You Want to Be Free?* All the plays employed dialect of various sorts and to varying degrees.

At this point, it seems appropriate to ask two questions: (1) Were there any advances made dramaturgically over earlier plays by Negroes? (2) Were the problems on which the plays focused persistent or limited to the thirties?

Hall Johnson's *Run, Little Chillun* was better constructed than any earlier plays of Negro authorship, and it was artfully supported by music. There is little doubt that Johnson learned a great deal about what is effective in the theatre by his association with the Broadway production of *Green Pastures* in 1930. He arranged and directed the music for Marc Connelly's play, attended rehearsals, watched the production grow. Three years later he wrote his own *Run, Little Chillun* and arranged the music for it.

Kenneth Burke was pleased that there was "no amusing picture of heaven here, nor 'backward superstition' . . . suggested by the unending nag of a drum-beat."[64] He credited Hall Johnson with being able to write about Negro religion powerfully because he was a Negro. It seems an oversimplification to say that the potency of the play comes from that source alone; the playwright's artistry was certainly fostered by his involvement with *Green Pastures*. An artist learns from art as well as from life.

The problem that is central to *Run, Little Chillun*, pagan versus Christian worship, is not a prevalent one in our society. The Negro's religious response, however, continues to be a very important part of his life. The spirituals that are at the heart of *Run, Little Chillun* are the freedom songs of more recent decades.

Frank Wilson, the actor, whose school was the stage, quite naturally wrote plays that were "shows." He knew what Negro performers had to do to be acceptable on a stage and let that be a guide to his writing. It is very likely that he wanted to be accepted in much the same way that Brother Mose did, not to make any trouble or ask any questions. Booker T. Washington's philosophy hovers over *Brother Mose* the way it did over *Caleb, the Degenerate* and *Appearances*.

The structure of *Brother Mose* is as loose as that of the earlier plays, the quality of the language as quaint, the characters as stereotypical, the ideas as broad and general. Like the earlier playwrights, Wilson gave the public what it wanted: songs, dances, gags, even some honest speeches on occasion. Like them he preached a message of optimistic faith. There may be fewer Negroes these days who defend the status quo so meekly, but they are still among us.

Rudolph Fisher can scarcely be held to account for the flaws in his play, *Conjur Man Dies*. With more experience in the theatre, this brilliant young man who wrote such dramatic stories might have written a good play, but he died before he had a chance to do so. The one play that we have is an awkward first attempt. A recent critic sensibly dismissed *Conjur Man Dies* in this fashion:

> Rudolph Fisher used voodoo and sorcery as a background for melodrama and horror. Although they have employed superstition for their dramatic purposes, most Negro dramatists have avoided picturing voodoo as a unique, important, or necessary part of the Negro's faith.[65]

Langston Hughes, as noted previously, was the first Negro playwright of any stature, a writer by profession, a man who traveled in his own country and abroad. It seems only fair to guess that, through these activities, he gained an objectivity that enabled him to interpret Negro life and, at the same time, to write a soundly constructed play.

There is a universality about *Mulatto* that other plays of the period lack. The play goes beyond the problem of miscegenation, which is still a real or imagined issue in our time. Bert symbolizes all educated Negroes when he demands his rights of Colonel Norwood, who so obviously symbolizes the old South. The Colonel educated Bert and then asked him to go back into the fields, to return to "his place." The South is just beginning to feel the results of Negroes coming of age, questioning their place in the scheme of things. The front door still belongs to the white man, but Langston Hughes predicted as early as 1935 the bloodshed that might occur if the Negro were not allowed to go in and out that door at will.

Critics have spoken of Langston Hughes's tolerance in dealing with characters, whites as well as Negroes: "In *Mulatto* it is not only Robert Lewis who suffers from tragic *hybris* and who involves our sympathy; it is also Colonel Norwood—trapped by the assumptions of his own society and too proud to defy them altogether."[66] Only recently has the public begun to realize that in abusing the black man the white man is doing terrible things to himself.

Finally, there is the one play considered here that can be called a protest play, *Don't You Want to Be Free?* Current as well as persistent problems of the Negro are the subject of this poetic agitprop play. Langston Hughes did not go far enough to the left to satisfy some critics, and yet he was never far enough to the right for others. *Don't You Want to Be Free?* was revised and brought up to date in 1963. The Young Man's answer to the Overseer who accuses him of being a Red could have been Langston Hughes's reply for himself in the sixties as well as in the thirties:

> Is it Red to want to live in a clean house on a decent street where the garbage trucks come by every day, not just when they feel like it? Is it Red to want a chance to work on any job like other Americans? Is it Red to want to vote in South Carolina? Or go to college in Mississippi? Or be safe from bombs in Georgia? Or get a fair trial? Or ride on a bus without Jim Crow? Or rent a house anyplace?[67]

The attitude exemplified in *Don't You Want to Be Free?* proved prophetic. Never again, after the thirties, were Negroes to write plays of acquiescence. Future playwrights were to protest rather than to accept the Negro's position in American society.

IV 🌱 THE FORTIES

Did somebody die?

THE POET who wrote about World War II that "blood was far away from here—Money was near"—and who asked at the end of another poem on the same subject, "Did somebody die?"[1]—was speaking ironically of gains made by Negroes during the war. He might have been speaking of the nation as a whole. This war that so involved us, so drained our resources, both human and material, also buoyed up an economy and brought strength and unity of purpose to the whole nation. What was amazing was not the dying, which is expected in war, but the fact that Americans took total war in their stride, adjusted to it, profited by it.

In idealistic terms that most Americans were willing to accept, President Roosevelt spoke of what he wished for the "little men and women ground under the Axis heel":

> When victory comes there can certainly be no secure peace until there is a return of law and order in the oppressed countries, until the peoples of these countries have been restored to a normal, healthy, and self-sustaining existence. This means that the more quickly and effectually we apply measures of relief and

rehabilitation, the more quickly will our own boys overseas be able to come home.[2]

If some Negroes were rather skeptical about help being sent abroad when they still found it difficult to lead "normal, healthy, and self-sustaining" lives at home, it is not surprising. When a high school class was asked to say what punishment should be meted out to Hitler, a Negro girl answered, "He should be let loose in America as a Negro."[3] This child was not alone in realizing the discrepancy between what we say is America and what in fact it is for those often classified as second-class citizens. The truth is, however, that her male relatives fought still another war for a dream rather than for actuality.

On the home front Negroes were not automatically welcomed into the labor force even in wartime. They learned to back up their demands for social reform with social pressures, to promise votes, to use the power they had been gaining painfully over the years. A. Philip Randolph, president of the Brotherhood of Sleeping Car Porters, organized the famous "March-on-Washington Movement" in 1941. He has since described it and its effects:

> *Thousands of Negroes throughout the country . . . mobilized for a 100,000-strong convergence on the nation's capital with a demand for equal employment opportunities in the defense industries. Many efforts were made to have the march called off, and on one occasion I was summoned to talk with President Roosevelt at the White House. When it became clear that we would not be cajoled, a reluctant President signed an executive order in June, 1941, reaffirming the government's policy of non-discrimination and establishing a Fair Employment Practices Commission to investigate violations of this policy in defense industries.*[4]

It was not enough, but it was a step toward security and a better position from which to bargain in the future.

Progress was made in behalf of Negroes by the FEPC before its demise in 1946. Strengthened industrial unionism helped the Negro, too, to make gains in civil and economic rights. But there were still the riots, still white opposition to Negro employment; and Negroes lost jobs more rapidly than did whites when the war came to an end. There were plenty of reasons for the NAACP to direct a 154-page petition to the United Nations in 1947. In the introduction, W. E. B. DuBois, still the critical Negro spokesman, wrote:

> If . . . the effect of the color caste system on the American Negro has been both good and bad, its effect on white America has been disastrous. It has repeatedly led the greatest modern attempt at democratic government to deny its political ideals, to falsify its philanthropic assertions and to make its religion to a great extent hypocritical.[5]

The scholarly DuBois stated his complaints in a petition to the U.N. Others fought in riots. Still others turned to art to try to express through one medium or another their dissatisfaction with the Negro's place in the American scheme.

It was partly their experience with the Federal Theatre in the thirties that gave Negroes the incentive to establish their own theatre companies in Harlem during the forties. These companies, however, were also in the tradition of early attempts by Negroes to have their own theatre: the Lafayette Players early in the century, the Krigwa Players in the twenties, the Rose McClendon Players in the thirties, to mention a few possible prototypes for the new ventures. The Negro Playwrights Company was founded in 1940; and the American Negro Theatre, organized in 1939, began actively producing plays in 1940. Three plays produced by these groups will be considered here. Since plays produced by the Committee for the Negro in the Arts (founded in 1947) were produced in the fifties, the CNA will be discussed in the next chapter.

Big White Fog by Theodore Ward was the one play produced by the Negro Playwrights Company. It had had a successful Federal Theatre production in Chicago in 1938, and the New York group chose it as a representative play by a young Negro playwright. It seemed to fit the qualifications they set forth in an elaborate brochure entitled A *Professional Theatre with an Idea*. In the lengthy "Perspective" contained in that brochure, which has been preserved by one of the founders, George Norford—others were Langston Hughes,[6] Theodore Ward, Powell Lindsay, Owen Dodson, and Theodore Browne—the emphasis was on a theatre for the Negro people that would foster "Negro literature of the drama comparable with reality or truth." The group was to present plays by Negro playwrights who would write with sincerity about the lives and history of the Negro people. The "Perspective" strongly opposed Broadway commercialism without calling it by name:

> These new writers recognize that they live in a real society . . . they will be writers worthy of the name only if they remain independent of the forces which have reduced brains to a commodity and driven weaklings and panderers to the practice of falsifying truth in order to make it conform to accepted beliefs and the tastes of those who tend to regard the Negro people as children or slaves placed in the world for their own exploitation or amusement.[7]

The Negro Playwrights Company acknowledged a debt to Federal Theatre units not only for their development of playwrights but also for their training of Negro technicians, designers, and theatre business managers. They stated their belief, too, in a public that the Federal Theatre helped to discover, Negroes who would attend the theatre if the productions were "characterized by sound professional stagecraft and honest realism." They indicated their intention to pattern themselves after the collaborative art of the Group Theatre. The "Perspective" concluded:

The company conceives itself as one which will foster the spirit of unity between the races, provide an outlet for the creative talents of Negro artists, encourage the development of marked abilities through the awarding of annual scholarships, and supply the community with an honest, vital, interesting, exciting, moving and colorful theatre, reflecting the historic reality of the life of the Negro people.[8]

Every sentence of the "Perspective"—every quotation from such famous associate members as Paul Robeson, Richard Wright, and Alain Locke[9]—vibrated with idealism, with a faith in the possibility of a people's theatre for Negroes and an equally strong belief in Theodore Ward's play. Richard Wright, expressing his conviction that the company was deserving of support, said of Theodore Ward: "There lives in America no playwright I know of who is better fitted for the launching of a people's theatre for the mirroring of Negro life in America than Theodore Ward."[10] And yet after sixty-four performances. *Big White Fog* closed. The length of the run would not constitute a failure, except that that was the last seen of the play and the end of the producing company. The Negro Playwrights Company announced that their next production, an intimate revue, would open in January. It did not open, and this brave attempt at a people's theatre became history.

Another Harlem venture, the American Negro Theatre, was organized late in 1939 by Abram Hill and Frederick O'Neal. The former was the Federal Theatre playwright who, with John Silvera, wrote the unproduced Living Newspaper, *Liberty Deferred*. Frederick O'Neal was at the beginning of his distinguished career as an actor. The theatre was housed in the basement of the 135th Street Library, where W. E. B. DuBois' Krigwa Players had had their headquarters almost twenty years earlier.

The American Negro Theatre was initially a smaller, less ambitious venture than the Negro Playwrights Company. The change in the theatre's direction, perhaps its purpose—although that was not spelled out much beyond Abram Hill's statement that "we're trying to discover something that could be called the *art* of Negro acting"[11]—came with the production of Philip Yordan's *Anna Lucasta*, originally a play about a Polish-American family, which was presented during the 1944–45 theatre season. Several Broadday critics saw it and praised it, and so a year later the production was moved downtown. There were two off-Broadway companies, one of which played for forty-four weeks in Chicago before going to California, while the other presented the play for many weeks in Philadelphia.

At first glance it would seem that with the production of *Anna Lucasta* the American Negro Theatre became less a community- and more a Broadway-oriented theatre. (Several persons who were working in the Negro theatre of that period have said just that in conversation.) But Frederick O'Neal recalls that

> *Anna Lucasta was produced in the early summer of 1944. There were a number of productions by the group since that date among which were Henri Christophe, Tintop Valley and several others, so that the assumption or impression that the Theatre became Broadway-oriented or identified is a mistaken one.*[12]

Loften Mitchell, with historical perspective, has called attention to troubles that have beset all the theatre groups in Harlem:

> *Since 1910, seventeen major groups have attempted to build a permanent Harlem theatre. All have been thwarted chiefly by the lack of local popular support, Broadway's ever-present influence and the lack of good native drama. There may never be a Harlem theatre that is supported by the people of the community.*[13]

One might go so far as to say that there will be no real support for ethnic theatre so long as the people of the community are striving to be successful, assimilated, middle-class Americans.

Of the plays presented by the American Negro Theatre, we

shall consider *On Strivers Row* by Abram Hill, produced in 1940, and *Natural Man* by Theodore Browne, produced in 1941 (and earlier in Seattle by the Federal Theatre). They are very different from each other, one a rather crude comedy of manners and the other a folk drama. They seem representative of plays then being presented at the Library Theatre, they are full-length plays, and they are among the few of Negro authorship.

During the forties Broadway produced more plays than usual on the subject of Negroes. There were the inevitable musicals, the most memorable being *Cabin in the Sky* (1940) and *Carmen Jones* (1943). There was wartime vaudeville—*Harlem Cavalcade* (1943), *Blue Holiday* (1945). The most successful play about Negroes by white authors was *Deep Are the Roots* by Arnaud D'Usseau and James Gow (1945). Only two plays by Negro playwrights were produced on Broadway during this decade: *Native Son* by Richard Wright (with Paul Green), produced in 1941; and Theodore Ward's *Our Lan'* in 1947.

Native Son did not fit the formula for Negro plays that are bound to succeed on Broadway. Enchanted by *Green Pastures*, Arthur Quinn had theorized earlier that "the Negro, in his wistful, exalted phases is much better suited to the stage than when he is being exploited as the symbol of a struggle for racial equality."[14] Bigger Thomas, the bitter young hero of *Native Son*, was neither exalted nor wistful; he was a symbol of the oppressed Negro, made flesh by Canada Lee's performance of the role.

Theodore Ward, whose *Big White Fog* had seemed awkwardly constructed and unduly laden with problems, had a play on Broadway during the 1947–48 season. This play, *Our Lan'*, which had been produced earlier off-Broadway, a play about the Reconstruction era, was praised for its dramaturgy, its dialogue, the beauty of its story, its sense of history. But critics who had praised the production on Grand Street in April felt that it lost important simplicity as it gained theatrical dimensions by the move to Broadway in September, 1947.

The author himself now feels that when he allowed a scene

of compromise to be cut he "sacrificed the belly of the play for Broadway. Also the director had a tenor sing offstage before the curtain and everyone expected a musical."[15] One wonders how the serious-minded Ward felt when George Jean Nathan chose to mingle with his praise of *Our Lan'* this comment on propaganda plays: "The natural tragic force of the theme is immeasurably greater and much more impressive than the artificial soapbox force of all the recent Negro Propaganda plays rolled into one."[16] Theodore Ward's thoughts may have gone back to the faith he and other Negro playwrights like Abram Hill and Theodore Browne had had at the beginning of the decade in *Big White Fog* and in the success of an ethnic theatre.

OFF-BROADWAY

On Strivers Row

Abram Hill, when he was interviewed in 1943 as a playwright-director and founder of the American Negro Theatre in Harlem, told the interviewer that his father had been a railroad fireman on the Atlanta-Washington run, and that his family had moved from Atlanta to New York City in 1925. Young Abram went to DeWitt Clinton High School, then to City College for two years, and to Lincoln University in Pennsylvania for the remainder of his college education.

In 1938 he became an assistant in the Drama Department at Lincoln, and later that year he went to New York to join the Federal Theatre as a consultant on plays about Negro life. It was under Federal Theatre auspices that he and John Silvera wrote the Living Newspaper *Liberty Deferred*, a frequently mentioned but never produced play. Later he studied playwriting at Columbia University and won a scholarship to the Dramatic Workshop of the New School for Social Research.

The title of one of his early plays, *On Strivers Row*,[17] tells us what ambiance to expect. Carl Van Vechten once described Strivers' Row in this way:

West One hundred and thirty-ninth Street, dubbed Strivers' Row by all and sundry in Harlem. This block of tan brick houses, flanked by rows of trees on either side of the way, had been designed in the early twentieth century by Stanford White, at the time when Harlem was a German section. Now they had been taken over by rich Negroes: a few, like Fletcher Henderson, the band-leader, and Harry Wills, the prize-fighter, of international fame, but most of them lawyers, physicians, real estate operators, or opulent proprietors of beauty parlors.[18]

Abram Hill chose to write about the class that E. Franklin Frazier named the black bourgeoisie. Of these middle-class Negroes Frazier wrote:

Since the black bourgeoisie live largely in a world of make-believe, the masks which they wear to play their sorry roles conceal the feelings of inferiority and of insecurity and the frustrations that haunt their inner lives. Despite their attempt to escape from real identification with the masses of Negroes, they cannot escape the mark of oppression any more than their less favored kinsmen. In attempting to escape identification with the black masses, they have developed a self-hatred that reveals itself in their depreciation of the physical and social characteristics of Negroes. Likewise, their feelings of inferiority and insecurity are revealed in their pathological struggle for status within the white world.[19]

Abram Hill's attempt to dramatize this class is only superficially convincing. The playwright dealt in comic strip characters and found himself putting masks over masks, caricaturing caricatures.

The entire action of the play takes place in the expensively and, we are told, discriminatingly furnished drawing room of the Van Strivens' home. Sophie, the Van Strivens' disrespectful maid, opens the play with comments on the newspaper she is reading. Mrs. Van Striven, or Dolly, comments on Negro newspapers and sets the tone for the play's comedy.

DOLLY: *Will you get rid of that awful Black Dispatch? Read a newspaper if you must, but that thing—*
SOPHIE: *Good 'nough for me. They got a powerful headline this week.*
DOLLY: *Powerful headline, give it here* (Reads) *"Three in Bed Causes Divorce"? t-s-s-s-sk!*
SOPHIE: (Casually) *They shouldah made it a foursome.*

Preparations are under way for Cobina Van Striven's debut. Mentioning neighbors who are not invited to the party, Dolly calls them "common nookies—an envious bunch of hoodlums. . . . The ones who always throw gin parties. Noise, the odor of chitterlings, whooie!" It is obvious that all things associated with Negroes (just as they are in prejudiced white minds) are ridiculed by the striving Van Strivens. But for all that they would dissociate themselves from Negroes of the lower class, these social climbers are constantly reminded that they are not white. Dolly and her friend Mrs. Petunia, Brooklyn "socialite," discuss servants:

DOLLY: *Something jumps out of gear when they have to serve us.*
PETUNIA: *Long as there is one ounce of vitamin I, in your face, they will insult us.*
DOLLY: *Vitamin I?*
PETUNIA: (Touching her face) *Ink, Dolly, ink!*

Education is held in great esteem by the Van Strivens. Cobina is home on vacation from Radcliffe, and a frequent house-guest is Professor Hennypest, who has degrees from Northwestern and the University of Pennsylvania. We are told that he is "quite an intellectual," but we have no way of knowing it from his dialogue. Cobina herself sounds scarcely human, which may be a comment in itself. The reluctant debutante cries out:

I am sad. I'm unhappy. I want to go to bed—Forget this debut business. Society, stuffed shirts and brilliant idiots. All spreading gossip like typhoid. I came home to enjoy my birthday. I don't want to be mulled, malled [sic], and stuck up at the head of a

*line for someone to make the highest bid. What are they going
to bid, anyway, N.Y.A. and W.P.A. checks?*[20]

Almost the entire first act is a recitation of black bourgeoisie
strivings, prejudices, and social cant. The tone is so light that a
Negro audience is invited to laugh easily at the foolish behavior
of these people who seem to have convinced themselves that they
belong to a very special "society." Frazier put it this way: " 'Society'
is a phase of the world of make-believe which represents in an
acute form the Negro's long preoccupation with 'social life' as
an escape from his subordinate status in America."[21] The Negro
press is filled with accounts of debutante parties and other mani-
festations of what Frazier calls the "carnival spirits" of Negro
"society." There will be a debut, whether Cobina wants it or not,
and by the end of the act it appears that the debut may be
something other than a calm and dignified affair.

Oscar Van Striven, Dolly's husband, comes home with the announcement that he has invited Ruby Jackson, a sweepstake
winner, to the party. He is selling Ruby some property in Jamaica,
Long Island (undesirable lots near the dumps), where she plans
to build a twelve-room house complete with tennis court and
swimming pool. She wants to join the "inner circle," and Oscar
has invited her to Cobina's debut for that purpose. Dolly swoons
at the very idea of "a plain, common, shabby cook" entering her
drawing room. There is no way out of the situation, however,
since the real estate deal hinges on Ruby's being invited to the
party. In reaction to Dolly's melodramatic announcement that
"one moment of unwise benevolence can tear down a life time
of prominence," Oscar turns on her for excessive spending. His
fulminations bring down the curtain on Act I.

Act II, in two scenes, is the debut itself. Dolly's snobbish, light-
skinned mother, Mrs. Pace, supervises the arrangements. Her
speeches come the closest of any in the play to being intelligent
observations, though they are as riddled with peculiar slang as
the others. (Most of the characters in the play use the same

brand of slang, which is surely a fault in dramatic diction.) Here
she is on the subject of eligible young men:

> In Boston they say—"Has he manners?"—In Philadelphia,
> "Who's his family?" In Chicago, "So what?"—In Atlanta,
> "What school did he finish?" In Brooklyn, they say, "How much
> money has he got?"—And New York—A big scarecrow, they
> say, "Let's take the sucker!"

When she is told of Negroes who succeed in "passing" downtown,
she remarks quietly, "You can't escape God and Africa."

With the entrance of Ruby Jackson and her friend Beulah, we
are treated to cartoons of lower-class Negro women suddenly
thrust into "society." They are familiar types, from movies especially—overdressed, swaggering, covered with feathers, speaking
ridiculous dialect, and always talking out of turn. They are well
matched with Beulah's boyfriend Joe, who is dressed in a zoot suit,
complete with pegged pants and high suspenders.

The Van Strivens' party features wild dances, quarrels and
schemes, a little love interest, a lot of laughs. Joe has been hired
by Petunia to ruin the party. The act ends in a full-scale brawl as
the guests take sides, Brooklyn against Harlem.

The air has cleared by Act III. The guests who are left include
an actress named Lily and the newly rich Ruby Jackson. Lily is
given the opportunity to take a crack at the Federal Theatre, commenting on "The Merchant of Venice in Jamaica" and doing a
burlesque of a speech from "the Swing version of 'Romeo' . . . laid
in Africa." Ruby, left alone with Dolly and her mother after Lily's
theatrical exit, accuses them of being snobs. Mrs. Pace, who seems
to be well acquainted with the writings of Oscar Wilde, answers
the accusation:

> She's a snob. I am a snob. Well, who isn't? Snobbery is a
> universal failing—or maybe it's a virtue. . . . And it isn't peculiar
> to our smart set, either—My dear, to live is to pose, and we all
> pose a little, we are all snobs. . . . We all stand in our little show-

cases charging the world admission to look over our own good points. . . . You are a snob of humility and modesty. Now, don't get me wrong. This snobbishness is a good thing—either in society, literature, or everyday life. It is a consciousness of one's difference, a decent self-respect, a healthy form of egotism.

Ruby is not convinced. She argues that "we all is pretty much the same brand." She will not be put off by their contention that she is "trying to jump at least a hundred years over night." When Dolly and Mrs. Pace make it clear that they will neither accept her nor try to understand her, Ruby has the only serious speech in the play:

I—get you—My mistake! I have stood over a hot greasy stove, rolling out biscuits, peeling onions 'til my eyes turned red. I never want to see another roasting pot! Have you ever had hot grease pop on you on a sizzling morning in August?—And home —to sit out on a stinking stoop with a pile of cussin' sickly men, lousing around like lizards in a pile of rotten logs!

Other characters break in, subplots are unraveled, and no one answers Ruby or even acknowledges her outburst. When, at the end of the play, Dolly and Mrs. Pace accept her, it is for no apparent reason. Mrs. Pace simply says, "We might as well finish this charitable deed," and invites Ruby to spend the night. The ending is happy if weak, resolved for the moment but left hanging in terms of both the play's construction and the various problems hinted at but never really faced.

Perhaps the most perceptive review of On Strivers Row was written by Louis Kronenberger when the play was revived in 1946:

This is a satire on Harlem's snobs and social climbers, and healthy proof that Harlem can laugh at itself. . . . Mr. Hill works on two levels: comic-strip burlesque and fairly harsh satire. He uses laughing gas on his uppity folk when they strike fancy attitudes, and on the more boisterous guests when they get too *happy or plastered. But he also squirts poison on the crueler aspects of snobbery, on an upper-class psychology that can be insolent and inhumane.*

The critic went on to say that the two varieties of satire do not mix well. His contention was that the play should provide "either the good-humored exuberance of a spoof, or the sobriety of real criticism."[22]

It would not be an easy task to do what Kronenberger asks, partly for reasons suggested by Frazier in a chapter entitled "Behind the Masks":

Despite the tinsel, glitter and gaiety of the world of make-believe in which middle-class Negroes take refuge, they are still beset by feelings of insecurity, frustration and guilt. As a consequence, the free and easy life which they appear to lead is a mask for their unhappy existence.[23]

Abram Hill stripped off some of the tinsel and allowed Ruby to disturb the world of make-believe with her presence and with one realistic speech, but he was not the playwright to go beyond these gestures. With Sterling Brown, we are still waiting for a "realist of vision" in the theatre to write a good play about the Negro middle class.

Natural Man

Beyond the fact that he wrote for the Federal Theatre and was briefly a member of the Negro Playwrights Company, very little is known about Theodore Browne, the author of *Natural Man.* He wrote this play originally for the Federal Theatre Negro unit in Seattle, Washington, where it ran for nearly a month in 1937. for that unit he also wrote a play entitled *Go Down Moses* and an African adaptation of *Lysistrata.*[24] *Natural Man* was listed in the thirties as a "full-length Negro opera,"[25] but by the time it reached New York in 1941 there was not enough music in it for it to be called an opera or even a play with music. Producers as well as critics described it simply as a folk drama based on the legend of John Henry.

Natural Man was the second production of the American Negro Theatre. According to Frederick O'Neal, it was "the best and most significant play" of those presented by the group. It opened on May 7, 1941, and was the first American Negro Theatre production to be reviewed by the daily press. Though the notices were good, the production was forced to close during the hot summer months. O'Neal explains further that "it was our intention to revive this show in the fall of the year (1941), but practically all of the man power was drained off for war services and we were never quite able to reassemble it."[26]

John Henry is one of the great subjects of Negro folklore. Although he lost his battle against machinery, pitting his steel-driving hammer against the steam drill, John Henry has become a symbol of indomitable human pride and an expression of the Negro's will to survive against seemingly impossible odds. In Theodore Browne's dramatic version of the legend, when the untamed natural man is in conflict with machine civilization, the Negro both wins and loses the battle. John Henry dies gloriously, having taken a stand not only against machinery but against a society that cares more for machines than for men.

The play is in nine episodes, the first two and the last in the present, the rest in flashbacks that define the man. In a sense, the legendary battle is a framework for the story of a vital man in a society that curbs his vitality because he is a Negro. Present action takes place before the entrance to the Big Ben Tunnel in West Virginia. At intervals during the opening scene the figure of John Henry using his hammer on the steel is silhouetted just inside the tunnel. The script indicates that he is singing, probably a work song, the kind that is punctuated by the rhythmic blows of his hammer.

The crew of Negro steel drivers is talking about a contest tomorrow in which John Henry is to stand up against a machine designed to drive steel better than men have been doing in the past. The betting is five to one on John Henry, with the white folks doing most of the betting. The Negroes are proud of their friend John Henry. Only one, Luther, is at all doubtful:

LUTHER: *How's any meat-man going whip something run by steam?*
HARD TACK: *Alright, you put your money where your mouth is!*
LUTHER: *White man smart. He sits up all night long, figuring out a way to put us all right back in slavery.*

The white boss, Captain Tommy, gives the men the afternoon off to celebrate the contest. When he says, "And see to it that you behave yourselves. Don't get mixed up in any shooting or cutting scrapes," he is the patronizing white man who has to take care of his charges. Not only does he affect a paternal air, he also assumes a pride in John Henry, promising to buy him a suit of clothes "as good as anything I wear myself" if he beats the machine. The first scene ends on an optimistic note with the Captain's blessing and John Henry's bragging:

Tomorrow at sunrise,
I'm going to be a natural man.
Tomorrow at sunrise,
I'm going to be a natural man.
Going to take that hammer, drive that
Steel the fastest in the land.

Scene two takes place before 4 A.M. the morning of the contest, which is scheduled to last from sunrise to sunset. Talking to the salesman whose steam drill is pitted against John Henry, the Captain boasts that his steel drivers are hand-picked:

I do the hiring and firing around here. I get most of them off the chain-gang. Pay their fines and then give them a chance to work it out. Some of them boys were up for life. . . . Yep, John Henry. Most valuable nigger I got. Wanted in Georgia for killing a white man. Was on the chain-gang. Killed one of the guards, then made a get away.

In view of the hold that he has over John Henry, the Captain puts pressure on him to win. He will see that the authorities find John Henry if he loses, but if he wins, the Captain will "fix it" with the Governor.

Even more revealing of the Captain's mentality is this speech about his preference for hand-labor over steam drills:

> With hand-labor, you play safe. You work 'em as long as you need 'em. Speed 'em up when it's necessary. Hire as many as you like when times are good. When things get bad, you can let as many go as you like, and nothing's lost. Play safe is my motto. I'll take cheap black-labor any day!

John Henry knows that he must win his battle with the machine or he will be returned to the white man's "justice." It does not matter that he killed a white man to avenge a Negro friend killed by the chain-gang boss.

Now the flashbacks, each symbolic of a problem faced by the Negro, begin. In a chain gang in Georgia the convicts sing their threats against the white boss and their longing for freedom. One commentator wrote this about work songs and their place in American music, so much of which when original has the Negro people as its central inspiration:

> They [work songs] embody not only the rhythmic swing of a hammer or axe, and the need to pool collective strength, but also an assertion of individual pride and defiance. . . . Whatever the words may say, the music says that a human being refuses to be broken, that he demands an unassailable respect just because he is a human being.[27]

After John Henry has listened to the other workers expressing their desire to be free, to destroy "every cracker down south," he bursts forth with this proclamation:

> Black man's easy to get along with, long as white folks'll treat him human. He do his work and never squawk. . . . Cause he talks back and stands up for his rights, white man don't like that.

Calls him a bad nigger. Nigger'll work his head off to please a white man. Try to be his friend, but Mister Charlie ain't going to let him. . . . Ain't going be no door-mat for white man to wipe his foot on.

In a mood of provoked defiance John Henry kills the white boss who has tried to flog the corpse of a Negro worker whose only crime was that he dropped dead of fatigue.

John Henry escapes, moving from place to place, scene to scene, trying to find refuge. At a camp meeting a terrified preacher says that he and his congregation cannot help a convict because the white folks would kill them all. He asks John Henry to go back to the chain gang to be judged first by the law of men and then by the law of God. John Henry runs away to be a natural man, to get some joy out of life.

On Beale Street in Memphis he meets the Negro underworld. A drunken streetwalker tries to console him, but he talks of nothing but his hammer. (The scene is the occasion for a trio of streetwalkers to sing "Love for Sale on Beale Street.") Even here in the underworld John Henry is rejected when it is discovered that he is the killer of a white man.

At a hobo camp white men do give him food, and John Henry moves northward in hope of using his hammer on steel again. Up North he is a "scab," accused by white men of stealing their jobs. The workers warn him:

FIRST: *We white workers can't get a living wage scale, for you goddamned niggers!*
JOHN HENRY: *Colored folks entitled to live same as you whites.*
SECOND: *They ain't entitled to buck no union.*
JOHN HENRY: *We ain't aiming to buck no union.*
FIRST: *No, you ain't! Not much!*
JOHN HENRY: *We just doing what we got a right to do—work. If you white folks had awanted us in your union, you'd asked us.*
FIRST: *We don't allow any niggers in our union.*

They tell him that he should go back down South "where niggers belong." If he stays in the North he had better be prepared to black boots or swing a mop. John Henry, the proud natural man, answers, "I ain't never black nobody's boots, ain't never swing nobody's mop, and you and nobody else's going to tell me what to do."

There is a fight, and John Henry lands in jail. Scene eight, in a Northern jail, is probably the most striking scene in the play. Voices of white "jailbirds" are heard taunting John Henry, the only man visible in the scene. They shout at him all the accusations and insinuations that white men have been calling out to Negroes whenever and wherever there was fear of losing jobs or status to these black men. There are the usual references to violence, gambling, and sex. When John Henry says that he is innocent, that he was minding his own business, the prisoners shout:

You hear that Fellows? He was minding his own business! (Laughter) How deep did you cut that guy? He didn't aim to cut him. His razor slipped! Did you leave your trademark on him, Boy? What did he do, pull some loaded dice on you? Maybe he caught him in bed with his gal! (Loud, side-splitting laughter)

John Henry, taking on a special magnificence under the sting of these tawdry accusations, gives his opinion of the white man's world in which, he has discovered, a Negro is forced to live:

White man's country. White man's world. Big Mister Great-I-Am! Makes all the high and the mighty laws and rules. Change everything to suit hisself. Black man got to bow and scrape to him, like he was some God Amighty hisself. Black man got to go to him with his hat in his hand and ask for the right to live and breathe, sleep, and eat, sweat and slave! . . . Even down when it comes to thinking. . . . Nothing he say or do what white man ain't got something to say about it.

The white prisoners amuse themselves at John Henry's expense and even allow themselves to wonder what it is like to be a "nigger." John Henry stands before the bars, faces the audience, and tries to answer, to say how he feels:

> Like a giant in a straight jacket! . . . Like a great king without a throne to sit on! . . . You tallow-faced sissies might be sitting on the throne, but that don't make you king cause you set there. Nossir! I built that throne. Built roads so you could travel from place to place. And I ain't asking you all to thank me for what I do. I ain't asking you to be my friend. Ain't wishing to eat at the same table with you. . . . All I ask is that you let me be.

The other prisoners answer with booing and hissing, which fades into the cheering of the spectators at the contest of the future-present of the play's last scene.

There is a robot on the landing, a "full-sized mechanical man." John Henry, weary to the point of utter exhaustion, wrestles with it. He throws the mechanical creature into the blackness of the tunnel, then staggers and falls from the landing to the floor. John Henry dies in his wife's arms. The robot can be heard, the steam drill at work in the tunnel. John Henry has put up a brave if losing battle with the machine.

Critics offered several interpretations of the play. Louis Kronenberger claimed that because "John Henry will recognize no laws but those of his own swaggering strength . . . he heads into a pack of trouble."[28] Kronenberger's guess was that the author of *Natural Man* was saying that the Negro cannot find his salvation through blind force. John Mason Brown came to much the same conclusion, commenting on John Henry's dying of his "own lack of discipline when the very rocks catch fire from the force of his hammer blows."[29] Not surprisingly, the *Daily Worker* critic wrote:

> From a thematic point of view, "Natural Man" speaks stirringly against outrageous Negro oppression and exploitation. Here the relationship between cheap slave labor, recruited from

prison camps, and the profit system is clearly shown. The rebellion against the machine becomes the Negro's outlet for his bitter anger.[30]

This critic did worry about the hatred of all white men expressed in the prison-cell scene but took hope from the scene in which white hobos offered John Henry a helping hand.

Brooks Atkinson felt that the American Negro Theatre deserved a better script, not just a scenario but a fully developed play.[31] In view of what the actors apparently did with this scenario (all the critics praised the production as a theatre piece), one questions the need for a fuller script. *Natural Man* is, after all, a kind of crude allegory, and the actors could fill in the spaces with expressions of their own frustrations as Negroes in America. For the theatre this sketchy script was sufficient; to survive as dramatic literature it would have had to be something more.

TOWARD BROADWAY: THEODORE WARD

Big White Fog

Big White Fog is a play about "a decade in the historical development of the Negro," the years between 1922 and 1932. For Theodore Ward this decade did not mean the Negro Renaissance, literary parties, or high living. Born in Thibodaux, Louisiana, in 1908, the eighth child of a mother who died giving birth to her eleventh, he was on his own by the age of thirteen, working at a variety of jobs that led him northward to St. Louis, Chicago, and other big cities where he barely made a living, usually as a bootblack. Here and there he went to school. He read all the time and indiscriminately. At home he had been exposed to his father's collection of books, "religious, practical, and classical works" that his father sold, along with patent medicines, from the back of his gig. "We had," Theodore Ward remembers, "the limited library of a religious family."[32]

For two years Ward studied at the University of Wisconsin,

winning the Zona Gale Fellowship in Creative Writing both years. He remembers that, when he wrote a play for one of his courses, it called to mind that his religious father had thrown his first play into the fire—"the work of the devil." When he left the University of Wisconsin, it was to go to Chicago, where he joined a John Reed Club, saw agitprop plays, and "got so mad I lined up a play to give them some material." A one-act play called *Sick and Tired* (or *Sick and Tiahd*) was the result. It won second prize in a contest sponsored by the labor movement. For the first time Theodore Ward thought that maybe he could write.

For a while he was a recreational director at Abraham Lincoln Center on Chicago's South Side. He joined the Federal Theatre unit in Chicago, and in 1938 his *Big White Fog* was produced there. Hallie Flanagan herself, according to Ward, led the fight to do this play, which many in the unit opposed because of the revolutionary tenor of its denouement and the bad publicity which it might cause. The play was radical in the same way that Clifford Odets' early plays were: it stated problems for two and a half acts and then proposed revolution as a solution. The newspapers, however, did not attack the Chicago production, and Ward insists that "American audiences did respond to an honest attempt to deal with Negro life." The play ran for ten weeks in Chicago and made money, though its author feels to this day that it was not adequately publicized by the Federal Theatre.

When the Federal Theatre came to an end, Theodore Ward was in the chorus of *The Swing Mikado* that had been sent from Chicago to New York. He stayed on in New York to become one of the founders of the Negro Playwrights Company. Here, among other things, was a chance to do *Big White Fog* for a Harlem audience.

Big White Fog is a three-act propaganda play about a Negro family living in Chicago in the twenties. The play's protagonist is Victor Mason, a Garveyite leader who sparks the play's activity, gives it form, states its problems. His speeches are made to bear the burden of a defense of Marcus Garvey. His earnestness in stating his position ensures interest in the arguments of the play even when the dialogue departs from everyday speech and moves into the realm of rhetoric.

Act I of *Big White Fog* is in two scenes and takes place during the summer of 1922. The setting, which remains the same in all three acts, is a "large, congenial room suggesting the fact that the house is one of those . . . which were vacated by better class whites, following the invasion of the district by Negroes during the period of the great migration and the World War."

From the beginning, family discussions revolve around "Marcus Garvey's jive," as Victor's disapproving sister-in-law calls the Back-to-Africa Movement. Victor has been asked to buy shares in the Black Star Line, but his interest in doing so is strongly opposed by his wife Ella, his brother Dan, and his mother-in-law, Mother Brooks. The last is the only representative of an older generation. She exclaims, in the single instance of Negro dialect in the play:

> Don't you mention no Affiki to me! I ain't no Affikin, I'm a Dupree! I was born in this country and I'm goin die in it, Vic or no Vic. . . . I done let that black crank root me up once with his fool talk about findin' freedom and happiness in the North. But he ain't goin suade me again. I'se too old for another transplantin'.

Dan, who works on the railroad, tells of meeting a Garveyite who calls himself "Duke of the Niger." To Dan it seemed that the Negro was playing right into the hands of white men.

VIC: *How do you mean?*
DAN: (Warmly) *By telling them just what they want to hear, that's what—Advocating segregation!*
VIC: (Defensively) *You don't understand the new spirit, Dan. We're out to wrest our heritage from the enemy.*
DAN: (Challengingly) *What our?—My heritage is here in America!*
VIC: (Quietly) *What?—a lynchrope? . . .*

DAN: (Heatedly) *Like hell. If those chumps down South haven't got sense enough to get out from under Mr. George, they ought to be strung up.*

VIC: (Reprovingly) *You talk like an imbecile, Dan, instead of an educated man.*

This kind of spirited dialogue that sounds like everyday speech is rare in the play. More common is the sort of poetic outburst that occurs when Victor supports his daughter Wanda's decision to leave school. After all, she is only learning "white folks' lies" and nothing about her own people.

Wanda's just reached the point where she sees what a girl her color is up against in this country! . . . We'll soon be out of this rut and on our way to Africa. Africa! I can see her now, like a mother weeping for her long lost children, calling us back to return into our own. . . . You're going to see the black man come out of the darkness of failure into the light of achievement, wearing the cloak of human greatness on his shoulders.

As the play continues, Les, the Masons' eldest child, learns that he will not receive a scholarship to college because, though he qualifies in every other way, the scholarship committee has discovered that he is a Negro. Victor's bitterness at this news helps him to decide to buy 1500 shares of the Black Star Line at a dollar a share. The act ends on this note:

LES: *Seems like the world ain't nothing but a big white fog and we can't see no light nowhere!*

VIC: (Fervidly) *Look to the East, Son, and keep on looking! Beyond the darkness and mist that surrounds us here, Africa, the sun of our hope, is rising!*

Though the quality of the play's language shifts back and forth from banal to ecstatic, the plot is clear enough and the characterizations sufficiently developed. By the end of the first act Victor Mason, a strong-willed Negro who wants an answer to insults received by himself and his children, thinks that he has found one in Garveyism.

Act II, scene one, a year later, opens on Victor Mason, still enthusiastic, rehearsing a paper he is going to deliver in New York. It is entitled "The Outlook for Cooperative Farming in Africa." One sentence from it will suggest the kind of speech it is:

> For just as the gigantic Pyramids of Egypt stand in eternal witness to our black forefathers' hands, so shall the New Africa, which shall have builded through this means, stand before the generations of tomorrow in final testimony to the black man's wisdom.

Marcus Garvey's own words had a similar sound: "Let the world know that 400,000,000 Negroes are determined to die for their liberty and that if we must die, we shall die nobly, we shall die gallantly, fighting up the battle heights of Africa to plant there the standard which represents liberty."[33]

The news that Marcus Garvey has been convicted of fraud does not sour Victor's optimism. He thinks that the white men who are running the country are trying to discredit a great Negro. He quarrels with his brother Dan, who has learned how to outwit white men on their terms and—what is more disgraceful in Victor's eyes—how to "bleed" his Negro tenants to pay for his $4,000 Cadillac.

The next scene, four months later, finds Victor out of work, the two little children sick, Wanda supporting the family. Victor has to ask Les to drop out of college for a quarter, but "by spring I know I'll be back on the job." His stubborn pride, however, will not allow Victor to sell his stock in the Black Star Line, at a loss, to his brother. His wife's bitterness grows as she urges him to sell the stock.

A turning point comes when a young Jewish student visits Les and tells him about socialism. He brings word from his professor that the best solution for all minority groups is to band together for justice and security.

> *Think of it Les—Security! It's what the whole world wants—*
> *Your people, my people—Freedom or security, it's all the same.*
> *It's what all the poor desire. Your father hasn't been able to*
> *find it here, so he wants to go to Africa. My Grandfather*
> *couldn't find it in the old country, so, like ten millions of others,*
> *he emigrated to America. But what good came of it? Why*
> *haven't they got together?*

His answer is an alternative to Marcus Garvey's answer.

Victor Mason, however, confronted with this sort of revolutionary proposal from his son, clings to the hope of the Back-to-Africa
Movement. Victor has been named "Lord of Agriculture," an office which permits him to wear a red, green, and black sash. He
persists in proclaiming the black man's place in the sun as "a
free man, honored and respected in the eyes of Nations of the
world." He is not ready, at this point, to cooperate with any white
men to achieve a social revolution.

The third scene of Act II is filled with acrimony, some of it
so strong as to seem an exaggeration—until we remember the frustrations that prompt it. Mother Brooks is dressing a black doll for
the Masons' two younger children. The grandmother shows her
impatience with, then her hatred of, "this black thing," symbol
of Victor's blackness and the whole Back-to-Africa Movement.

Later Victor overhears his mother-in-law refer to him as "dat
evil, good-for-nothing, black fool." (In the typescript the word
"Nigger" is crossed out and "fool" penciled in.) In the ensuing
argument he shouts at the lighter woman that she envies him his
black skin. He resents what he calls her dishonest attitude:

> *She's got nothing against me, and she knows it. But she's like a*
> *lot of others who let the color of their skin drive them to think*
> *black people are some kind of dirt beneath their feet, when*
> *nothing could be more idiotic than the pride they take in the*
> *blood of their raping ancestors!*

The family argument builds to a climax when Ella lets her
husband know that she is tired of his idealism and the poverty

that has engulfed them. She will stay only in order to be with
her children, but she is through with Victor. She hopes that he
will go to Africa. "Maybe you'll find the company of your own
kind in the jungles," she calls to him as she leaves the room.
Left alone, Victor says, "Prejudice . . . everywhere you turn . . .
nothing but prejudice. A black man can't even get away from
it in his own house."

The nature of this kind of domestic quarrel among Negroes
may come as a surprise to some. It would not have startled
Wallace Thurman, who wrote: "You can't blame light Negroes
for being prejudiced against dark ones. . . . White is the symbol
of everything pure and good, whether that everything be concrete or abstract."[34] Victor Mason's stand against his mother-in-
law is a good example of the counteracting chauvinism and pride
in blackness preached by Marcus Garvey. It is significant that all
the Garveyites who appear in the play are described as black men,
but brother Dan, who cheats and steals from his brothers, is a
mulatto.

By Act III it is 1932, and the Masons are about to be evicted.
A Jewish used-furniture dealer does not offer enough money for
their furniture, and Wanda calls him a disgrace to his race. When
Uncle Dan adds that it is "no more than you can expect from a
Jew," Les reminds him that white men speak that way about
Negroes. The boy is accused of having communistic ideas when
he says that Jews have contributed more to civilization than most
people have. "It didn't take the Communists to find that out," he
replies. "The whole world's been aware of it ever since the coming
of Christ."

In the final scenes Les comes forward with the Communist
answer. He and his friends are planning a protest march on the
state capitol. He urges his father to resist eviction. In one speech
he predicts that "the disinherited will never come to power without bloodshed!"

When Victor Mason is confronted with the news that his
daughter has been prostituting herself with a white man and has

been caught in a raid—"You had to have the money, Mama. What else could I do?"—he is moved to ask the Reds for help in resisting eviction. When he stands up to the police, voices off-stage are singing, "Mine eyes have seen the glory. . . ." The police warn him, "We're not going to stand for no more of this Red interference." Vic is brought down by their guns, as Les says, "Shot in the back." Ella falls on Vic's lifeless form, but only after Les has reminded everyone that his comrades are a light in the big white fog—"my comrades, Papa . . . they're black and white."

Richard Lockridge once said of Clifford Odets that he could not see how things are because he was so sure how they ought to be; that his characters were more a product of revelation than of observation.[35] The same might be said of Theodore Ward. No one can deny that all the problems dealt with in the play were present in reality, that Negroes gained and lost hope with Marcus Garvey, that young people became cynical and/or radical in the face of economic and educational frustrations, that the Depression hit the Negroes early, that feuding among themselves grew out of the various bitter disappointments they faced. It would seem that Theodore Ward put every problem he had ever witnessed or thought about into his play in an attempt to "express man's economic, social everyday life." Perhaps the flavor of the play was, as a result, too bitter and the propaganda too blatantly expressed for it ever to be popular.

Today Theodore Ward admits that his play did not reach Harlem audiences as he had hoped it would. According to the *Daily Worker*, 24,000 white New Yorkers and only 1,500 Negroes saw *Big White Fog*.[36] The playwright says in retrospect, "We thought that the Negro audience was ready for the theatre in 1940, but the group needed a larger sense of understanding."[37] *Big White Fog* remains a good example of a bold play in the politically conscious genre by a Negro who made no concessions to the white man's theatre tastes, but whose revolutionary solution was either too strong or too dated for many members of his audience, white or black.

Our Lan'

When asked how he came to write the historical play *Our Lan'*, Theodore Ward answered that he wanted to find out "how far back in American history there was the clearest expression of the Negro's comprehension of what was necessary for his own salvation." His reading of Negro history led him to the Reconstruction era, a period of hope and betrayal when the Negroes, "emerging from slavery, grasped the reality of their time; they sharply understood the political and social situation."[38]

Ward wanted to write about their courage in the face of betrayal, a worthy subject for heroic drama, especially if at the center of the story is a man of heroic stature. Joshuah Tain is that man in *Our Lan'*. One critic wrote of him: "Negative and destructive characters abound in literature but convincing 'good' or 'positive' characters are rare. We get one in Joshuah Tain, the blacksmith who leads the farmers in *Our Lan'*."[39]

In 1941 Ward had tried to get an early version of *Our Lan'* produced in Chicago. He organized a company, found a theatre, but could not persuade the manager to move an air conditioner off the stage.[40] In 1942 he offered his services to the Writers' War Board in Washington, D.C. He had an idea for a play about Frederick Douglass which might have helped the morale of Negro troops. The Board found it too serious. He went from shining shoes in Chicago to inspecting motors in a war plant, where he made notes for a labor play. By 1945, Ward was with the waning Office of War Information, writing scripts for overseas broadcasts, "but Congress dumped the OWI as it has massacred the Federal Theatre," and he was again out of work.[41]

In 1945 the Theatre Guild gave Theodore Ward a scholarship, on the basis of his draft of *Our Lan'*, and membership in a playwriting seminar conducted by Kenneth Rowe. He rewrote the play in this seminar. In 1946 a week's run of the play was arranged in the 400-seat Henry Street Playhouse.

The off-Broadway production of *Our Lan'* was so successful that several producers competed for the rights to present it on Broadway. Eddie Dowling opened the play at the Royale Theatre in September for a run of five weeks. The critics were still enthusiastic, but most of them preferred the earlier simple production to the more elaborate one at the Royale. Commenting on the fact that *Our Lan'* had a respectable but not a "hit" run on Broadway, Kenneth Rowe said that it was "one of the not infrequent examples of the fact that length of run and the quality of a play do not always correspond, and that opportunity to experience a play is an occasion for individual judgment."[42]

Our Lan' is dramaturgically sound, historically accurate, and theatrically moving. To consider each of the ten scenes of this two-act drama is to become acquainted with a group of ordinary people who rise to heroic heights under the leadership of Joshuah Tain. The characters are sufficiently individualized, especially Joshuah and Delphine, to invite the audience to understand Negroes as persons worthy of attention, sympathy, and admiration.

The opening scene takes place in a cave on the road to Savannah in January, 1865. Three ragged Negroes named Edgar, Emanuel, and Peltier, in their twenties and early thirties, are gathered around a campfire, waiting for sweet potatoes to bake. They are freedmen with their former bondage very much on their minds. Emanuel says to Edgar, "If it wasn't fer de Yanks, whar'd yuh be?—Still in de Quarters, duckin n' dodgin ole Marster!"[43] Even though they are cold and hungry, they are glad to be free. When an older couple joins them and Edgar calls the woman "Anty," he soon learns that she knows her new station.

WOMAN: *Now hold on, Sonny!* (Brushing by him, she turns and admonishes him sharply) *If yuh want t' git along wid me, don't call me "anty"!*

MAN: (Meanwhile—Placatingly) *Now, Patsy; de boy didn't mean no harm.*

PATSY: (Emphatically) *It's time these youngsters learn we're free* (Parentally, turning to EDGAR) *Ah's titled t' a handle on mah name, Sonny—Ahm Miz Patsy Ross, 'n thas mah husband, Mister Joseph Ross.*
ROSS: *Jes call me "Uncle."*

Patsy realizes that a name is a label, and she wants hers to say who she is personally. Her husband is content to be an "uncle."

Throughout the scene other freedmen arrive at the cave, their homely activities and conversations characterizing them and their situation. They are all engaging, this group of freedmen, some sure and others doubtful about their future. They tell each other stark tales about children sold to traders by their masters and weep together; just when they need release from sadness and a sign for the future, they hear voices singing in the distance. The approaching group sings of going to "Heabem," and a scout reports back the news that "Gen'l Sherman given everybody lan!" The whole company of freedmen is ready to go then.

Before following the joyful singing into the next scene, it might be well to remind ourselves of the historical reality of freedmen at this time. The Thirteenth Amendment had been approved early in 1865 and was in process of ratification during the remainder of the year; it went into effect on December 18, 1865. Even before approximately four million slaves had been officially freed, a tenth as many had been either manumitted or born free. Only a few of these freedmen had either property or education. They knew only the ways and the orders of plantation life; they marched into freedom wearing their possessions, the rags on their backs. Former masters gave some of them temporary support, and Freedmen's Aid Societies helped others. These societies, many of them affiliated with Northern churches, were private, voluntary organizations. The greatest numbers of ex-slaves were cared for by agents of the Bureau of Freedmen, Refugees, and Abandoned Lands—commonly called the Freedmen's Bureau. This agency of the War Department was created by Congress near the end of the war (March 3, 1865).[44]

At the center of Theodore Ward's play is the problem that confronted the victorious Union in 1865: what to do with the ex-slaves who had been set free in a society that was ill prepared to redefine their status. It seems obvious that relief for these people had to come before reconstruction could take place in the South. General Sherman's offer of forty acres of land for each freedman was one attempt at relief;[45] it sparks the initial activity of Ward's play.

Arriving at their destination, an island off the coast of Georgia, the freedmen rejoice in their "lan' of Canaan," choosing, at first, to overlook signs of disuse and decay. "Remnants of old farm equipment, an overturned anvil, and several tufts of weeds are scattered like dumb witnesses remarking the vanished prosperity of this former slave kingdom in the sea." But even broken things are beautiful in sunlight, and the freedmen arrive on a dazzling day. This light in contrast to the play's dark opening surely suggests hope, belief in the future. If further symbolism is needed, there are laughing, shouting, dancing men and women. Young children dart in and out as the newcomers proclaim their possession of the land.

Joshuah, earlier only a baritone voice in the distance, is now a leader moving with assurance among the crowd. He and his band of freedmen find "a rusty-black old fellow of 70," Daddy Sykes, still living on the abandoned property, waiting for his master to return from war. With him are Roxanna, a girl of 16, and her sister Delphine, "an extremely attractive brown young woman of 23." The arrival of a ragged band of Negroes who announce that they are "de new owners" comes as a shock to these trusted house servants, who have been awaiting word from a master who always prescribed their fate. Daddy Sykes's first reaction introduces a note of foreboding when he says, "Ole Marster ain't goin like this!" The women are young enough to be intrigued by the new turn of events. Delphine soon identifies with the new owners but maintains an initially suitable reserve.

Even though Joshuah refuses to accept the honor of being

"Gubner," stating his preference for work with his hands, there is no doubt that he is the group's leader. Although some of the young men are in Union Army uniforms (the war is, after all, still going on, and Negroes are being conscripted), and an aristocratic mulatto, Ollie Webster, has joined the group in Savannah, it is Joshuah Tain who commands attention.

> He is an expression or symbol, if you will, of the best traits of his people. There is a sure sense of dignity about him and his very physical strength bespeaks something of the restlessness and courage which characterized the bulk of the vilified black men of the period—a people conditioned by the terrors of ruthless oppression and communicating their spirit from generation to generation; not by precept but by example—now graphic, now more or less obscure; now passive, now insurrectionary, but always passed on . . . in a word, one senses that here is a man![46]

Joshuah and Ollie meet Delphine, and both express an interest in her. Ollie, it turns out, is the son of a free man who helped persuade General Sherman to let the freedmen have land. The contrast between the styles of these two men, Joshuah and Ollie, is evident in the way they first speak to Delphine.

JOSHUAH: *Mah name's Joshuah Tain—What might be yores?*
DELPHINE: *Delphine.*
JOSHUAH (Smiling): *Delphine. Thas sure is er pretty name. But Ah reckon yuh kin wear it!*
DELPHINE (Pleased): *Ah speck t'wouldn't do t' try to spute yore word.*
JOSHUAH (Laughing): *Take a blind judge not t' back me up.*
OLLIE (Joining them): *I agree with you perfectly, Mr. Tain!*
JOSHUAH: *This is Mr. Ollie Webster—*
OLLIE (to Delphine): *Had I known you were here, I would've visited this island sooner.*

Poetry is on Joshuah's side even though he is a practical man. When the new owners of the island begin to inspect their property in earnest, they find few provisions, huts that are crawling with spiders and lizards, leaky roofs, everything in need of repair. They are soon grumbling about their promised land. When they want to move into the Big House, Joshuah reminds them gently that General Sherman gave them only the land, though he agrees to let the children stay in the house for protection until the huts are repaired. Complaints fill the air, and, after trying to present some simple encouragements, Joshuah is moved to speak sharply to his followers. His leadership is revealed in his sternness that both chastises and sustains his people:

> Now listen, everybody. There's sompen we got t' git straight right now. We didn't come heah t' have no barbecue. Jus yistiddy we had bout ez much chance ez er housefly in de winter time. But today yuh kickin. Yuh got lan. Yuh got de chance t' look forward t' yore own bale of cotton; yore own ca'iage n' span. 'N yet yuh kickin! What yuh think this is?—A lil ole measly patch of ground? This is er whole ilun!

Then he coaxes them to work for the future. It is, after all, the first time they have had a future to call their own.

Plans are made to repair the huts—Ollie's father, who owns half interest in a sawmill, will lend a steam-donkey and bandsaw— and a few go off to war while the others settle down to the work of making the island habitable. Then just as the group recovers its courage, the overseer, Saunders, returns to the island to reclaim his master's property. Described as a "wiry, leathern-faced white man of perhaps 40," he lets it be known immediately that he has no respect for the Negroes and will not acknowledge their claim to the land. He laughs at the idea of their having tickets from General Sherman to prove their ownership—"Well, ah suppose the Gen'l must have his little joke." When Joshuah says that the freedmen will receive deeds to the land after the war and that meanwhile they will raise a crop, Saunders is at first scornful, and then he offers to hire the Negroes rather than drive them off the island as he had originally intended. Joshuah's answer is irrevocable: "We ain't wukin fer no white man!" The freedmen seem determined to find a way to raise a crop on the land that they feel is rightfully theirs.

Saunders expresses succinctly the viewpoint of many defeated white Southerners when he says to the freedmen:

> *This land belongs to John Burkhardt, and there ain't a Yankee living who can turn it over t' you. Why, condfound it, there ain't a white man South of the Mason and Dixon Line who wouldn't rather be dead than live under such topsyturvy conditions. By Gawd, it's the same as makin us slaves and yuh masters. But perhaps that's what yuh want?*

Joshuah's answer is no less dramatic as an expression of the Negroes' feelings after generations of slavery: "You couldn't pay me t' be nobody's stinkin master. 'N furthermore, Ah'd advise you t' git on way from heah 'n leave us erlone." Not just two individuals have clashed here. The old and the new order have met, and the major dramatic question has been posed: Will the freedmen be able to keep their land?

At the opening of the third scene of Act I, pairs of freedmen are drawing a plough to which they have harnessed themselves by means of a long rope. Prescribed, nearly choreographed movement is indicated in the stage directions; it matches the rhythmic work song that the men sing. Here is one of many instances in the play when music sets a mood, helps to characterize, and provides shifts in the play's tempo. The previous scene closed on a song of hope, "Didn't my Lawd deliver Daniel," and during the blackout the change to "Hoe, Boy, hoe!" provides a continuity that is effective theatrically. The songs alone make it clear that the settlers are proving their ability to work the land successfully. A crop is being planted, the donkey engine has arrived, houses soon will be built. Throughout the play music bridges serve to move the action forward, toward the future, while contributing to a definition of the present.

Ollie finds Delphine alone and forces his attentions on her.

When she resists his flattery and lets him know how much faith she has in Joshuah, Ollie's response reveals his sense of superiority.

DELPHINE: *When Joshuah git through wid this island, Ah reckon yuh city ristocrats goin be wantin t' move ovah heah.*

OLLIE: *That's rich! Joshuah—Prospero disguised as a clod-hopper. He waves his magic wand, and, presto, he transforms the whole island! But, after all, you're not to be blamed. You've no way of knowing what life is like in Savannah—for people of my standing and culture—free men, who've never known what it is to call another "Master," who for generations have been educated abroad—in the best schools on the continent—as I was. Otherwise, you'd appreciate your chances and make an effort to get above this, this living like a common field hand!*

Ollie ridicules Delphine's background, praises her beauty, and soon loses her respect when he proposes that she let him set her and her sister up in an apartment in Savannah. She politely, but coolly, declines the offer.

This interlude of flirtation is in interesting contrast to the next incident, a brief but powerful one involving several of the freedmen. Here Joshuah himself, neither a Prospero nor a clodhopper, is defined further both by his words and by his actions. The men are resting after plowing. They speak of their children who, one of the men says, will never know the barefoot days that the fathers have known. The conversation then turns to talk about Daddy Sykes, the old retainer who lives off the labor of these freedmen, but who has no sense of being a part of their movement. He stopped living, it seems, when his master left him.

At this moment in the play there occurs what Kenneth Rowe describes as "a knot of emotion," one that has been well prepared for by the talk of youth and age. Lem, too young to be in the army, a boy really, begs to be excused from work, saying, "Mah shoulder's killing me." The others are resentful and Joshuah turns on him in righteous anger:

Yuh's de youngest in de gang. Yore muscles hard as er hickry jint. But from sun up t' sundown heah lately, all yuh been doin is stallin'! (Harshly) *What yuh miss is de bullwhip! Yuh's free 'n yuh got yore own patch o lan. But in yore heart yuh still ain't nothin but er trifling slave! Now if yuh want-er go, git!*

Nothing more damning than these last statements could be said by one ex-slave to another.

When Lem takes his shirt from his shoulder to reveal a flesh-less collarbone, the skin all rubbed off by his labor, Joshuah begs the boy's forgiveness and makes arrangements to take him to Savannah to get help from the army doctors there. It is a scene that shows Joshuah as a fallible human being, a man capable of losing his temper, but one also ready to apologize for a mistake. It is a scene that indicates, too, the courage of the coming generation.

Joshuah's emotional apology to Lem is cut off by the arrival of Captain Bryant and a lady. Joshuah teases the Union Army captain about a wedding, supposing the young lady to be his bride. In youthful embarrassment, the captain blurts out her identity: "This lady, Joshuah, is Miss Libeth Arbabanel, of Hartford, Connecticut, the teacher you sent for."

The excitement and awe of the freedmen in the presence of a teacher is very touching. The children cluster about her, while their parents stand respectfully by, and Joshuah welcomes Miss Libeth to the island. His greetings, expressed with humility and dignity, move her to respond with equal sincerity.

JOSHUAH: *Well, Miss Libeth . . .* (Carefully feeling his way, but with gravity) *'Low me, Mam, t' bid yuh welcome. Ah dunno jes what Ah kin say, cept'n deep down in de hearts of ebery one of us . . . there's er well of gladness 'n pride t' see yuh heah mongst us. Ah reck'n there ain't be one way to put it. Yuh's like father Abraham, de way we see yuh. He broke ouah bonds 'n sot us free. 'N yuh's come t' hep us break de chains of ignance.*

LIBETH: (*Moved*): *Mr. Tain, you make me feel very proud and very much ashamed. When I accepted your invitation, I did so thinking it was the only charitable thing a God-fearing woman could do. But you give me a new sense of responsibility. Since listening to you, I know now, I should've gone down on my knees and offered thanks for the opportunity you were giving me. . . . I shall consider it my God-given privilege to do all in my power to help you, as you've so wisely said, break the chains of ignorance.*

Captain Bryant watches this scene with obvious pleasure, and then he comments on the Negroes' progress in clearing and planting the land. He tells the group that General Sherman will be proud to hear of their activities. "To put it bluntly," he tells Joshuah and his followers, "you're going to justify your emancipation in the eyes of all!" A corporal appears with a telegram announcing the end of the war, and the scene reaches its climax when the Negroes realize that they are truly free. Some drop to their knees in grateful prayer, others shout their joy, and Joshuah begins to sing the triumphant old spiritual, "Go Down Moses." For a while he sings alone, and then the entire group joins him. The whole scene has been one of hope and faith in the future. With the war over, the land theirs, and a teacher in their midst, the freedmen are filled with confidence.

The fourth scene of Act I is, for the most part, a love scene between Joshuah and Delphine. A transition from the preceding crowd scene to one involving only two persons is provided by the schoolteacher and her pupils. A week after her arrival, Miss Libeth is discovered sitting with the children under a tree in the April sunlight, reading from Longfellow's poem "Paul Revere's Ride." She reminds them that the man who was "first to fall, . . . pierced by a British musket-ball," was Crispus Attucks, "a Negro citizen of Concord . . . the first to shed his blood for *liberty and freedom for all* in our native land." Her impromptu lesson in history over, she leads the children back to the classroom in the Big House, correcting their grammar on the way. Meeting Joshuah as she is leaving, Miss Libeth reminds him that she expects the grownups to attend class, too. He promises that "everybody'll be there tonight."

The episode is brief, but it tells a great deal about this New England "schoolmarm." Her reading of this particular poem, her insistence upon keeping to a schedule and involving young and old alike in the educational process, mark Miss Libeth as one of the missionary teachers once described by Horace Mann Bond:

> The missionary teachers from New England, fresh from the then-recent victories of Horace Mann and Henry Barnard in the battle for a free school, encouraged the freedmen in their conviction. At no time in America has there been exemplified so pathetic a faith in education as the lever of racial progress. Grown men studied their alphabets in the fields, holding the "blue-back speller" with one hand while they guided the plow with the other. Mothers tramped scores of miles to towns where they could place their children in school. Pine torches illumined the dirt-floored cabins where men, women, and children studied until far into the night.[47]

The episodic nature of Our Lan', the need to get on with a courtship more crucial to the plot than Miss Libeth's class, no doubt forced the author to leave the "schoolmarm" the least developed of all the characters in the play.

Among the most charming episodes in Our Lan' is this first love scene between Delphine and Joshuah. That they are recently freed Negroes is not what matters here. This is a universal confrontation of youth and age. Joshuah's hesitation to speak his heart to a willing Delphine confirms her early suspicion. He doubts the wisdom of a marriage between a man of his age and a young woman.

When Delphine persuades him to tell her about the home he plans to build, he describes a place of comfort, a "refuge."

Delphine's response shows her character; she stands up to him in defense of her own view of marriage.

DELPHINE: *Yore house is too gloomy.* (Earnestly) *Er house ought t' be like er wedding feast, bright 'n cheery; wid friends comin 'n goin.* (Carried away by her deepest instinct and hopes) *It ought t' have chillun, runnin everybody crazy, rompin 'n squealin from mornin till night—Don't you gree wid me?*

JOSHUAH: (Moved and smiling) *Well, Ah admit hit's er mighty pretty picture—specially de part bout de chillun.* (Sobering) *But Ah still say, first we got t' git out de rain 'n try t' stay out. Once we git set, hit'll be time nuff t' set out de jug in friendship-whole-'n-hearty—!*

Delphine might have found a way to turn this imagery to her own uses, but the two are interrupted in their playfully serious courtship by the arrival of a girl to tell Joshuah that "de pig done fell in de well." A scene that began with learning and then moved to love now ends in homely humor as Joshuah runs out to rescue the pig, and the girls laugh together at the prospect of "pork chops fer supper."

The final scene of Act I, which takes place on the evening of the day just witnessed, is introduced in the stage directions with this statement: "Prior to visibility it is clear that something in the nature of a catastrophe has struck the life of the freedmen." That something is news of the assassination of Abraham Lincoln. Between the girls' laughter at the end of the previous scene and a rich contralto voice singing at the opening of this one, "They crucified mah Lawd, 'N he never said er mumblin word," there is an ominously silent blackout.[48]

The whole crowd is singing the profoundly sorrowful spiritual when Joshuah arrives and is told of the President's death.

CROWD: *He gone, Joshuah!*
They done shot President Lincoln—
They done laid him low!
Ouah best friend gone, Joshuah. He gone!

Joshuah joins them in their mourning. Fear and bewilderment spread through the people. When Mr. Webster speaks of their need to compromise, Joshuah stands up to him, saying, "We got this lan' 'n anybody who speck t' be er leader round heah got t' fight for ouah right t' hang on t' it!" Like the biblical Joshua after the death of Moses, Joshuah Tain, after the death of Lincoln, is willing to fight to gain the Promised Land. The difference is that the "law" was on Joshua's side in the Old Testament; it is on Burkhardt's side in the nineteenth century. Joshuah will listen to no arguments from Webster or Miss Libeth, who both speak of the Negroes' need to gain political power through the ballot. Instead, he gives an eloquent speech in which he indicates that he will lead his people into war, if need be, to keep their land. Although history may seem to support Mr. Webster, Joshuah's speech is dramatically powerful, informed by suffering, and calculated to touch his own people very specially.

It's easy fer anybody t' prize somepen they ain't got. Ah remember tha bout Freedom. But votin—this much Ah know about tha. Votin ain't much. Ah's seed it all mah life, here in Gawgie 'n down in Lusana too. De man what holds de land holds de office—Look at de poor white folks. They vote. But what do they git out-er it? A gallon or two of corn likker come lection day, 'n attar tha, nothing but de same ole struggle 'n de same ole shack full of rawbone babies.—Ah sayd it once 'n Ah say it ergain; let dem what have de ears t' hear, let em hear: We got this land, 'n votin or no votin, we tend t' keep it!—We's lost Father Abraham. But we ain't going let tha discourage us. We goin moan his loss. But we goin do it in sorrow, 'n not in despair. Ah say tha cause despair 'n hope don't mix, 'n hope was de first big thing he give us. The planters might skeer some. But not us— not us, who's felt de lash, who know what tiz t' see er brother's brains dashed out, er father shot down in de middle of de field, 'n er mother hanged for liftin her hand gainst de Overseer. No! They don't skeer us, cuz we was brought up in de house of horror! (Suddenly pausing, he looks over the group and his eyes

soften and a note of tenderness marks his tone) *Now t' git back
t' Father Abraham. He's lyin up yonder in Washington. Soon,
they'll be puttin him in de cold, cold grave. . . . To some folks
thas goin be de end of him. But not t' me 'n yuh—*

With this speech Joshuah Tain is revealed as the classical tragic
protagonist possessed by a single idea, admitting to no compromise, doubtless doomed, but glorious in his determination to
make his actions suit his beliefs. The only possible response to
his words is support from his followers. It comes in the form of
"Amens" from the crowd and a spiritual led by Delphine, dedicated to the memory of Lincoln, "Steal away, steal away, Steal
away home t' Jesus." Act I ends on a sad note, with only a suggestion of the troubles these people are yet to know.

The death of Lincoln does not constitute the play's crisis, however, because the coming act does not move from this turning
point down to disaster. Instead Act II moves in waves of hope
and defeat; every advance is met by a setback as outside forces
close in on the freedmen. The crisis of *Our Lan'* occurs four fifths
of the way through the play (Act II, scene three) with the return
of the plantation's former owner, Mr. Burkhardt.

In the first scene of the second act, Ollie tries to warn Joshuah,
as his father had earlier, about Washington's attitude toward the
dispossessed planters. The island could be returned to its former
owner by a court of law. No talk of protecting the land "wid
blood" would keep a judge from awarding it to Burkhardt. But
Ollie's voice of reason is not what the freedmen want to hear.
They turn on him, spurning his caution for Joshuah's courage.
Joshuah stands silent and does not defend the well-intentioned
Ollie. The scene ends with lightning and thunder. Hurricane
winds are rising, and everyone, even Ollie, must be sheltered in
the Big House for the night.

The next scene, six weeks later on a sunny morning, is filled
with personal concerns. Although members of the community
open it, this is a scene that belongs to Joshuah and Delphine.

Joshuah discovers Delphine sitting beneath an oak, weeping softly as she sings. He can no longer restrain his emotion. He confesses his love.

Delphine's reaction is surprising in view of her earlier interest in Joshuah. She firmly refuses his proposal. She cannot marry him, she confesses, because it is too late; she is going to have Ollie's child. Delphine's account of the night of the storm suggests that Ollie took her by force, although superstition leads her to add that she was probably the victim of a love powder. Joshuah is stunned, angry, bitter toward Ollie and Delphine. But when he accuses her of being a "wanton woman," she rises to her own defense with a magnificence that reveals not only her self-respect but also her love for Joshuah. And yet, as soon as she observes that he is convinced and crushed by her arguments, Delphine softens. "On the other hand," she says, her eyes brimming with tears, "Ah still think yuh's de finest man Ah's ever known!" Then she leaves Joshuah alone, sitting "focused in pain and regret." Though the scene has shown no reversal in the fortunes of the group, the suffering reflected in the personal story of Joshuah and Delphine relates the mood of this scene to that of those still to come.

Scene three of Act II opens on success. It is October, and the freedmen have had a good harvest. All is hope and high spirits. In 1865 Elizabeth Botume wrote that "some of the finest cotton brought to market on the islands" that year was raised by a group of freedmen who "worked independent of any white superintendent."[49] She and other white observers of the period reported that the Negroes worked better and harder for themselves than they ever had for their white masters. Theodore Ward's characters, handling bales of their own cotton, discussing market prices and what they will do with the money earned, are true to history as it was reported by the Negroes' friends, especially those missionary teachers who worked on the sea islands before and during the Reconstruction era.[50]

What should be cause for excitement and an occasion for

rejoicing—the news that Congress has passed the Civil Rights Bill with the Stevens Amendment that gives the freedmen their land— is no more than an abortive announcement because the new captain from the Freedmen's Bureau brings further word of President Johnson's veto. Captain Stewart puts it this way:

> The President felt the Bill was a mistake. I'm not here to lie to you. General Howard sent me here to represent your interest. He is my superior, and the President told him to make arrangements to restore the land to its former owners. . . . I know you expected the Government to give you the land. But that is not to be. It's not my duty to question why. All I can do is tell you, if you want to remain here, you must come to an agreement with Mr. Burkhardt, the rightful owner. Those contracts in his hand were drawn up by General Howard himself to safeguard your interest. You've already shown yourselves to be wise and industrious people. . . . If you remain the same, in three years you will be privileged to purchase your own forty acres if you so desire.[51]

If the captain thought that this sort of honesty would win the freedmen's respect and cooperation, he was mistaken, Joshuah stands ready to defend the land that "we already got," and his men will stand with him. When Ollie, ignorant of Delphine's condition and unaware of Joshuah's personal enmity, seeks to advise the freedmen, Joshuah damages his position in Captain Stewart's eyes by attacking Ollie physically. Refusing to cooperate in any way with Burkhardt, Joshuah angrily proclaims, "We'll be slaves till every man can raise his own bale of cotton 'n say, 'This is mine!'" Sides are drawn. The soldiers retreat as Joshuah orders his men to hold their fire, and for a moment at least there is a relaxation of tension.

The next to the last scene of *Our Lan'* is short. Its purpose is to establish the mood of men waiting for battle, to indicate the tension that grows when nothing happens, and to suggest the desire for action in the face of unbearable suspense.

The initial activity of the play's final scene is caused by the arrival of supplies from the mainland. Later Joshuah announces that he and Delphine are "goin git married." His decision has not been an impulsive one, as we learn when he tells her of the thinking he has been doing.

JOSHUAH (Explaining): *De chile ain't mine. Thas so. But look back er ways, 'n what yuh see?*
DELPHINE: *Ah don't follow yuh.*
JOSHUAH (Gazing into the distant past): *Take yore Mammy 'n mine—'n Ah reckon pretty near everyboy else's Mammy—Ain't none of em ever had no sayso bout de father of thar chillun.* (Turning to her gently) *So whether it's er case of er high-yaller wid love powder, or ole Marster's whip, it's all de same in de end.* (Her eyes swimming in response to his humanity, she creeps into his arms. For a moment they are silent, as he strokes her hair) *Yuh feel better?* (She nods) *Den Ahm glad. Mighty glad.*

The poetry of this love scene is extraordinary. And the poignancy of these moments before battle is heightened by Joshuah's knowledge that he is asking his people to take a stand that means sacrificing the present for a distant future. When the Yankees arrive, Joshuah reminds his followers:

We ain't many. 'N it's hard t' stand yore ground when yuh know deep down in your heart de best yuh can do is serve as er lesson. Remember John Brown. Him 'n his lil handful stood up for ouah freedom 'n they sot de whole country on fiah! Git t' yore post now, 'n hold your fiah till yuh heah from me.

Captain Stewart brings Burkhardt to the island in a last-minute attempt to make a deal. Burkhardt volunteers the information that the country's "leading niggers" are opposed to the idea of confiscation. Joshuah, empowered by the freedmen to speak for them, humbles himself to the extent of asking for "jes er few acres," but Burkhardt will take nothing less than the entire island. Joshuah's answer then to those who are asking him and his men to surrender to Burkhardt's greed is one that is inspired by racial memory and filied with racial pride:

Ah see yuh ain't mean t' be fair. (Bitterly) Yuh think yuh got de ups on us. But don't let tha fool yuh. 'N don't let what happen heah today fool yuh neither. (Looking off, his eyes sharp with inner pain) Cuz neither yuh nor all de rest of de planters put together going ever kill de thing we's after. We know what's what. Yuh think if we ain't got no lan, we have t' wuk for yuh for nothin. But yuh never git way wid it. This is ouah lan. We done wukked 'n paid for it. Not only here, but all ovah this cruel South. De graves . . . ovah yonder is mah witness. De slaves sleepin in em declare Ahm right fore Gawd. It was us what first did de tillin t' make it give up de sweet sustenance of life, 'n yuh kin mark mah word: Though yuh won't even sell now, the same sun yuh see yonder goin yit rise 'n find dem what does de tillin gatherin in de harvest—Yuh kin go, Cap'n. We'll hold ouah fiah till yuh git back t 'yore men.

The rifle fire begins, and the stage is plunged into blackness and silence to suggest the passage of time. Then the last movement of the play begins. There is no hope for the freedmen. By the end of the afternoon the few remaining men learn that Captain Stewart gives them until sunset to surrender; if they do not, he will use a cannon that he is putting ashore. Though Joshuah says that a couple of his men may accept the offer, he makes it clear that he himself will remain on the island.

Delphine joins Joshuah, waiting for the sunset and death, and they talk about the time before their first meeting. In this tender interlude they define themselves for each other. When Joshuah tells Delphine that she carries herself "like yuh mount t' sompen in de world," she answers after a moment, "Ah reckon if things had er been diffunt, maybe me 'n yuh'd both been somebody, wouldn't us?" He agrees, and as he puts his arms around her to warm her—"Winter jes er-round de corner"—she asks him to sing. In the fading light, he sings "Deep River." The sound of a bugle interrupts the song, a white soldier appears on the porch, and Delphine tries to protect Joshuah but fails. The soldier fires, and Joshuah is hit. Dying, he says to Delphine, "Now . . . it's yore time . . . t' sing . . . Sing . . ." She does. Ignoring all else, she cradles Joshuah in her arms and concludes his song.

To read *Our Lan'* is to realize that here is a nearly perfect play. There may be, as Kenneth Rowe points out, a few trite sentences from "non-folk characters," and too little is done with Miss Libeth after her first entrance; but even a reading of the play supports general critical opinion (based on theatrical productions) that *Our Lan'* is remarkable. It may be the finest play ever written by an American Negro. That it was written by the same man who wrote *Big White Fog* at the turn of the decade is greatly to his credit as an artist. Theodore Ward—through research, study, and experience in the theatre—learned how to write an effective play.

He learned, too, how to use history well in writing about his people. No doubt he gained objectivity by choosing a period through which he had not lived except perhaps in racial memory. He wrote a play that is well informed by historical evidence and yet not overwhelmed by historical detail. He wrote about Negroes so truthfully that they gained universality; he made his hero, Joshuah Tain, noble—without sacrificing his humanity.

Reading about Joshuah, one is impressed by the fact of his existence, not by the significance of that fact. Alfred Kazin, speaking to and about Negro artists, once said that, because the Negro is so central to our experience today, artists tend to deal in significances, to assume that we will know what a man means because we know what he stands for. The critic reminded the artists that this last is not so, because "it all goes back to one house, one street, one uncle or grandmother, or whatever."[52] Theodore Ward had the good sense to go back to one ex-slave, one leader who by his actions helps us to understand American Negroes.

BROADWAY

Native Son

Richard Wright died in Paris at the age of fifty-two on November 29, 1960. Born on a plantation near Natchez, Mississippi, he moved to Memphis, Tennessee, at the age of six, when his father deserted the family. He worked at menial jobs in Memphis and then went to Chicago by himself when he was nineteen years old. In the early thirties he was on relief, and it was at this time that he joined the Communist Party. In 1937 he worked with the Federal Writers' Project. His four novellas, published under the title *Uncle Tom's Children*, won him a $500 prize from *Story* magazine in 1938. A Guggenheim grant in 1939 enabled him to finish *Native Son*, a novel which became a Book-of-the-Month Club selection in 1940. At the time of Wright's death, the New York *Times* declared:

> His greatest success, both financial and literary, was "Native Son," a harsh, realistic, brutal, angry novel . . . based partly on Wright's own experience and partly on the case of Robert Nixon, a Chicago Negro who was put to death in the electric chair in 1938 for the murder of a white girl.[53]

The novel was adapted as a play in 1941. In Argentina in 1950 it was made into an unsuccessful film, with Wright himself in the leading role.

Wright's autobiography, *Black Boy*, appeared in 1944 and was also a Book-of-the-Month Club selection. After the war (1945) he moved to Paris with his white wife, whom he had married in 1940. In the late forties he broke with the Communists, although, according to the New York *Times*, he "remained leftist, materialist and atheist."[54] His disavowal of the Party appeared—along with those of Gide, Koestler, and others—in *The God That Failed* (1950). Under the influence of Sartre, Wright wrote an existentialist novel, *The Outsider*, in 1953. A novel entitled *The*

Long Dream, considered generally to be his feeblest work, was published in 1958 and unsuccessfully dramatized for Broadway by Ketti Frings in 1960. His novel *Lawd Today,* written before *Native Son,* probably in 1937, had the clumsiness of an apprentice work while hinting at the power that was to come. It was published only posthumously in 1963.

This kind of rehearsal of events does not begin to suggest the real place of Richard Wright in the history of American literature. It is too soon to say how this Negro writer will be judged when time and custom allow him to be judged simply as an American writer. His ideology, his aesthetics, his sociology, his psychology, all are still the subject of a continuing discussion among writers such as James Baldwin, Ralph Ellison, and Irving Howe.[55] None of Wright's critics question the power of *Native Son* and all would agree with Nelson Algren that "Bigger Thomas forced recognition by an act of murder, Wright by an act of art."[56]

Native Son, whether in novel or play form, is the story of Bigger Thomas a twenty-year-old Negro living in the Black Belt of Chicago in the late thirties. James Baldwin has suggested that we cannot separate the book from the social climate of the period in which it was written:

> It was one of the last of those angry productions, encountered in the late twenties and all through the thirties, dealing with the inequities of the social structure of America. It was published one year before our entry into the last world war—which is to say, very few years after the dissolution of the WPA and the end of the New Deal and at a time when bread lines and soup kitchens and bloody industrial battles were bright in everyone's memory.[57]

Bigger Thomas represents every unemployed, restless, bitter Negro living in a rat-infested slum, with little hope of finding a way out of this socioeconomic trap.

A man of whom little has been said and to whom surely some praise for the dramatic version of *Native Son* must go is Paul

Green, Wright's collaborator. Recently Green wrote these recollections on how his collaboration with Wright came about:

> I had been studying the novel, and finally I wrote [Paul] Reynolds [Wright's agent] that I would be glad to try my hand at making a play from it provided I could do certain things with the material. One was that I should be allowed to poke some fun at the gravity of communism and its claims. Another was that I would be allowed to make Bigger Thomas partly responsible and consciously so for his "lost" condition and the murder of the white girl. I didn't subscribe to the old familiar whine that the reason "I'm a dead-beat or I'm mean, or I can't get anywhere in the world is that the world treats me wrong." No. Every man has something to do with what he becomes. . . . Reynolds got in touch with Wright who was in Mexico and he agreed. Then since I was rushed . . . I asked if Wright could come up and stay by while I wrote the play. I would need his advice here and there as certain points for discussion would certainly arise. Wright did come to Chapel Hill shortly after that and I set to work. Then since he was giving so much of his time and had come all the way from some satisfaction in Mexico to a rather arduous session in the south, it seemed fair to ask him in as collaborator. I did the dictation to a secretary, then revised, and Wright revised some too. Though he would say again and again that he knew nothing about writing a play, his suggestions were most helpful. I remember once asking him to try his hand at writing a scene. He did. It was beautiful, but completely novelistic. I couldn't use it. I wish now I had kept it as part of my memory of him—a wonderful and hurt man.[58]

A native of North Carolina, Paul Green has probably written more sympathetically and honestly about Negro life than has any other non-Negro playwright in America. Most of his plays have been about folk life in the South, about Negroes and the tenant white class. His play In Abraham's Bosom, which was produced in 1926, won the Pulitzer Prize for drama in 1927; it remains one of the finest and least sentimental of the plays written about American Negroes. Lajos Egri has commented on the simplicity of Paul Green's dialogue and has called it "the vehicle for cutting satire of character and situation."[59] Green once wrote about the nature of the dramatic struggle:

> Any character who is awry with any or all of his three worlds—himself, his neighbor, the outside universe—is the subject matter for drama if he struggles to dissipate this awryness. There must be struggle, and wherever that occurs there is drama. If the struggler fails or pays too big a price for what he gains, we have what we call tragedy.[60]

There can be little doubt that Bigger Thomas is awry with all his worlds, that he struggles, and that he pays a high price while making small gains.

Only an examination of the play, scene by scene, can reveal the problems that feed the overwhelming frustration which erupts into violence in such a way that Bigger Thomas gets the attention of all his worlds. The very setting of Native Son confronts the reader with a problem known to Negroes in all the large cities of America: the slum existence they are forced to endure in urban ghettos—in this case, Chicago. The Thomases live in a crowded apartment, so small and sparsely furnished that Bigger and his brother Buddy sleep on quilts on the floor. The mother, Hannah, and sister, Vera, in an effort to have a little privacy, dress under their robes, asking the boys to turn their heads. Tenement living affords no real privacy: this family, for example, shares a toilet off the landing with other families in the building. It is a wrathful Bigger who returns from the hall, having discovered that an "old woman with the toilet trots" is ahead of him. His first angry outburst places the play in a period and lets us know that Bigger does not have the patience and forebearance of his hymn-singing mother.

Relief didn't say more'n forty people got to use the same toilet every morning—lining up like women to see Clark Gable. (With sudden viciousness as he flings his arm around) *It's the way the white folks built this building.*

Bigger and Buddy chase a rat around the apartment, cornering it in great excitement. Bigger kills the rat, holds him up by the tail, and names him "Mr. Dalton" after the owner of all the houses in the neighborhood. Unnoticed by the Thomases, Miss Emmet, a white social worker, has entered the room in time to witness the ritualistic killing of "Mr. Dalton." Ironically enough, she has come to tell Bigger that he may get a chance to be the Daltons' chauffeur.

Miss Emmet, a fair-minded woman who has probably had more than one psychology course, makes no mention of the rat incident and wishes Bigger well with his application for the job. For his part, Bigger seems to care little about what others think or feel. He mocks his mother's faith in God and Miss Emmet's reference to him as the "head of a household." What does Bigger have faith in? Not "the white folks' God." Left alone, he takes his gun out of a hiding place, looks at a picture of Christ, and says defiantly, waving the gun, "Here's what you didn't have —but I got it!"

Simply in terms of theatre the opening scene is strong. Everything that Hannah does, from singing hymns about salvation to making preparation for doing a wash in the basement, reveals her acceptance of life as it is. Everything Bigger does shows him to be someone filled with anger and resentment at his position in society. "Bigger says we got nothing to smile about," Buddy tells his mother. "Says that's what wrong with the niggers—always smiling, and nothing to smile about."

Bigger's character is known by the end of the first scene, but that his environment has affected him far more than his family has is not readily apparent. There was a revealing observation made very early in the novel:

He hated his family because he knew that they were suffering and that he was powerless to help them. He knew that the mo-

*ment he allowed himself to feel to its fullness how they lived,
the shame and misery of their lives, he would be swept out of
himself with fear and despair. So he held toward them an attitude of iron reserve; he lived with them, but behind a wall, a
curtain. And toward himself he was even more exacting. He
knew that the moment he allowed what his life meant to enter
fully into his consciousness, he would either kill himself or someone else. So he denied himself and acted tough.*[61]

This is the insight that Louis Kronenberger and other critics felt
was missing in the theatre.

The second scene of the play is a street scene. Bigger and two
of his friends engage in horseplay, plan a robbery, and end at
odds because of Bigger's wild talk and emerging violence. All
three aspects of the scene help further to define Bigger, showing
us sides of his personality that tie him to his fellows, and others
that separate him from them. The dialogue of the scene often
relates specifically to current events.

Early in the scene Jack and Gus act out a telephone conversation between the President and the Secretary of State. The latter
says that he is preparing to send "that old Hitler" another note,
and the President starts to comment on "them Japs." But Bigger
(as Wendell Willkie) breaks into the conversation to tell the
President that he had better wait with the war, because "the
niggers is raising sand all over the country. You better put them
down first." Jack, as the President, is quick to pick up the message. He replies, "Oh, if it's about the niggers, Mr. Willkie, we'll
wait on the war!" The Secretary of State (Gus) puts an end to
Willkie's interference with the war effort, and the boys "bow
about in sudden and rich physical laughter, slapping their thighs,
their knees easy and bent."

Bigger takes part in the joking and the laughter, but later, when
he turns on Gus for not wanting to join them in robbing Mr.
Blum's store, he refers back to his (Willkie's) being put out of
the game. He makes their fun an excuse for violence. He does

not know how else to deal with what he calls Gus's cowardice. If he once confronted that cowardice and examined it, he might find that it was natural fear and that he felt it too. Rather than face this possibility, he attacks his friend.

Bigger is eager to fight anyone, though he would prefer "to take a gun and pop off a few of these white folks." He tells Jack that he feels Blum "gnawing round my liver here." Jack adds, "and in your lung and throat too—like fire. We gonna spit him out in a few minutes now." The fact that their intended victim has a Jewish name may be significant. For decades the "ironic historic confrontation of Jew (as landlord, merchant, housewife, businessman) with Negro (as tenant, customer, servant, and worker)" has brought about hatred on the part of the poor, uneducated Negroes.[62] James Baldwin observes that the Negro hates the Jew "partly because the nation does and in much the same painful fashion that he hates himself. It is an aspect of his humiliation whittled down to a manageable size and then transferred."[63]

Airplanes overhead distract Bigger and his friends from robbing Mr. Blum. Instead the boys look up in wonder at what Bigger calls "the white man's sign."

BIGGER: Go on boys, fly them planes, fly 'em to the end of the world, fly 'em smack into the sun! I'm with you. Goddam! (He stares up, the sunlight on his face.)

GUS: Yessuh! If you wasn't black and if you had some money and if they'd let you go to that aviation school, you might could be with 'em.

The voice of reason, reminding him of some of the prices he pays for his color, does not reach Bigger's ears. He is caught up in a pantomime of bombing, a game that the others soon join. They bomb white folks and their property. Bigger is in an ecstasy as he destroys a turbine tower: "Look at the fires—things flying through air—houses—people—streetcars—hunks of sidewalk and pavements. Goddam!" In his excitement, Bigger takes out his pistol. The others are frightened by it. It was one thing to plan to hold up Mr. Blum's store with a stick poked in the old man's ribs; a real gun can mean trouble of the kind that Jack and Gus do not want to risk.

Buddy arrives with the news that Bigger has the job as the Daltons' chauffeur. Bigger is riding high; he has a gun and the promise of a job that means driving a high-powered car. To celebrate his good fortune, he terrorizes Gus with his knife, threatens the owner of Ernie's Kitchen Shack, and then, as he is leaving, throws the boys a fifty-cent piece that he has stolen earlier from his mother. Lines spoken toward the end of the scene are prophetic, born of all that has occurred in this scene and pointing toward what follows:

ERNIE: *Somebody gonna kill that fool yet.*
JACK: *Or he's gonna kill somebody. Take more'n a job to kill what ails him!*

The next scene, the interview in the Daltons' sun-filled breakfast room, shows Bigger in the alien world of white folks. Mr. Dalton has the manner of an old-fashioned businessman who also teaches Sunday school. Mrs. Dalton is blind and carries a white cat in the crook of her arm. Mr. Dalton reads Bigger's application form aloud. Among other things there is a statement that Bigger's father was killed in a race riot in Jackson, Mississippi, in 1930. Dalton's only reaction to what he is reading comes when he chuckles at the words: "Knows how to obey orders but is of unstable equilibrium as to disposition." (It is easy to imagine Miss Emmet using this jargon in all sincerity.) Only the first part of the statement has any real meaning for the Daltons; they have still to learn about the second. Mr. Dalton also dismisses a reference on the application to Bigger's term in reform school, saying, "I was a boy myself once, and God knows I got into plenty of jams." Mrs. Dalton knows, however, that the comment is inappropriate here, for she says softly, "But he's colored, Henry." Nevertheless, Bigger is hired after a painful interview with Mrs. Dalton alone. She speaks to him about bettering himself and concludes her comments with an invitation for him to use the library if he wishes.

Bigger's position in this white world is clarified by the Irish maid, Peggy, who tells him about his duties—tending the furnace, watering plants, driving all the members of the family, but especially "looking after Miss Mary," the Daltons' college-age daughter. Peggy characterizes Mary with the observation that she "runs around with a wild bunch of radicals. But she's good-hearted—she'll learn better."

The scene builds to the entrance of Mary, who appears in a flowing red robe, her hair tousled, her face heavily made up. Wright's stage directions emphasize Mary's boredom and disillusionment, qualities which, despite Peggy's preparation, Bigger may not have expected to find among the privileged whites.

Mary begins to talk about Negroes and the Negro condition, moving from the observation that her mother's inevitable attempts to reform Bigger will be useless because "you've got no chance to be anything. None of you colored people have," to a confession that her own opinions are founded on her general sense of hopelessness rather than on familiarity with the Negro:

> You know, some time I'd like to meet some colored people . . . sometimes I drive down South Park way, and I look at all those buildings crowded with black people, and I wonder what's going on inside them. Just think, I live ten blocks from you, and I know nothing about you. I've been all over the world, and I don't know how people live ten blocks from me.

The sentiments may seem forced and pretentious, but the speech is more credible than a comparable one in the novel:

> Never in my life have I been inside of a Negro home. Yet they must live like we live. They're human. . . . There are twelve

*million of them. . . . They live in our country. . . . In the same
city with us.*[64]

Bigger is, in a very real sense, in Mary's power because part of
his job as chauffeur is to drive her whenever and wherever she
wishes to go. She pursues the subject of Negroes with the relent-
less honesty of the young liberal. Focusing on the black man who
must listen to her, Mary asks him a series of questions:

*Bigger, how do you colored people feel about the way you have
to live? Do you ever get real mad? Why don't you talk? Oh,
maybe I'm not saying the right things, but what are the right
things to say? I don't know. . . . How is it that two human
beings can stand a foot from each other and not speak the same
language? Bigger, what are you thinking about? What are you
feeling?*

Nothing about their lives up to this moment has prepared
either of them for communication with each other. The scene
ends in mutual confusion; Mary seems as uneasy being white
as Bigger is being black. It is evident that she dissipates her
power in drink as surely as he bolsters his weakness with a gun.
Environment possesses them both.

Without an intermission the next scene follows; it is the crucial
scene, so well prepared for and so terrible in its consequences.
Bigger is trying to steer a drunken Mary safely home in the middle of the night. Finding himself alone with her in her room,
Bigger is frightened. "This your room, Miss Dalton? They kill
me—kill me—they find me—." (Elsewhere Richard Wright has
written of a Negro bellboy being castrated when he is discovered
alone with a white prostitute.)[65]

The pathos of Mary's last fairly coherent speech, before she
stumbles and falls to the floor, is surely lost on Bigger. It is the
summation of her frustrations:

*I am what the Russians call "the penitent rich"—I feed the
poor—And I'm drunk—an I'm dead—drunk and dead—inside I*

am—I'm just a girl falling to pieces. . . . I want to talk—Trouble
with the world, Bigger—Nobody to talk to—Mother and Father
—they—talk up to God in the sky—I talk down—way, way down
to you at the bottom—Oh, I wish I was black—Honest, I do—
Black like you—down there with you—to start all over again—
a new life—

Marxism may have assuaged her conscience for a time, but Mary
craves something more. Nothing describes the confusion of this
wealthy American girl more clearly than this honest cry in the
night, when she asks to be allowed to take on Bigger's blackness
—and the degradation that goes with it.

When Bigger picks Mary up and carries her to her bed, she
touches him, tries to get through to him physically. She tells him
that she wants to suffer, but having said it and feeling his arms
around her, she is frightened and calls out, "Mother!" Then she
passes out, and Bigger places her on the bed.

The blind Mrs. Dalton answers her daughter's cry, coming
eerily into the room where a Negro stands in agony by a white
girl's bed. When Mary stirs and seems about to speak, Bigger
puts a pillow over her face to keep from revealing his presence.
Mrs. Dalton leaves, convinced by the heavy smell of alcohol
and the silence that her daughter is unconscious. When Bigger
discovers that Mary is dead, he says, "They'll say I done it—I'm
black and they'll say I done it." He hears the sound of the
furnace draft, picks up the body, and carries it out of the room
toward the monstrous roar.

In the novel Bigger decapitates the corpse as he prepares to stuff
it into the furnace. Such action, of course, is unsuitable for the
stage. Whatever theatre audiences may have imagined in the
moments between the fourth and fifth episodes was dictated by
their own imaginations. The loss of explicit violence is no great
one, for, as James Baldwin has pointed out, one of the severest
criticisms of Wright's work is that the violence in it is "gratuitous
and compulsive." Baldwin would have had Wright examine the

rage at the root of his violence, would have had him recognize that he was protesting the sexual myths with which Negro men have persistently been burdened by white people. In other words, Bigger Thomas' violence, according to Baldwin, is an expression of his rage against the white world that has castrated him and made him the object of its sexual paranoia, an expression of its sexual hates and fears and longings.

> Thus, when in Wright's pages a Negro male is found hacking a white woman to death [sic], the very gusto with which this is done, and the great attention paid to the details of physical destruction reveal a terrible attempt to break out of the cage in which the American imagination has imprisoned him for so long.[66]

As reader of novel or play, one is struck by the fact that Bigger himself seems never to have thought of white people as persons. They have been for him an oppressive presence, a natural force, but not individuals. As long as he stayed in the part of the city prescribed for Negroes, he did not have to know white people as anything but a force. Mary was only briefly an individual, and when she was dead Bigger knew that he had killed something more than this one girl—"he felt a lessening of tension in his muscles; he had shed an invisible burden he had long carried."[67] He had acted out a dream of revenge on the whole white race.

When a detective questions Bigger about the disappearance of Mary Dalton, the Negro at first puts the blame on her radical boy friend, Jan Erlone. It is a natural move for him to make, especially since the police suggest that they are delighted to implicate the Reds. Ironically, Bigger himself is not suspected at first by the Daltons or their maid because he seems to know his place. "He's just like all colored boys to me," says Peggy when she is asked about Bigger's behavior. This slighting observation initially diverts attention from Bigger and allows him freedom of movement.

Scene VI takes place in the one-room apartment of Bigger's

"sweetheart" Clara. The novel's comments about their need for liquor and sex as means of escape from the drudgery of their daily lives are lost in the play, but Bigger does protest that he hates having to come to Clara for comfort and sex. His seeking her company at this time, shortly after the murder, invites some psychological speculation. Surely he is looking for a "possible" outlet for his thwarted sexual drive. It is weakness, Bigger feels, that forces him to bed with Clara. It is weak to admit to loneliness and a need to share. At this point he shares only the knowledge that Mary Dalton is missing, and then Clara plants the idea of a kidnaping by mentioning a recent one in the Daltons' part of the city. Bigger becomes excited at the very idea of money and fame coming to him:

> Money! Goddamit. Everybody talking about it—papers with headlines, telephones ringing. Yeh, let 'em ring—ringing all over America, asking, asking about Bigger. The bells ringing; they'll sound the sirens and the ambulances beat their gongs.

He prints a ransom note, marveling the whole time at his newly discovered power to turn the world upside down. Exultant, he concludes the scene with a mad peroration:

> Twenty years, up and down the dark alleys, like a rat. Nobody hear us—nobody hear you, nobody pay any attention to you, and the white folks walking high and mighty don't even know we're alive. Now they cut the pigeon wing the way we say—like bars falling away—like doors swinging open, and walls falling down. . . . the big churches and the bells ringing and the millionaires walking in and out bowing low before their God—Hunh-huh. It ain't God now, it's Bigger. Bigger, that's my name!

There is a false courage, an overcompensation for fear, in these lines. Such bravado never lasts long. Bigger's cannot endure beyond the boundary he crosses when he returns to the white world. Consequently in the next scene, which takes place the following night in the basement of the Dalton home, Bigger is overcautious, his wariness betraying his anxiety to one of a visiting delegation of newspaper men. When the others have left, the suspicious reporter (having examined the premises and learned of the existence of a ransom note) stays to question Bigger about the furnace. The scene leads to the reporter's discovery of Mary's earring in the ashes.

Scene VIII reveals Bigger on the edge of madness, hiding out in an empty room at the top of an abandoned house. He is wrapped in an old blanket, trying to keep from freezing. He mumbles to himself, and then out of the incoherence emerge these comments on a revolving beacon he sees flashing in the night sky:

> Look at that old Lindbergh beacon, shining there 'way out through the darkness—Old Lindbergh—he knowed the way. Boiling icy water below him, the thunder and lightning, the freezing and the hail around him. Keep on driving—riding through. . . . Yes, he made it, got there. And all the people running and shouting, and the headlights switching and sweeping the sky! He not scared! . . . Aw, I ain't scared neither!

Earlier Bigger identified himself with white pilots flying overhead, straight into the sun—away from the world as it is into the unknown. Now he relates the courage that made him kill and that keeps him alive in hiding to that of Charles Lindbergh. He prays to a hero for sustenance. The irony is particularly poignant when we remember the wealthy Daltons who, like the Lindberghs, waited for news of a kidnaped child—only to learn of its death. To Bigger, as to all American boys, Lindbergh was a hero, not a man or a father, just a hero. Again there is the contradiction between American dream and reality.

It does occur to Bigger, however, that his welcome will not be like Lindbergh's: "When I light, ain't goin' be no lot of people running to *me* with flowers! Hell, no! When I come, they run! Run like Hell!" The memory of newsreels showing Lindbergh's welcome probably runs together in Bigger's mind with scenes from movies about trapped gangsters shooting it out with the police. His paranoia makes it possible for him to take as much pride in being a villain as in being a hero; he is a hero to himself in his own terms. In his wild dreams he is above even Clara's reproach. He tells her about the murder when she joins him in his hideout, and he boasts that he is not afraid. "Maybe you ought to be scared," says Clara with rare perception. "Scared maybe 'cause you ain't scared."

The questioning of his courage and the implied criticism of his acts lead Bigger to turn on Clara. He beats her, hurls her against the wall, and kicks her. One of her last utterances is very like one of Mary's: "My heart's all heavy like a lump of lead—and dead." Clara pleads with Bigger to kill her, to kill them both— "no more worry, no more pain"—but Bigger lets one of the white policemen kill her for him when they break in and capture him. He holds Clara in front of him when the police start shooting. This moment is perhaps the lowest point to which Bigger sinks, although in the novel he throws Clara's half-dead body into the alley. His action in the play is psychologically sounder. To let a white policeman kill Clara is, from Bigger's point of view, to let him kill someone already dead, destroyed by the white world to which she daily sacrificed herself.

The courtroom scene, Bigger Thomas' trial, consists of two monologues. Edward Max, counsel for the defense, engages in the longer one. David A. Buckley, state's attorney, does not need much time in which to ask for the death penalty. Max's speech, one of the strongest indictments of white society that exists in American literature, asserts that, when a crime is committed by a man who has been excluded from society, society itself is on trial as an accomplice to the crime. He begins his defense of Bigger:

> I say that this boy is the victim of a wrong that has grown, like a cancer, into the very blood and bone of our social structure. Bigger Thomas sits here today as a symbol of that wrong. And the judgment that you will deliver upon him is a judgment

delivered upon ourselves, and upon our whole civilization. The court can pronounce the sentence of death and that will end the defendant's life—but it will not end this wrong!

Then he leads the jury into a consideration of Bigger's childhood and adolescence. As a small boy Bigger saw his father shot down by a Southern mob because he was trying to protect other Negroes from violence—the kind of violence that now threatens to break down the doors of the courthouse. When Bigger, his mother, sister, and little brother moved to Chicago, hoping to find a freer life, they found "poverty, idleness, economic injustice, race discrimination and all the squeezing and oppression of a ruthless world." The city meant increased frustration, new cruelties.

Having sketched Bigger's short biography, Max asks why this boy rebels against being left out of the society described to him in school as a free one. The lawyer's answer is that of a sociologist (not necessarily that of a radical, though Edward Max is a Communist:)

> With one part of his mind, he believed what we had taught him—that he was a free man! With the other he found himself denied the right to accept that truth. In theory he was stimulated by every token around him to aspire to be a free individual. And in practice by every method of our social system, he was frustrated in that aspiration. Out of this confusion, fear was born. And fear breeds hate, and hate breeds guilt, and guilt in turn breeds the urge to destroy—to kill.

The Communist side of the lawyer's argument is more evident in his comments on Mr. Dalton, the wealthy capitalist who rents tenements to thousands of Negroes. Max reminds the court that, although Mr. Dalton gets proportionately high rents for these tenements that are among the worst in the city, he is held in high esteem, "because out of the profits he makes from these rents, he turns around and gives back to the Negroes a small part as charity." The Negroes, Max insists, have no say about how they live or where they live, and they must accept the crumbs of this white man's charity. This is the dishonest, futile sort of bribery which Bigger has rejected, and in doing so he is crying out for a multitude of Negroes who ask to be treated as men.

Referring to Bigger Thomas as a living corpse, counsel for the defense summarizes his indictment of white America and asks that Bigger's life be spared:

> You cannot kill Bigger Thomas, for he was already dead. He was born dead . . . among the wild forests of our cities, amid the rank and choking vegetation of our slums—in the Jim Crow corners of our busses and trains—in the dark closets and corridors and rest rooms marked off by the blind and prejudiced law as Black against White. And who created that law? We did. And while it lasts we stand condemned before mankind—Your Honor, I beg you, not in the name of Bigger Thomas but in the name of ourselves, spare this boy's life!

This speech is almost word for word from the even longer one in the novel. Of the original speech James Baldwin has complained:

> It is addressed to those among us of good will and it seems to say that, though there are whites and blacks among us who hate each other, we will not; there are those who are betrayed by greed, by guilt, by blood lust, but not we; we will set our faces against them and join hands and walk together into this dazzling future when there will be no white or black. This is the dream of all liberal men, a dream not at all dishonorable, but, nevertheless, a dream.[68]

The play does not keep the message in its pure state (John Mason Brown resented the fact that the lawyer's Communism was only "suggested" on stage). Although the speech is too long for a play presented in a period that does not expect set speeches or sermons in the theatre, it is undeniably moving. Its power derives from a passionate use of sociological data. Though state's attorney Buckley criticizes Max for suggesting that "the American nation and its methods of government," not Bigger, are on trial, there can be no doubt that members of the theatre audience (the jury) were disturbed by Max's accusing words.

Buckley puts the state's case against Bigger in these terms:

> If thine eye offend thee, pluck it out; and if the branch of a tree withers and dies, it must be cut off lest it contaminate the rest of the tree. Such a tree is the State through whose flourishing and good health we ourselves exist and carry on our lives. The ruined, the rotten and degraded must be cut out, cleansed away so that the body politic itself may keep its health. . . . I pity this diseased and ruined defendant. But as a tree surgeon . . . I repeat that it is necessary that this diseased member be cut off—cut out and obliterated—lest it infect us all unto death.

Biblical quotations and cadences lend an air of impressive sanctity to his remarks. He points out, too, that Bigger has pleaded guilty and that the state asks only that he die justly for the brutal murder of Mary Dalton. The radical Max has made a passionate plea for mercy. Buckley demands Old Testament justice, a life for a life.

Stage directions at the conclusion of this, the play's penultimate scene, indicate that the judge's voice can be heard in the thickening gloom of the courtroom as he says, "Bigger Thomas, stand up." No verdict is announced. The audience had to wait until the opening of the next scene to do more than speculate on the judge's verdict. Dimming lights, the voice of authority, the mob muttering outside—all of these effects were well calculated for theatrical suspense.

When the lights come up on the last scene, they reveal Bigger Thomas in the death cell a few weeks after his trial. The greatest climax having occurred in the courtroom, the rest of the play ties up loose ends, particularly the strands of Bigger's search for an understanding of what has happened to him and through him. When he killed, he tells Max, he experienced a great sense of relief. He established his identity and in a sense began to live at that moment. The time in prison gives him a chance to think about the world in which he has moved and of which he has had so small a share. In the novel we read:

> He would not mind dying now if he could only find out what this meant, what he was in relation to all the others that lived, and the earth upon which he stood. Was there some battle everybody was fighting, and he had missed it?[69]

When Max describes the battle in terms of a world that will come, when "there are no whites and blacks, only men," Bigger is puzzled. He is also resentful that Max has prompted all these hard questions, considerations beyond his comprehension.

Although Bigger admits that it was crazy and wrong to kill, he confesses that he did feel "like my own man" right after the murder. He adds, "I don't feel that way now. It didn't last." "It never lasts, Bigger," says Max.

But even the understanding he gains about the meaning of violence leaves Bigger frustrated, because he must face death without having had a chance to live. He can come only to the unsatisfactory conclusion that the world neglected him, yes, but he did not give *himself* a chance to live, only to die.

In the midst of his last talk with Max—ironically, his only friend is this white man—Bigger hears an airplane flying high above the prison. He listens, and then he shouts:

> Fly them planes, boys—fly 'em!—Riding through—riding through. I'll be with you! I'll—(Yelling, his head wagging in desperation) Keep on driving!—To the end of the world—smack into the face of the sun! (Gasping) Fly 'em for me—for Bigger—

Again airplanes draw his attention upward, away from the unfair world with its lack of answers—up, out, into the unknown.

Bigger walks out of his cell when the time for his execution arrives; the door of the death house opens with a flood of light, and he "moves toward its sunny radiance like a man walking into a deep current of water." The door closes behind him, shutting out the light. The audience is left in darkness, but Bigger has walked "smack into the face of the sun."

More than one critic, while praising Canada Lee's performance of Bigger as an honest portrayal of a suffering human being, took exception to the director's virtuosity, which heightened the violence, and the dramatists' words, which they felt did not always ring true. "Bigger," Richard Lockridge wrote, "explains himself with uncharacteristic eloquence—the stage's unsatisfactory substitute . . . for the novel's analysis of character."[70] Nor was Lockridge alone in preferring novel over play. John Mason Brown went so far as to ask why anyone would even dream of turning *Native Son* into a play when it was such a superlatively well realized novel and would unavoidably suffer from the limitations of a new medium.[71] Though Louis Kronenberger found *Native Son* "a vivid evening in the theatre," he complained that the play lacked the "richness and subterraneous power of the book."[72]

Only Brooks Atkinson, among the daily newspaper critics, praised Richard Wright and Paul Green for making out of a powerful novel an equally powerful play. He gave the authors credit for having "translated a murder story into a portrait of racial fright and hatred and given it a conclusion that brings peace to a taut and bewildered mind."[73] He especially commented on the dynamic use of the stage to represent convictions about life.

In some ways the play is better than the novel. The latter suffers from trying to say too much, especially in trying to provide a final glorious answer from the Communist lawyer. The play focuses on a human being, Bigger Thomas, and for all the theatricality of its ending, it is truly tragic when Bigger goes to his death bravely after wrestling with the implications of his useless, blighted life. Bigger has struggled, as Paul Green put it, to dissipate the awryness of his worlds.

Of the plays considered in this chapter, only *Native Son* and *Our Lan'* have been found worthy of publication, the former almost immediately and the latter thirteen years after its production. The dramaturgy of both plays is sounder than that of earlier ones by Negro playwrights, and both stand up as literature as well as theatre pieces. Richard Wright's choice of Paul Green as his collaborator and Theodore Ward's chance to put himself under the discipline of a playwriting seminar surely contributed to the success of their work.

It would be a mistake, however, to give all the credit to craftsmanship gained through joint cooperation and study. Langston Hughes has said that "craftsmanship enhances the creativity of a serious playwright, but it is never the whole answer."[74] Theodore Ward and Richard Wright (and to a lesser extent Theodore Browne) had something to say, cared passionately to say it, and had talent that could be trained to that end. Only Abram Hill, among the Negro playwrights of the forties, had little to say and little will to discipline what talent he possessed.

Perhaps the best way to summarize the dramaturgical advances made and the Negro problems reflected in the plays of this decade would be to compare the plays with each other and, where possible, with plays of the past. Not surprisingly, plays of the forties were concerned with the Depression rather than with World War II, with persistent more than with current Negro problems. The American theatre had soon rejected the Living Newspaper—if indeed it had ever accepted it—and returned to the customary time lag between life and art in the theatre. The best plays considered in this chapter, while fastening on recent and distant history, have a timeless quality. John Henry, Bigger Thomas, and Joshuah Tain are all memorable characters. They come out of periods in American history, but they are born into the eternity of art.

Theodore Ward has always maintained that the theatre should belong to everyone, not just to a privileged few; that it should really express man's everyday life. "We must," he said in 1940, "get the people to see it is an error to assume that some discrepancy obtains between a vital theatre and a theatre of amusement."[75] In 1963, commenting on his apprenticeship in Federal Theatre, Ward stated that "national theatre must be of this kind, not a prestige theatre only."[76] Today, as he did twenty years ago, he blames playwrights for choosing subjects too remote from the lives of their audiences. About Negro playwrights specifically he once wrote:

> Surely there can be no drama more compelling, more vital, more exciting, more interesting than that which manifests a coming to grips with life without evasions and affirms with candor the warm aspirations of a people who have come of age and demand their immediate freedom![77]

This passionate pronouncement may be true, but Harlem audiences did not support *Big White Fog*, which was a failure in 1940. And yet the press generally had given the company and the play excellent advance notices, some of them based on knowledge of the Federal Theatre production in Chicago. From such diverse journals as *The Voice of Ethiopia*, the New York *Times*, the *Daily Worker*, and the New York *World Telegram* there were encouraging articles expressing hope for the play's success. The names of Paul Robeson and Richard Wright were used to arouse interest; the advertisements called special attention to Perry Watkins, a Negro designer who had been responsible for several Federal Theatre and Broadway productions. Neither wishful praise nor the sponsorship of famous men could save the play from failure.

Was Theodore Ward too radical? Did his idea of a people's theatre smack of the kind of left-wing thinking for which many people condemned the Federal Theatre? *Big White Fog* does have an ending reminiscent of the final moments of Clifford Odets' *Awake and Sing!* It will take a revolution, both plays tell us, to correct the evils of our society. New York journalists, however, seemed as sympathetic to Ward's attempt to put his answer on stage as a Chicago writer had been in 1938, when he made this defense of the play:

> Only recently there have been letters passed around suggesting that the mayor do something about stopping the production of

"Big White Fog" on the grounds that it is "communistic" (which it probably is) and that it excites race prejudice (which it probably does not). And we disagree with these objections more than with the moral of the play, for the pure and simple reason that we believe in free speech whether on stage or off.[78]

If radicalism killed the play, it did so by its absence in the audience. The ticket buyers in New York were upper- and middle-class Negroes and whites; if they had ever considered the Communist answer to poverty, racism, and other American socioeconomic problems, they had rejected it some time ago.

Several theatre critics, having seen the New York production of Big White Fog, did feel that the regulation Communist ending weakened it aesthetically. The answer was "tacked on," not part of the play's totality. Some critics applauded Ward's sincerity while finding fault with his dramaturgy. John Mason Brown, for example, felt that "Mr. Ward struggles ineptly to give dramatic statement to what is heart-breaking in the Negro's life."[79] Brooks Atkinson found the play monotonous and objected to the Communist finish, but he still thought that within the boundaries of social significance Big White Fog was the "best serious play of Negro authorship about race problems that this courier has happened to see."[80]

We have to add, in all honesty, that another reason for the play's failure, in spite of critical interest and the proper sort of publicity, was the play's unimaginative language. Ralph Ellison analyzed Big White Fog with more insight than did any of the other critics. He felt that the theme of the play, with its emphasis on Garveyism, was dated. More important (because Garveyism, digested, may one day make a great play), Ellison expressed his disappointment with the language of the play:

> The impact of American life upon Negroes is so immediate and sustained that their expressed feelings are cloaked in quite graphic and realistic imagery—even their idealism. This imagery is missing . . . from Ward's dialogue in general. . . . Its inclu-

sion would have given "Big White Fog" a poetic shimmer similar to that of the best work of Odets.[81]

The authors of On Strivers Row and Natural Man, Abram Hill and Theodore Browne, had in common the facts that they were Negroes and that they had both worked in Federal Theatre units. Their plays, presented mostly to Negro audiences but reviewed by both the Negro and the white press, do not stand up well as literature. Of the two, Natural Man is better constructed, has less improbable dialogue, shows a concern for more than merely the black bourgeoisie. On Strivers Row, limited to making a comment on the Negro middle class, suffers from a narrowness of vision, especially when the characters are the stereotypes that Abram Hill's are.

A statement by Sterling Brown appears on the title page of the script of On Strivers Row:

> There is certainly place in American fiction for treatment of the Negro middle-class. The precarious situation of this small group could well attract a realist of vision, not only to satirize its pretense, but also record its dogged struggling. But to approve it in proportion to its resembling white middle-class life, is not the way of important realism.[82]

The play does not succeed in answering this plea for "important realism," but one has the sense, reading it, that the author tried, within his artistic limitations, to satirize the obvious pretensions of the black bourgeoisie. The fact that productions of the play have been successful and that it has often been revived in Harlem is sufficiently indicative of the author's ability to record his people's pretenses with good-natured humor if not with wit or real vision.

While On Strivers Row is a special play for a specific audience, Natural Man has a larger sphere of concern. Theodore Browne made good use of the John Henry legend to call his audience's attention to many injustices suffered by Negroes. He wrote of

Southern chain gangs; they exist to this day. He wrote about a Negro who proclaimed his humanity with the words, "I'm going to be a natural man," a Negro who stood up to his white tormentors when they kept him out of their union or locked him in their jails. John Henry will not be put down. He will die rather than submit to the white man's rule in which he does not believe. His heroic stance cannot be denied.

The robot is a symbol of the white man's power (by extended implication, automation) and, true to history, defeats John Henry. This Negro's gestures are as futile as those of Bert in Langston Hughes's *Mulatto*, but they are as necessary also to the sustenance of his people. John Henry is related to Bert and to Joshuah Tain of Theodore Ward's later play. They are Negroes who oppose injustices for themselves and others.

It is not easy to include Bigger Thomas in this company because he acted with so little consciousness of his acts except in retrospect. It is difficult to accept Bigger as the sympathetic protagonist of a protest drama. Perhaps what Darwin Turner has to say about Wright's creation of Bigger will help us to understand the author's intentions:

> Recognizing the unreality of both the "noble-savage" drawn by Negro polemicists and the "savage-beast" drawn by Dixon and other Negro-phobes, Wright blended in Bigger the weaknesses for which the race has been criticized. Then he charged non-Negro America with the responsibility of breeding such individuals. Although he offered a stereotype . . . Wright evidenced the new confidence of the Negro writer in revealing the vices of race, not in comedy, but in work intended to evoke sympathy.[83]

While Bigger may not represent all Negroes, he seems to symbolize a violence that may reside in all of them as a result of social circumstances in America.

Wright himself tried to explain Bigger in a pamphlet entitled *How "Bigger" Was Born*. He claimed that there have always been Bigger Thomases. In the South they are the Negroes who have consistently broken the Jim Crow laws and gotten away with it "at least for a sweet brief spell." Most of them ended up shot, maimed, hanged, or simply among the living dead, their spirits broken by the Southern white man's restrictions. Why did Bigger Thomas of *Native Son* revolt? Wright tells us:

> *First. . . he had become estranged from the religion and the folk culture of his race. Second, he was trying to react to and answer the call of the dominant civilization whose glitter came to him through the newspapers, magazines, radios, movies, and the mere imposing sight and sound of American life.*[84]

He is ashamed of the submissiveness of Negroes, and he is frightened by the power possessed by whites. He kills by accident, but his whole life has been a preparation for the act.

James Baldwin may be right, however, when he says that it was useless for Richard Wright to present Bigger as a warning to America—to ask judge, jury, and spectators to feel guilty for the creation of this monster. Bigger has always been a warning, Baldwin reminds us, but we will not heed it, because we want to hate him, not to forgive him, to keep him in his place or to kill him for stepping out of it.[85] This is a strong condemnation of *Native Son* as a work of art and of America as a democratic society, but it is a condemnation with a basis in psychology.

According to Edith Isaacs, audiences supported the play as no one in the theatre world ever dreamed they would. Most theatre people who knew Richard Wright's novel doubted the wisdom of putting it on the stage; it was too strong, too filled with violence to be a success. "But give a theatre audience the roughest possible material," she observed, "and if it is fast-moving, well acted and directed and has a heavy coating—either farce or melodrama —and nine chances out of ten the theatre will swallow it without strain." She attributed much of the play's success to Canada Lee's interpretation of Bigger Thomas as both a real man and a symbol of the frustrated Negro in American society. She concluded, too, that "*Native Son* had a very real effect on the social conscience of its audience."[86]

There may be fewer reasons to believe her statement about

the audience's social conscience than there are ways to substantiate Baldwin's contention that *Native Son* appeals to our need to keep the Negro in his lowly place. It is impossible to measure an audience's social conscience, certainly not by the applause it gives to a magnificently staged drama. There were stories circulated about members of the audience who went home and fired their Negro chauffeurs. On the other hand, a quotation from a letter written by one of the actors, John Randolph (non-Negro), in the touring company of *Native Son*, does suggest that Mrs. Isaacs' comment on the social impact of the play was not unfounded:

> When we reached the old American Theatre in St. Louis on opening night, the square in front of the theatre was filled with police motorcycles with sidecars containing tear-gas guns, riot sticks, etc. It seems there had been a racial incident in a trolley-car a few days before and the police expected more trouble with our play. Further tension existed because the theatre management refused to change the Jim Crow seating arrangements; Negroes were permitted to sit only in a roped-off section of the balcony and limited to twelve seats. We had to use every gift of persuasion to get the editor of the St. Louis Call (a Negro newspaper) to attend the play because he had vowed never to attend a segregated theatre. Afterwards he told the cast that when Bigger Thomas' defense attorney mentioned that men like Bigger Thomas were "brought up in the Jim Crow corners of our trains and busses—yes, even in our Jim Crow Army and Navy, it was black against white," he, as a Negro, had never felt more vindicated, sitting in the roped-off section of the balcony, as a living example of what the white audience was hearing on the stage. By the time we left St. Louis, the theatre owner had given in to the local cast and producer pressure to temporarily eliminate segregated seating in the balcony and mezzanine.

Randolph also comments on the strain that the Negro members of the cast were under. There was a constant battle against discrimination in hotels and restaurants in Detroit, Pittsburgh, and Chicago. Posters and pictures were ripped off the front of theatres. But the actor writes, "What sustained us all—Negro and white—were the audience reactions, the tears in the eyes of the people who came backstage, the lessons in inter-racial cooperation we gave to many communities, and the lessons we learned ourselves of the need to work together and fight against discrimination twenty-four hours a day."[87]

Richard Wright would have been pleased to learn what, in this instance, his art achieved; for he was always aware of the propaganda value of what he wrote. It would be unfair, however, to attribute Wright's and Ward's penchant for propaganda to their leftist stance. It would be more accurate to say that they, along with many Americans who had lived through the thirties, sensed the need for reform of our economic and political system. As Negroes who had not bought the American Dream outright, Wright and Ward suspected that reform would have to come through revolution. This belief in revolution diluted the effectiveness of *Big White Fog*, was not evident enough in *Native Son* to offend most observers, and appeared in *Our Lan'* only by implication.

Not careful construction, beautifully developed characters, nor subtle message can fully account for the success of *Our Lan'*. By choosing to write a historical play—the *first* historical play of Negro authorship produced on Broadway—Theodore Ward gained a perspective useful to art, while bringing to his writing the same deep concern for his people that he had earlier evidenced in *Big White Fog*. Once, speaking of his admiration for Chekhov, Ward said, "He cut across class lines and focused on aspirations."[88] It seems fair to say that Ward focused on aspirations during Reconstruction in order to stir in contemporary audiences, of all classes, the same or similar dreams.

The Negro problems presented in *Our Lan'*, those related to ownership of property, the possession of the ballot, the need for education, are still with us and of concern to large areas of the rest of the world. It is significant that Mrs. Chen Jui-lan of the

University of Peking has asked permission to translate *Our Lan'*. She wrote to Ward that she thinks he is "very much of the people."[89] Her letter attests to the universality of the ideas in *Our Lan'*. It is a reminder, too, that revolutions are related, because people have similar problems at different times in history.

By the end of the forties we seem to have left behind plays about the submissive Negro, plays straining for laughs (often at the Negroes' expense), and those—like *Appearances* and *Conjur Man Dies*—that featured stereotypes and little else. The professional Negro playwright, by the end of World War II, was coming of age. Spirituals were not sung for their charm alone but as an integral part of the play's action and for purposes of characterization. Language, whether dialect or not, was more human than in earlier plays about Negroes. By the time of *Our Lan'* audiences could watch love scenes between Negro characters, an unheard-of occurrence in earlier plays. Finally, critics did not have to make excuses for Negro playwrights writing crude plays of necessary protest, for these artists were beginning to shape their propaganda skillfully, to write with a great awareness of dramatic technique and of the theatre itself, from which they had so long been barred.

V ❦ THE FIFTIES

A dream deferred

IN HIS POEM "Montage of a Dream Deferred," Langston Hughes asked some provocative questions about the Negro's reaction to his long wait for freedom and equality:

What happens to a dream deferred?
  Does it dry up
  like a raisin in the sun?
  Or fester like a sore—
  and then run?
  Does it stink like rotten meat?
  Or crust and sugar over—
  like a syrupy sweet?
  Maybe it just sags
  like a heavy load.
Or does it explode?[1]

Here are all the possibilities: despair, decay, acceptance, resignation, and revolution. The emphasis is on revolution, on explosion, and in this Hughes proved to be a prophet. As William Brink and Louis Harris have observed, Negro protest in the form of direct action became an accepted part of the American scene during the fifties:

> From half-hidden depths of impatience and anger the Negro revolution began rising to a crescendo of protest in the middle of the twentieth century. During the 1950's there were sporadic incidents, a handful of Negro children here and there seeking entrance to white schools in the South. There were ugly and ominous trouble spots, such as Little Rock. But as yet the real proportion of the Negro's revolt were not clearly visible.[2]

American Negroes wanted, as Sterling Brown had said years before, "to be counted in . . . to belong."[3]

There are those, of course, who are not persuaded that integration is the whole answer, who wonder about the value of the society Negroes are trying so desperately to enter. The Black Muslims are perhaps the most obvious example of a group which denies the need or desire for integration. And yet one cannot assume that the great majority of American Negroes of the fifties or even of the sixties belong in one of two camps, some favoring integration, others opposed. Desperate attempts to claim racial pride may lead one man to a kind of black racism, while at the same time he wants the vote and a share in the common values of American society. There are dedicated Black Muslims, devoted SCLC and SNCC workers; but still there are many Negroes in between, bearing no label and yet part of what has been called a Negro revolution.

If some commentators have stopped short of calling this movement truly revolutionary, it is because, as Harry Ashmore has observed, most of its members "do not seek to remake the community, only to join it. . . . The drive seems to be to obtain only what has been denied."[4] (Even though there is still truth to this observation, especially in economic terms, one should add that the uprisings or rebellions of recent summers have begun to pose questions that cannot be answered except by radical changes in

America as we know it.) It is as understandable as it is ironical, this desire on the part of Negroes to be "counted in" as Americans. Somehow before the sixties they had always sensed, under the fog of discrimination, a promised and possible shape of the future. According to Louis Lomax, one of the most vocal of young Negro spokesmen:

> Whatever else the Negro is, he is American. Whatever he is to become—integrated, unintegrated, or disintegrated—he will become it in America. Only a minority of Negroes have ever succumbed to the temptation to seek greener pastures in another country or another ideology. Our lot is irrevocably cast, and whatever future awaits the Negro awaits America. . . . It is true that we are angry about our present plight, for we measure America by her potential rather than by her achievements. . . . It has never occurred to us that the Negro Revolt will not, in the end, succeed. This fundamental optimism is, I submit, a resounding faith in the American dream.[5]

The effects of the social stirrings that presaged a Negro revolution were felt in the American theatre as early as the mid-forties and increasingly in the fifties. Changing attitudes toward Negroes meant, for one thing, that Negroes could buy tickets to Broadway shows, and not only for seats on the aisle or for certain sections of the theatre. Also Negro actors were occasionally employed for their talent, not just their color, although they continued to play stereotypical roles in many productions. In the late forties several white playwrights wrote plays about the postwar adjustments of the Negro, among them were On Whitman Avenue by Maxine Wood (1946), Forward the Heart by Bernard Reines (1949), and How Long Till Summer by Sarett and Herbert Rudley (1949). By the early fifties—at the same time that Negro performers were appearing in revivals of Green Pastures (1951), Shuffle Along (1952), and Porgy and Bess (1953)—Negro playwrights were finding a way to exhibit their own plays on Broadway, off-Broadway, and in Harlem.

Of the six plays examined in this chapter, only two were strictly Broadway productions; three were done off-Broadway, and one in Harlem. It should be noted, however, that this is no real indication of the number of plays produced in Harlem, but rather a comment on the present availability of scripts. Especially after the organization of the Council on the Harlem Theatre in 1950 there were many plays written and directed by Negroes. That most of the scripts have disappeared is not surprising in view of the fact that "a number of Negro-written plays appeared in library basements, in community auditoriums and lodge halls, financed quite often because the group collected money from its members and launched a production,"[6] a process that rarely leaves traces.

The Committee for the Negro in the Arts had been formed in 1947, and it joined the Council on the Harlem Theatre in 1950. The CNA, as a producing unit, was responsible for several important plays, concerts, revues, and lectures. A fair idea of the committee's aims can be gained from reading its organizational report, which states a belief in "the integration of Negro artists into all forms of American culture on a dignified basis of merit and equality" and a determination to wipe out persisting racial stereotypes in the various arts.[7] In a later CNA Bulletin there is a reference to the 1951 revival of Green Pastures, which the committee viewed as an example of the continuing "refusal of Broadway producers to present a true and honest picture of Negro life."[8] (Since jobs were scarce, the Bulletin added, actors were not being asked to boycott the production of Green Pastures.)

In 1950 Alice Childress, who had been an actress in the American Negro Theatre company, adapted Langston Hughes's Simple Speaks His Mind for the stage, calling it Just a Little Simple. This "dramatic-musical-revue" was produced at the Club Baron on Lenox Avenue and, according to CNA, played to a "total audience of 8,000 New Yorkers and out-of-towners."[9] (In 1956–57 Hughes himself wrote Simply Heavenly, which was produced both on and off Broadway.) Then, in 1951, CNA produced William Branch's first play, *A Medal for Willie*. Another Alice Childress play, *Gold Through the Trees*, ran from April 7 to May 19, 1952, at the Club Baron. Advertised as a "dramatic review," it was apparently an attempt to make American Negroes proud of their past history. Incorporating an Ashanti warrior's dance, modern dance, the Blues, sketches about Harriet Tubman and about the present-day freedom movement, *Gold Through the Trees* was further proof of Miss Childress' creative talent in the theatre.

In the early fifties, the Club Baron and other Harlem theatres began to suffer from a socioeconomic blow that hit many community theatres in New York City, such as the famous Yiddish Theatre that had been thriving for so long on Second Avenue. People were moving out of the city to Long Island, Brooklyn, the Bronx, and Westchester. Negro artists who had fought for a community theatre in Harlem were faced with the fact that many of the people whom they had been educating to the idea of a Negro theatre were leaving Harlem. Middle-class Negroes who could have supported an ethnic theatre were eager for social integration with the whites, sensing that a society defending uniqueness defends also a measure of discrimination. To move away from Harlem seemed to many Negroes a step toward Americanism or toward what Nathan Glazer has described as "the final homogenization of the American people, the creation of a common nationality replacing all other forms of national connection."[10]

When audiences began to move away from New York City, producers were no longer willing to maintain theatre buildings. They began to rent, not own, property, and playwrights lost places in which to show their wares even to a diminished audience. In the case of Negro playwrights, few theatres were ever available to them even in Harlem. The two large theatres, the Apollo and the Lafayette, have more often than not housed vaudeville. Old movie theatres that might have become legitimate theatres were more likely to become churches in Harlem.

In 1951 the Apollo contributed rather directly to the determination of Negro playwrights to find theatres for their plays.

The management sponsored productions of *Detective Story* and *Rain,* and when these "white" plays were unsuccessful both artistically and commercially, the theatre issued a public statement to the effect that Harlem did not care for serious drama. The Council on the Harlem Theatre answered with the following statement:

> The owner of the Apollo has insulted the Negro people by bringing to this community two inferior pieces with little meaning to our lives. Ridiculous prices were charged and, when we exercised the buyer's right [of withholding patronage], we were accused of lacking taste.[11]

Unfortunately, those Negro playwrights who wanted to bring honest, meaningful plays before the Harlem public had neither an audience nor a theatre. It is not surprising that they turned their attention increasingly to Greenwich Village and, of course, to Broadway.

The Greenwich Mews Theatre at 141 West 13th Street in Greenwich Village has often been characterized as an interracial theatre, but this is only one aspect of its generally experimental nature. Sponsored by the Village Presbyterian Church and the Brotherhood Synagogue, this small theatre has taken a chance on first plays by untried playwrights and on other plays that might have been neglected by larger theatres. Three Negro playwrights had their plays produced at the Greenwich Mews in the 1950s: William Branch, *In Splendid Error* (1954); Alice Childress, *Trouble in Mind* (1955); and Loften Mitchell, *A Land Beyond the River* (1956). Reviews of all three plays indicate that they received careful staging and thoughtful direction.

The American theatre of the fifties was more conscious of Negroes than ever before because the nation as a whole was being made more conscious of them. The theatre was just one of the institutions, along with schools and churches, which reflected this newly awakened concern. Also Negroes were in the theatre audience in greater numbers than they had been formerly, and so

Loften Mitchell was not exaggerating when he wrote about Louis Peterson's *Take a Giant Step*, his own *A Land Beyond the River*, and Langston Hughes's *Simply Heavenly* that "Negro theatre goers were directly responsible for the financial success of these plays."[12] In a theatre that rarely becomes passionate about ideas, Negro playwrights did well to get an audience to hear their protests and to become aware of their problems. This is not to say that enough people heard the voices raised in protest or even that those who heard gave sufficient attention to the Negro's plight. But the following plays, among others, did put the problems before the public, black and white alike; they were part of the brewing Negro revolution.

HARLEM AND OFF-BROADWAY
A Medal for Willie

Born in New Haven, Connecticut, in 1927, the son of a Methodist minister who changed his parish every four years or so, William Branch lived in various towns in the East—among them Poughkeepsie and Mamaroneck, New York—before his family moved to Charlotte, North Carolina. Young Branch was sent to high school in Washington, D.C., received a B.S. degree in speech from Northwestern University in 1949, and, after serving in the army, went on to graduate school, receiving an M.F.A. from Columbia University in 1958. In answer to a question about his education as a playwright, Branch replied that he had had one semester of playwriting as an undergraduate and another at Columbia, but that he had found that "far more helpful were extensive reading of plays and seeing plays on and off Broadway."[13] He has been writing for stage, radio, films, and television since 1951.[14]

His first play, *A Medal for Willie*, was produced by the Committee for the Negro in the Arts and directed by Elwood Smith. It opened in October, 1951, at Harlem's Club Baron, and ran through January, 1952. William Branch was then twenty-four years old. The day after his play opened, he was inducted into

the United States Army. He was to serve, shall we say, between
the wars, but, as a Negro, he no doubt endured a variety of
humiliations. He could most certainly understand the bitter sentiments expressed in a poem by another Negro soldier:

Uncle Sam
I'm dark
From Alabam
You asked me to carry this gun
For you and freedom:
But Uncle Sam
How 'bout me?
I'm dark
From Alabam
And if I live through this war
For freedom
Can I carry some home to Alabam?
Answer: When you are ready for it, boy. [15]

The poet anticipated the soldier's return. William Branch, in A
Medal for Willie, anatomized the grief of a dead Negro soldier's
family and friends in the stultifying atmosphere of a Southern
community's hypocrisy.

A *Medal for Willie* is a short play in seven scenes, plus Prologue and Epilogue in which are shown the preparation for and
dismantling of an assembly in the auditorium of the Booker T.
Washington High School in Midway, a town in the South. The
school assembly will be "a memorial service and presentation
ceremony" in honor of Corporal Willie Jackson, who died a
hero's death fighting for his country. Now the community will
honor him with the public presentation of a medal to his mother.

The play really gets under way with a scene in the Jackson
home, where Willie's sister Lucy Mae is doing her mother's hair
(using pomade and a hot iron), helping her to get ready for the
memorial service. Mrs. Jackson remembers that this same boy
who is being praised today was called "no-count" by his own

father, that he was always in trouble, and that he was expelled from the school that now honors him. Recalling her son's decision to shine shoes in a barbershop rather than return to school, Mrs. Jackson says that Willie was stubborn but not rough. Perhaps to take her mother's mind off past troubles, Lucy Mae reminds her that today's gathering in Willie's honor will be unsegregated. "Anybody can sit where they want," she explains, "whether they're white or colored. That's makin' history!"

Mrs. Jackson is somewhat less than enthusiastic about the unsegregated audience and a "colored park" that may be named after Willie. Even when Lucy Mae says that the Jackson family is going to sit on the platform with the Mayor, the Superintendent, and a General from Washington, the mother does no more than agree to sit there. Asked if she will be thrilled, she answers in words that must have been in the hearts if not on the lips of countless bereaved Negro women:

> Yes, Lucy Mae, I'll be thrilled, I guess. It's all very nice what everybody's doin' and I'm proud, very proud. Only—where was everybody when Willie was alive? Where was they when your father and me was strugglin' to feed him and put clothes on his back and bring him up decent? Where was everybody when he needed help in school, but they put him out instead 'cause they didn't have time to fool with him. An' where was they when he was walkin' the street lookin' for work. It's all very nice to give him a program he can't come to, and a medal he can't wear, an' name a park after him they ain't built yet. But all this can't help Willie now! It ain't doin' him no good.

With a gesture reminiscent of scores of plays and movies about strong Negro mothers, she blows her nose, dabs the corner of her eyes with a towel (in some plays it is an apron), and turns toward what must be faced.

The play's next three scenes serve to demonstrate the attitudes of white members of the Southern community. In scene two the Mayor of Midway (one wonders if the name makes a spatial or a temporal reference) talks to the visiting General in an effort to make sure that the latter will not say or do anything that will give the Negroes too much encouragement. "We have to kind of pat 'em on the wool a bit one minute," he reminds the General, "and then make sure they don't get any fancy notions about gettin' out of their place with all this talk about fightin' for freedom and democracy and all." The General, it turns out, is quick to understand the Mayor; he is from South Carolina himself. A Jewish captain from the Bronx who is also present does not accept this way of thinking, but he is not in a position to do more than state his disagreement, which is pointedly ignored by his superiors.

In scene three, the white barber, who owns the shop where Willie used to work, brags about him to a customer who says, "All these young bucks look alike to me." It is to William Branch's credit that he does not stack the cards against the white race by having all white men, even in the South, in agreement. Just as the Jewish officer had a good word to say for Negroes, so the barber states his opinion that there is something wrong in Willie's fighting and dying for men who do not even recognize his existence. The barber knew Willie as a hard-working boy, and he wants now to give him due praise for bravery in battle. The customer, who cares only about keeping his own son out of the war (by fair means or foul), becomes angry at the talk of Willie's bravery. "To hell with this Willie Jackson!" he explodes. "He ain't nothin' to me but another nigger dead." The barber, however, has the last word in the scene, calmly announcing that he is on the draft board and will not miss the next meeting.

Scene four is very short. It takes place in a newspaper editor's office in Midway. The editor is assigning a reporter to the ceremony at the high school. What he wants, he informs the reporter, is a sob story with a patriotic theme:

> Little colored boy from the shanty town slums went over there and fought and died for his country, his native land, to preserve the American way of life and give the lie to those subversives

who continually try to stir up trouble between the races by harping on equality.

The editor even considers calling the boy's mother *Mrs. Jackson*, which would be a real concession from a Southern newspaper. If the story is good enough, he tells the reporter, he will send it to the AP and even to the Voice of America. The irony of the scene needs no underlining. It concludes the portion of the play in which no Negroes appear.

Scene five is a bitter episode. It involves Willie's girl friend, Bernice, and a white boy who, rather too coincidentally, turns out to be the son of the customer in the barbershop. Bernice, who is eighteen years old, is waiting at a bus stop, on her way to the memorial service. The white boy asks Bernice to join him on a bench. The bench is for white folks only, but he lets her know that he is liberal and does not object to her sitting by him. She refuses his invitation. The more he talks to her, the more she bridles at his familiarity.

Bernice is apparently neither pleased with the white boy nor frightened of him. When he persists, she lashes out at him, "I don't want any part of any white trash like you!" His response is to slap her, to call her a "black bitch," to try to kiss her. He demands that she show respect "when white folks speak to you!" She silently refuses. He advances toward her, and she scratches his cheek. He throws her to the ground and leaves her alone sobbing, "Oh, Willie—Willie—Willie!" Their struggle is a paradigm of black and white struggles over the centuries.

A brief scene follows in which Mr. Torrence, the Negro principal of Booker T. Washington High School, tells Mr. Taylor (the teacher who served as narrator in the Prologue) that he has prepared a speech for Mrs. Jackson to read. It is clear from his comments about the speech that the principal is asking Willie's mother to humble herself before the white community, to express gratitude and a willingness to serve white interests. Young Mr. Taylor, who has not been teaching very long, is shocked to discover that his principal is willing to play Uncle Tom rather than use this occasion as a step toward desegregation.

The principal, growing expansive, announces that he is soon to become state supervisor of Negro schools. He boasts of his venality:

> I am supposed to travel around and make speeches and all—a general public relations thing, you know—Pointing out how progress is being made and keeping down criticisms. I'll consult with Negro leaders throughout the country and advise them to go slow, that gradual improvements will be made if they keep their mouths shut. You see, it's a snap! Ten thousand a year plus expenses.

With the Negro teacher the Negro principal is a braggart, but it is easy to imagine him licking the boots of his white superiors, enduring the special humiliation that is reserved for Southern Negro professionals.[16] Mr. Torrence gains more than a shred of sympathy when he remarks that the teachers who call him a "White Folks Nigger" have no way of knowing how he must literally beg for equipment and books and dollars for the school. "They don't know," he tells Mr. Taylor, "how I've had to humiliate myself before the Board, how I've been laughed at, cursed at, called 'boy.' "

A large part of the last scene of A Medal for Willie, the ceremony itself, is given over to the General's speech. It is a classic rendition of the patriotic speech that is designed to wring the heart and cloud the mind. Having praised the town for its "basic grand old traditions of gracious old Dixie," the General expresses his pleasure at being able to participate in a family gathering and his deep regret "that I come to you under quite these circumstances, with their overtones of tragedy in the death of our young honoree." He tells the audience that Corporal Jackson served nobly and has won "the thanks and appreciation of a grateful and admiring nation." The part of his speech that really sounds

like every patriotic speech ever uttered, and the part that carries
the most striking ironies, is this paragraph:

> We are engaged today in a struggle which tests the very vitals
> of the people of our great nation. The question is whether we
> shall be free to continue on in our great national heritage of the
> American way of life, or whether we must allow the alien
> ideologies of an imperialistic power to devour our country and
> our heritage. This bitter struggle requires of us the stamina, and
> the courage and the loyalty of every citizen of this land. We
> may not all be called upon to make the supreme sacrifice that
> Corporal Jackson so willingly made, in order to protect the
> freedoms that are ours. But the inspiration and the example of
> Corporal Jackson ought to fire every heart and soul with a
> burning zeal to meet the test and weather the storm. Our
> homes, our children, our traditions, our industries, and our very
> existence in the world as a free and independent nation lie at
> stake. But I have little doubt that, as evidenced in the heroism
> of Midway's Willie Jackson, we Americans are going to meet
> the challenge and emerge victorious! (Applause)

Mrs. Jackson accepts the Distinguished Service Medal for her
son, and then she tries to read Mr. Torrence's prepared speech.
She stammers when she comes to a statement about Willie's
sacrifice not being made in vain. Departing from the script she
asks, "Or was it, son? Was it? Did it really mean anything to
them, Willie?" She regains her composure and resumes:

> I want to thank you all for this medal—on behalf of Willie, an'
> —an' (She stops again and shakes her head slowly from side to
> side) No, Willie. I just can't do it, son! (She looks up quietly
> and announces) I can't read this speech.

Mr. Torrence, the dishonest man shocked by another's honesty, tells her, "I typed it myself." Mrs. Jackson answers simply,
"Yes, I know you did. That's just why I can't read it." Her last

line, addressed to the principal and to most of the audience as well, is "You'll never understand." Her exit is quiet, calm, and dignified. Implicit in her silence is the still unanswered question, "Where was everybody when Willie was alive?"

A *Medal for Willie* is annoyingly episodic, and there are too many extended monologues for such a short play. Still it must be admitted that William Branch gave an interesting shape to his play by putting an auditorium scene at the beginning and at the end of the play, thus establishing a temporal pattern while allowing for exposition in the Prologue and a strong climax in Mrs. Jackson's heroic stand. The six scenes that take place concurrently in the space of time between Mr. Taylor's preparations in the Prologue and the ceremony itself in scene seven might be fuller, their characters more developed, but possibly the kaleidoscopic effect that is essential to the temper of the play would then be lost. The long monologues, especially Mrs. Jackson's in scene one and the General's in scene seven, while theatrically unwieldy, contain some of the best writing in the play.

Appropriately Mrs. Jackson and the General are the most fully developed characters and epitomize two responses to the racial question. The Negro woman speaks simply and movingly. The white officer speaks in clichés. The quality of their language suits these persons as they are in life as well as in art. There is not a false note in what they or other characters (even the barber's customer) say or do. If their words and actions are anticipated, it is because we have become steeped in accounts of racial injustice, and William Branch rarely makes a new statement of old truths.

In 1942 Ralph Ellison wrote, for *New Masses,* "The Way It Is," a record of an interview with a Mrs. Jackson of Harlem whose son Wilbur was in the army. "Wilbur's got a medal for shooting so good," says his little brother. After listening to this mother's brave but confused words about her son, her doubts about housing and health in Harlem, the author concludes:

The Mrs. Jacksons cannot make the sacrifices necessary to participate in a total war if the conditions under which they live, the very ground on which they must fight, continues its offensive against them. Nor is this something to be solved by propaganda. Morale grows out of realities, not out of words alone. Only concrete action will be effective—lest irritation and confusion turn into exasperation, and exasperation change to disgust and finally into anti-war sentiment (and there is such a danger). Mrs. Jackson's reality must be democratized so that she may clarify her thinking and her emotions. And that's the way it really is.[17]

William Branch may or may not have read this essay that first appeared when he was fifteen years old, but his Mrs. Jackson is certainly among the Negro women demanding our attention; their sons deserve more than a medal for shooting or dying for democracy.

In Splendid Error

William Branch wrote the first two drafts of his play *In Splendid Error* while he was in the army (1952–53), stationed in Germany. "As a matter of fact," he recalls, "I began the first few pages on the troopship during the trip over. It was originally titled *Frederick Douglass* and received its subsequent title during a rewrite done after my discharge from the service late in 1953."[18] This change is understandable in view of the fact that a play about Frederick Douglass, when it is also about John Brown, needs a title that suggests their relationship. *In Splendid Error* is, in a sense, Douglass' epithet for the man he so greatly admired even when he found it necessary to disagree with him. (As *In Splendid Error* the play opened at the Greenwich Mews on October 26, 1954; it ran through January, 1955.)

With him in Europe Branch had at least three books: the famous autobiography, *Life and Times of Frederick Douglass*

(1892); Shirley Graham's *There Was Once a Slave* (1947), a fictionalized biography of Douglass; and *God's Angry Man* (1932), a novel about John Brown by Leonard Ehrlich.[19] The autobiography furnished "the core of the story-line itself," Branch says, "although . . . certain dramatic licenses were taken in order to more effectively dramatize what I consider to be the basic conflict: that of two ways of fighting for a cause."[20] This contrast, contest if you will, provides *In Splendid Error* with dramatic conflict which is both true to history and symbolic of the present division in Negro action.

The entire action of this three-act play takes place in the parlor of Frederick Douglass' home in Rochester, New York, between 1859 and 1860. The characters who appear on the scene are men whose names are familiar from history, antislavery men from various walks of life. In the first scene of the first act, Negro and white abolitionists gather on a spring afternoon to share news and opinions. They are also, it turns out, a welcoming committee for an escaped slave. Early in the scene the Reverend Jermain Loguen boasts to Mrs. Douglass that thirty-three free souls have passed through "our little station on the Underground Railway." The one who arrives this day is named Joshua. He is welcomed into the fraternity of free men and sent on to Canada.

George Chatham, a white businessman, tells his friend Theodore Tilton, editor of the New York *Independent*, that Rochester is fortunate to have a man of Douglass' prominence choose this city for his home. "And to think of it, Mr. Tilton," Chatham adds in awe, "a scant twenty years ago this man was a slave—a chattel, a 'thing.' " Now he is a journalist and pamphleteer, editor of a newspaper, and a forceful orator. The way is thus prepared for the entrance of Frederick Douglass.[21]

After graciously greeting his visitors, Douglass engages Tilton in an argument about abolitionist strategy. Not all abolitionists were in agreement. Some, like Garrison, championed moral force and passive resistance. Others, led by militant New Yorkers, ad-

vocated political action. Only John Brown and his followers under-
took direct revolutionary action. When Tilton is critical of John
Brown, accusing him of hindering the abolitionist cause by his
"self-appointed crusade to keep Kansas free," Douglass has this
to say about slavery:

> Slavery is like a spawning cancer; unless it is cured at its core,
> then despite all precaution it will eventually infect the whole
> organism. It must be stamped out entirely, not merely pre-
> vented from reaching other parts of the body.

By implication he says that John Brown has not been radical
enough. Tilton trusts the federal government to deal with slavery;
others do not because they feel that President Buchanan is swayed
by Southerners, and so the argument continues. The talk is as
congenial as it is serious, and the visitors are optimistic when they
leave, though still divided in their opinions.

Only the Douglass family is present when John Brown arrives,
traveling under the name of Nelson Hawkins (a pseudonym
which he did frequently employ). He is the latest arrival on the
Underground Railway. He asks if he may stay for a few weeks, a
request to which Douglass immediately accedes.[22] When the two
men are alone, Brown says that his work in Kansas has not freed
a single black soul. "I must," he says, "get back to my true work:
to free enslaved black folk, and not further waste my energies on
political partridge like Kansas."

Old John Brown, as he was called, though he was only as old
as the century, outlines his plan to hide men in groups of five
in the Virginia mountains. There he wants to drill them in the
art of guerrilla warfare, and then to have them steal down to the
plantations and drive the slaves into the hills in great numbers.
When such valuable property disappears, he contends, the plantation owners will have to consider a system more economically
secure than slavery. "We attack the slavery system at its core,"
Brown explains, "and that is its pocketbook." When Douglass
expresses concern that it will take too long to defeat slavery in

this fashion, Brown disagrees, saying that he has spent years planning not just minor skirmishes but a large operation that will extend far into the South. The Negro leader feels that the risk involved is too great, that failure in this undertaking might destroy all that the abolitionists have accomplished to date, and yet he compliments John Brown, saying, "There is one thing that cannot be denied: you have not just talked about slavery, you are doing something about it." The orator feels compelled to lend his support to the man of action. The last speech of Act I is John Brown's:

> Oh, Douglass! Douglass!
> I knew I could count on you! It's coming . . .
> I can feel that it's coming! As Moses led the
> children of Israel from Egyptian bondage to the
> land of Canaan, so shall we lead the
> children of Africa from Southern bondage
> to the land of Canada. It is God's will!
> Together—together we will free the slaves![23]

Act II is a long act in three scenes. Beginning with the implied and then the overt treachery of Hugh Forbes, the act rises to a peak of intensity in scene two when Douglass and Brown quarrel about Harpers Ferry. The third scene brings news of John Brown's defeat. The pyramidal pattern of the act indicates what the important action is: the clash of two men's convictions in an argument over the means to an end.

In reality Colonel Hugh Forbes, an Englishman and a former lieutenant of Garibaldi, was commissioned by John Brown in 1857 to write a manual of guerrilla warfare and to help drill a company of soldiers. Forbes did indeed write a "Manual for the Patriotic Volunteer," but he was soon asking for $100 a week more than the $600 a week that Brown was paying him,[24] and he eventually went to prominent Republicans with information about the proposed uprising. W. E. B. DuBois has summarized Forbes's actions in this way:

He had all the foreigner's difficulty in following the confused threads of another nation's politics at a critical time. He classed Seward, Wilson, Sumner, Phillips and John Brown together as anti-slavery men who were ready to attack the institution vi et armis. This movement which he proposed to lead had been started, and then, as he supposed, shamelessly neglected by its sponsors while he had been thrust upon the mercies of John Brown. He was angry and penniless and he intended to have reparation. He first sought out Frederick Douglass, but was received coldly. He appears to have been more successful with McCune Smith and the New York group of Negro leaders. He immediately, too, began to address letters to prominent Republicans.[25]

Branch's play is true to the spirit of history, although there is some dramatic license taken in telescoping events into the years 1859-60. In the first scene of the second act, Forbes visits Douglass, who is handling John Brown's finances, and threatens to go to the authorities if he does not receive more money. In scene two the other abolitionists urge Brown to delay his plans now that Forbes has informed the authorities, but Brown will not be discouraged by this turn of events. He is at a fever pitch, and, when he and Douglass are alone, he lets slip his intention of getting arms at Harpers Ferry.

Douglass, greatly disturbed at this plan to capture a United States government arsenal, tries in vain to get Brown's attention long enough to express his alarm.

DOUGLASS: Brown! What are you thinking of?
BROWN: (speaking fervently now): Can't you see it, Frederick? The word traveling from lip to lip . . . the slaves rallying to the call . . . the mountain passes sealed with bullets . . . liberty spreading southward like a trail of fire!
DOUGLASS: John!
BROWN: The nation roused—
DOUGLASS: Do you know what you're saying?

BROWN: *The chains dropping—*
DOUGLASS: *It's mad. It's madness, I tell you!*
BROWN: *Free men rising from the muck of enslavement!—*
DOUGLASS (shouts): *John!! Listen to me. You cannot do it!*

Brown rushes on to a passionate defense of the necessity of bloodshed when moral suasion has failed. He cites the Bible, the shedding of blood of the firstborn of Egypt. There is, he says, no remission of sins without bloodshed. Douglass breaks in to ask, "John! Do you think you are God?" After a pause, Brown replies:

God? . . . *God is different things to different men, Frederick. To some He is a separate entity, dispensing wrath or reward from philanthropic heights. To some He is watchdog conscience, gnawing at the marrow. To me . . . God is simply the perception and the performance of right. And so I am a little bit of God. Or trying to be.*

When Douglass refuses to argue further, because it is obvious that he cannot change his friend's mind, Brown asks him, "Then you're coming with me, Frederick?" To which Douglass replies, "I cannot." Here is the great moment of decision for Frederick Douglass, the climax of the play.

In his autobiography the historical Douglass wrote: "The taking of Harpers Ferry was a measure never encouraged by my word or by my vote. . . . My field of labor for the abolition of slavery was not extended to an attack upon the United States arsenal."[26] And, perhaps even more significantly, he wrote, "My discretion or my cowardice made me proof against the dear old man's eloquence—perhaps it was something of both which determined my course."[27]

In the last moments of the second scene of Act II, Brown taunts Douglass, asks the Negro if he has forgotten the lash or if he is afraid of a gun. As if struck, the former slave and ardent abolitionist answers slowly:

I have never questioned it before, John. If it would do good . . . if it would do good, this moment I would die, I swear it, John!

But I cannot cast away that which I know I can do for that which I know I cannot do. I have no right to do that. I should rather fail you, John, than feel within myself that I have failed my people. For them . . . I believe it is my duty to live, and to fight in ways that I know I can succeed.

Again John Brown has the curtain line, as he turns at the door to say, "I shall miss you, Frederick."

Scene three takes place a few weeks later, early in the morning. First a telegram comes from Douglass, who is away on a trip, instructing his son Lewis to secure all his papers at once. (He has letters and a constitution written by John Brown locked in his desk.) Then Chatham brings news of Brown's defeat at Harpers Ferry. Douglass returns and tells of arguing with Brown at Chambersburg, Pennsylvania. Some of that argument, as recorded in the autobiography, was used by the playwright in the second scene, but it is repeated here to reinforce Douglass' opposition to Brown's way of fighting for their mutual cause.

It is soon evident that the Negro leader is troubled by his inability to follow old John Brown into battle. He turns to Loguen with these unanswered questions:

Then tell me, Loguen—how long this night? How long this dark, dark night when no man walks in freedom, without fear, in this cradle of democracy, no man who's black? How will it happen, what will we have to do? Nat Turner tried it with guns, and he failed. Dred Scott went to the high courts, and they handed him back into slavery. Old John said it must be by blood, and tonight he lies wounded in a Virginia prison.

Loguen and the others persuade Douglass to go to England to avoid being implicated in the investigation of Harpers Ferry. The scene ends with Anne Douglass alone, singing, "Didn't it rain, children/ Rain, oh my Lord."

When Act III opens, six months have passed, the investigation has been dropped, and Douglass has just returned from England. Chatham and Tilton, before Douglass' entrance, speak of the

politics of a little-known legislator named Lincoln who has a real
chance of defeating Seward for the presidential nomination at the
Republican convention in Chicago. But when Frederick Douglass
enters the room, all talk is of John Brown. Tilton tells of being
at the trial and even at the hanging of Brown. Douglass listens
and soon reveals that he is still tortured by the thought that he
did not go to Harpers Ferry. He feels unworthy of the people of
Rochester who are gathering outside his house to welcome a hero.

He confesses a lack of faith in the stand he took in opposing
John Brown:

> I have discovered that it is possible for a man to make a right
> decision, and then be tormented in spirit the rest of his life
> because he did not make the wrong one. There are times when
> the soul's need to unite with men in splendid error tangles
> agonizingly with cold wisdom and judgement. . . . Then in
> London, when the news came . . . how brave the old man
> was . . . how steadfastly he refused to name or implicate any-
> one . . . how he died upon the gallows, it came to me in a rush
> that John, in his way, had succeeded! In splendid error he had
> startled the sleeping conscience of the nation and struck a blow
> for freedom that proves stronger every hour.

Refusing to address the rally, Douglass says that he cannot look
an audience in the eyes without hearing John Brown's challenge:
"Are you afraid to face a gun?"

After several attempts, Chatham forces Douglass to listen to
him. He has, he reports, been to see John Brown's widow, Mary.
She has sent a package to Douglass. Chatham produces a canvas
parcel, and Douglass unwraps it, revealing a tarnished musket and
a torn American flag. Chatham also has a message that Brown
wrote in prison. Douglass reads it aloud slowly, quietly: "Tell
Douglass I know I have not failed because he lives. Follow your
own star, and someday unfurl my flag in the land of the free."
The silence that follows is broken by the sound of a distant drum,
signaling the beginning of the rally. Douglass agrees to go; he will

speak to the crowd. Outside the parade passes, and a fife-and-drum corps plays "The Battle Hymn of the Republic."

In Splendid Error is a historical play of considerable merit, especially when one considers that it came from the pen of a twenty-six-year-old playwright, and that it was his second play. Critics agreed that the writing was impressive and generally praised the Greenwich Mews production, giving special credit to actors William Marshall, as Frederick Douglass, and Alfred Sandor, as John Brown. After calling William Branch's writing eloquent and vigorous, however, the New York *Times* critic felt constrained to add that the playwright had tripped on an obstacle that frequently blocks the way of those attempting to re-create history in the theatre.

> *In the play history speaks with strength but the characters of history, for all their flesh and bones, lack the inner spirit of human beings. Neither John Brown nor Frederick Douglass comes completely alive in spite of all their words and outer anguish.*[28]

One might add that they lack life, credibility, because of too many words and too much anguish. *In Splendid Error* suffers from a message repeated too often and too eloquently.

Rather specific criticism was leveled at the play by left-wing critic Harry Raymond. He felt that the play dwarfed both Brown and Douglass because the tactical differences between the two men were exaggerated.

> *By failing to present Brown's tactical reasons for the Harper's Ferry venture, Branch's John Brown emerges as a man driven by wild fanaticism rather than a skillful tactician in guerrilla warfare and a man zealous in the fight to rid the land of slavery.*[29]

William Branch has recently stated his intentions in detail:

> *I saw in the Douglass-Brown story certain parallels—remarkable and uncanny parallels—between the climate and events of the*

1850s and those of the 1950s. Like Douglass, I found it hard to discard an ingrained belief that change could somehow take place without the necessity of outright overthrow of the government. . . . Like Douglass in the play, I found myself taunted by more revolutionary souls and inwardly agonized over wanting to join in more active methods to speed legitimately needed reforms, and yet unwilling to accept joining the Communist Party—especially with its undeniable links to International Communism—as a personal alternative. (It so happened that all of these friends later became disillusioned with the Party and left it as well, but at the time, they thought of themselves as the only truly brave souls and sometimes were particularly vicious in excoriating their friends who declined to "go all the way" with them.)

Thus In Splendid Error eventually became (during final drafts) more and more of a personal statement in contemporary terms as to the differing roles people could play in a revolutionary movement. I believed then, and believe now, that society needs both its fiery souls and its more reasoned thinkers, both its id and its super-ego.[30]

Trouble in Mind

Born in South Carolina, Alice Childress was raised in New York City and educated in the New York public schools. She did not go to college. What contributed to her interest in theatre? Her grandmother, she says, was a great storyteller. The Bible, Shakespeare, and Paul Laurence Dunbar were part of her early experience. In Harlem she went to Negro church programs at which concert artists and readers appeared. Her first recollection of a theatrical experience is of hearing an actress named Laura Bowman reciting scenes from Shakespeare. "A lot of Shakespeare is done in the Negro community," Miss Childress has observed. "We are more identified with his flamboyancy than with a more restricted kind of theatre." The first role that she herself remembers playing, at an early age, was that of Titania in A *Midsummer Night's Dream*.[31]

All during the forties, when she was in her twenties, Alice Childress was an actress. One of the original members of the American Negro Theatre, she appeared in *On Strivers Row* (1940), *Natural Man* (1941), and *Anna Lucasta* (1944). She wrote her first play in 1949. Written overnight, *Florence* was an effort to settle an argument with fellow actors (Sidney Poitier among others) who said that, in a play about Negroes and whites, only a "life and death thing" like lynching is interesting on stage. *Florence* is a one-act play about what happens when a Negro woman and a white woman in the Jim Crow waiting room of a Southern railroad station try to communicate. It is perforce a rather static play, but Miss Childress did prove that everyday situations can be dramatized. She also showed that she had a good ear for dialogue and a fine sense of characterization. *Florence* was produced by the Committee for the Negro in the Arts in 1950 and again in 1951. Also in 1951 she received twenty dollars for its publication in *Masses and Mainstream*.

Alice Childress has been, from the beginning, a crusader and a writer who resists compromise. She tries to write about Negro problems as honestly as she can, and she refuses production of her plays if the producer wants to change them in a way which distorts her intentions. In defense of this stand, she has said:

> Most of our problems have not seen the light of day in our works, and much has been pruned from our manuscripts before the public has been allowed a glimpse of a finished work. It is ironical that those who oppose us are in a position to dictate the quality and quantity of our contributions. To insult a man is one thing, but to tell him how to react to the insult adds a great and crippling injury.[32]

A case in point is *Trouble in Mind*, her first full-length play, which was produced off-Broadway in 1955. It was subsequently optioned for Broadway, but quarrels about theme, statement, and interpretation led Miss Childress to withdraw her work. The producer kept asking for changes in the script that would have made it a "heart-warming little story," something that it most assuredly is not.

The title, *Trouble in Mind*, comes from a blues song of the same name. Alice Childress chose to tell about trouble in a milieu that she knows well—the theatre. The three acts of *Trouble in Mind* take place during rehearsals in a Broadway theatre, between Monday and Thursday of a week in 1957. The play being rehearsed is one about Negroes and whites; the cast of the play-within-a-play consists of two Negro actresses, two Negro actors, a white actor, and a white actress. The remaining characters— director, stage manager, and doorman—are white. What happens to all of them as they react to the play they are rehearsing and to each other is the substance of Miss Childress' play, which opened November 4, 1955, at the Greenwich Mews Theatre and ran for ninety-one performances.[33]

Trouble in Mind opens with the entrance of a middle-aged Negro actress named Wiletta Mayer, a former musical comedy singer. When John Nevins, a young Negro actor, arrives, she soon begins giving him advice about the theatre or, as she prefers to call it, show business. "It's just a business," she reminds John. "Colored folks ain't in no theatre." When he mentions that he has studied at the Actors Studio, she warns him, "Don't let the man know that. . . . They want us to be naturals . . . you know, just born with the gift." He may, she says, tell the director that he was in *Green Pastures* when he was a little boy. (It is an old joke that all Negro actors have been in at least one of the *Green Pastures* productions.)

Next she advises John to laugh at everything that the white director (a Mr. Manners) says; it will make the white man feel superior. What she suggests seems "Uncle Tommish" to John. Wiletta agrees but adds that being an Uncle Tom is no different from being a white "yes man." Both have to lie, to pretend, and to hold back honest opinions in order to survive in show business.

These lessons in diplomacy are interrupted by the arrival of other members of the cast. Millie, a handsome Negro actress, about thirty-five years old, is well dressed and seemingly at ease in the world. Sheldon Forrester is an elderly Negro character man who wants nothing more than to stay out of trouble. Judy Sears, a young white actress, is fresh out of Yale Drama School and quite in awe of Broadway.

While they are waiting for the director to appear, the Negroes forget Judy's presence and talk among themselves about Negro problems in the theatre. Millie says, "I'll wear them baggy cotton dresses but damn if I'll wear a bandanna." Sheldon's comment that bandannas are fashionable, that even white folks wear them, does not dissuade her. She goes on to joke with Wiletta about playing "every flower in the garden"—Gardenia, Magnolia, Chrysanthemum. And if they were not flowers, they were jewels—Crystal, Pearl, Opal. The two women laugh heartily at this state of affairs, and Sheldon, worried that they may complain to the director, warns them to be careful and to "keep peace." Wiletta's response is wryly philosophical: "I always say it's the man's play, the man's money and the man's theatre, so what you gonna do?"

Sheldon reminds the others of Judy's presence, and so they all turn their attention to the white girl. Trying to make conversation, Judy says that she hopes that people will learn something from the play. When urged to say what, she blurts out, "That people are the same, that people are . . . are . . . well, you know . . . that people are people." The dialogue begins to separate in a way that it frequently does throughout the play:

SHELDON: *There you go . . . brotherhood of man stuff! Sure!*
WILETTA: *Yes, indeed. I don't like to think of theatre as just a a business. Oh, it's the art . . . ain't art a wonderful thing?*
MILLIE: (Bald, flat statement to no one in particular) *People aren't the same.*

It is easy to sense who is "acting" and who is not.

Director Al Manners arrives. He is described as a man "in his late forties, [a] hatless, well tweeded product of Hollywood. He is a bundle of energy, considerate and understanding after his own fashion; selfish and tactless after ours." He waits for applause, begs laughs, and generally lives up to the picture of a director as depicted in countless Hollywood movies. He is, in short, a stereotype.

When Manners tries to tell the cast about the play, "Chaos in Belleville," and about his dedication to the production, there is interesting contrast between their meaningful reactions and his platitudinous talk.

MANNERS: *When I read it bells rang. This is now, we're living this, who's in the headlines these days?* (Eloquent pause)

SHELDON: *How 'bout that Montgomery, Alabama? Made the bus company lose one, cold, cash, billion dollars!*

JOHN: *Not a billion.*

MANNERS: *Here was a contribution to the elimination of . . .*

SHELDON: *I know what I read!*

MANNERS: *A story on Negro rights that . . .*

SHELDON: *How 'bout them busses!*

JUDY: *And they're absolutely right.*

MILLIE: *Who's right?*

MANNERS: *A contribution that really . . .*

JUDY: *The colored people.*

MANNERS: *. . . leads to a clearer understanding . . .*

MILLIE: *Oh. I thought you meant the other people.*

MANNERS: *A clearer understanding.*

JUDY: *I didn't mean that.*

MANNERS: *Yale, please!*
(All silent)

Once he has regained their attention, Manners lets them know that he believes in the play, in the cast, and of course in his own good judgment.

The rehearsal begins. Losing his temper with Judy for not

knowing one stage area from another, Manners crumples a piece of paper and throws it onto the floor. Then he catches Wiletta off guard when he insists that she, not one of the men, pick it up. She is so shocked that at first she refuses—"Hell! I ain't the damned janitor!"—and it is with great difficulty that she regains her submissive composure. Manners stops the scene and, out of embarrassment at what he has revealed about himself, says to the cast:

> What you have just seen is . . . is . . . is fine acting. Actors struggle for weeks to do what you have done perfectly the first time. You gave me anger, frustration, movement, er . . . excitement. Your faces were alive! Why? You did what came naturally, you believed . . . that is the quality I want in your work . . . the firm texture of truth.

Only Judy is convinced that Manners was playing a trick. A tension enters the play that never quite leaves it.

Manners calls the Negro characters in the play-within-a-play "tenant farmers," which Wiletta translates to Sheldon as "sharecroppers." In the scene read by the actors, these Negroes want to hold a barn dance, but the white boss is reluctant to give them permission, because he is disturbed by a rumor that they intend to vote. Judy plays the boss's daughter who intervenes on behalf of the Negroes. The actress balks at having to say, "Papa, let the darkies have their fun." Manners questions the cast to discover whether or not they are bothered by the word "darkies." John is very politic, stating that he does not like the word himself, but "it is used, it's a slice of life." Since it seems to bother no one but Judy, the word is left in the script. (It might as well stay, since most of the dialogue harks back to Edward Sheldon, or even Dion Boucicault.)

Later they rehearse a scene leading up to a lynching, and Wiletta, as Ruby, is to set the scene by singing a song. It is a sad song that she remembers from childhood, Wiletta tells the cast. It begins:

I must walk my lonesome valley,
I got to walk it for myself.
Nobody else can walk it for me,
I got to walk it for myself.

The cast is moved by her singing, but Manners has decided to uncover her motivations.

MANNERS: *What were you thinking?*
WILETTA: *I thought . . . I . . . er, er . . . I don't know, whatever you said.*
MANNERS: *Tell me. You're not a vacuum, you thought something . . .*
WILETTA: *Uh-uh.*
MANNERS: *And out of the thought came song.*
WILETTA: *Yeah.*
MANNERS: *What did you think?*
WILETTA: *I thought that's what you wanted.*

When he gets nowhere with this approach, he tries word association. The word he gives her is "Montgomery," which calls up "Alabama" and "Reverend King." Reaching for something more profound, he tries the word "colored." Her first association is with the colored lights that used to play on her as she sang. Then she remembers a question that Sheldon asked the stage manager about his apartment building: "They got colored in that building?" Manners presses on.

MANNERS: *Children, little children.*
WILETTA: *Children . . . children . . . pick up that paper! Oh, my . . .*
MANNERS: *Lynching.*
WILETTA: *Killin'! Killin'!*
MANNERS: *Killing.*
WILETTA: *It's the man's theatre, the man's money, so what you gonna do?*
MANNERS: *Oh, Wiletta . . . I don't know! Darkness!*
WILETTA: *A star! Oh, I can't, I don't like it . . .*

MANNERS: *Sing.*

Apparently it is difficult for the white man to understand that her racial responses are not as readily articulated as her personal ones. Whatever he liked in her singing came from too deep to be verbalized except in the song.

His intellectual bullying creates such anger in Wiletta that she now sings the song almost belligerently. The flood gate is opened, and all her customarily repressed racial feelings are poured into the song. This is not what Manners wanted. He is puzzled that her singing seemed perfection when she did not know what she was doing. He will settle, he says, for her original interpretation of the song. Wiletta, at a loss, answers, "I said I knew what you wanted."

Act II of *Trouble in Mind* takes place during the morning of the fourth day of rehearsals of "Chaos in Belleville." It opens with Bill O'Wray, the white character actor, doing a set speech on tolerance. As old Mr. Renard (Bre'r Fox?), the actor intones his lines passionately. The climax of Renard's speech, with its citation of Dickens and the Bible, may seem rather old-fashioned to anyone unaccustomed to Southern oratory:

> Oh, friends, moderation. Let us weigh our answer very carefully when the dark-skinned Oliver Twist approaches our common pot and says, "Please, sir, I want some more." When we say "no," remember that a soft answer turneth away wrath. Ohhhh, we shall come out of the darkness, and sweet is pleasure after pain. If we are superior let us show our superiority!

It is soon apparent that Bill O'Wray is nothing like Renard. With characteristic playfulness, Miss Childress has him portray a wicked and purposive Renard, though he himself is a sweet man, a worrier who "sees dragons in every corner." One of his current worries is that his not mingling with the Negro members of the cast may be misunderstood. His problem, he tells Manners when they are waiting for the others to arrive, is not prejudice but ulcers. He cannot bear to have people stare at him while he eats, and they do, for example, if he eats with Millie. He has the feeling that people in the restaurant are accusing him of lechery because he is with a pretty Negro woman.

When the actors arrive for rehearsal, there is the usual small talk, all expressed in multiple levels of dialogue so that observations on life and death mingle authentically. It is significant that just before the rehearsal begins, the talk is of the death of an actress, a talented woman who lived and died alone. Wiletta has to move from that conversation into a scene that has little reality for her, something that she increasingly resents. The characters in "Chaos in Belleville" are waiting for news of Job (John), waiting to find out if the lynchers have caught up with him or not. Ruby (Wiletta) is ironing, Petunia (Millie) is looking out the window, and old Sam (Sheldon) is whittling a stick—stock actions for characters in a play about Negro life in the South. These Negroes are even being comforted by the presence of the white boss Renard's daughter, Carrie (Judy). Other familiar devices employed in the scene are a prayer, fragmentary responses, and a spiritual.

When Job arrives, having escaped the lynch mob, he asks for help to get out of town. His mother (played by Wiletta) cannot understand why he is running away if he has not done wrong. And yet she is the one who urges him to confess to voting, which in the eyes of the lynch mob is his crime. Job says pathetically, "I wasn't even votin' for a black man, votin' for somebody white same as they." The old folks say that they have never voted and have no interest in who gets into office—"Don't make no nevermind to us." Job counters with, "When a man got a decent word to say for us down here I gonna vote for him." His elders tell him that a decent word is too small a thing to die for. The white girl says that her father will put him in the county jail to keep him safe. (The hero in Edward Sheldon's "The Nigger" [1910] does the same for one of his tenants.)

When Renard arrives, Ruby pleads with him to protect her

boy, who, she says, did not understand the wrong he was doing by voting. Renard agrees to take care of Job and then suggests that a white man named Akins is behind this voting business. Maybe Akins is the man with "a decent word" for Negroes. Job does not say. He follows Renard out into the night as his mother sings a spiritual and goes back to her ironing. All in all, the scene is right out of an old melodrama, with the one difference that the Negro is accused of voting rather than of rape.

During a rehearsal break following the scene, Manners tries to clarify the remaining action of the play for Sheldon:

> Renard drives him toward jail, deputies stop them on the way, someone shoots and kills Job as he tries to escape, afterward they find out he was innocent, Renard makes everyone feel like a dog . . . they realize they were wrong and so forth.

Sheldon wants to know in what way Job was innocent. He did vote, after all. Manners reminds him that the boy was not guilty of any "wrongdoing." The cast then tries to discuss Job's innocence or guilt, but there is great difficulty in communication.

Wiletta finds it particularly difficult to justify the play. She cannot understand why Job has to be killed for the audience to learn that violence is wrong. Nor is she satisfied with John's contention that these characters are uneducated, humble people who cannot fully comprehend what is happening to them. When Manners steps in to say that they are human beings, she is quick to let him know that she is aware that Negroes are human.

"It does not matter to me that they are Negroes," Manners insists. "Black, white, green or purple, I maintain there is only one race . . . the human race." Sheldon applauds, but the cast proves that there are Negro and white individuals among human beings—or, as Miss Childress has put it elsewhere, that "human beings are more than just people."[34]

In an effort to get back to "Chaos in Belleville," Manners asks the cast to imagine the horror of a lynching. It seems that Sheldon saw a lynching when he was nine years old. Manners asks him to try to recall his feelings so that the cast can profit by hearing about them. Sheldon tells his story simply in a long speech that is filled with the kind of homely reference that moves a story of the past into the present.

> *A sound come to my ears like bees hummin' . . . was voices comin' closer and closer, screamin' and cursin' . . . and the screaming' was laughin' . . . Lord, how they was laughin' . . . louder and louder. . . . Then I hear wagon wheels bumpin' over the wet, stony road, chains clankin'. . . . Chained to the back of the wagon, draggin' and bumpin' along. . . . The arms of it stretched out. . . . A burnt, naked thing that once was a man . . . and I started to scream but no sound came out . . . just a screamin' but no sound.*

Sheldon says of the man who was killed that folks thought he was crazy because he was "quick to speak his mind."

Act III of *Trouble in Mind* has much the same pattern as the first two acts. The cast, returning for afternoon rehearsal, indulges in talk of this and that; the rehearsal begins, only to be interrupted by Wiletta's questioning of the play's validity, and there is an argument involving the entire company. This particular argument is a revelation to all the participants and provides the denouement of Miss Childress' play.

The rehearsal of "Chaos in Belleville" is broken by Wiletta at the moment when, as Ruby, she is called upon once again to urge her son Job to give himself up to his white "protectors." The actress refuses to portray this woman who is willing to send her son to his death. She cannot believe what she is being asked to do and say in the play. She presses Manners for an answer to the question, "Why don't [Job's] people help him?" The director rises to her challenge:

MANNERS: *Why this great fear of death? Christ died for something and . . .*
WILETTA: *Sure, they came and got him and hauled him off to jail.*

His mother didn't turn him in, in fact, the one who did it was a so-called friend.

MANNERS: *His death proved something. Job's death brings him the lesson* . . .

WILETTA: *That they should stop lynching innocent men! Fine thing! Lynch the guilty, is that the idea?*

There is no halting this kind of argument, filled as it is with long-repressed and rarely articulated accusations.

Manners tries to justify the play in terms of its author's talent. Wiletta then accuses the director of not listening to her because he is prejudiced. With this accusation she sets the white man's arguments in motion. He presents his case in a long speech that is broken only by fragments of unheeded protest. It is not, Manners assures the cast, so wonderful to be white. He has troubles, too. Being white has not saved him from having to "crawl and knuckle under step by step" in order to get ahead in the theatre world. Negroes, he says, have a way of thinking that there is a white conspiracy, "one great, grand fraternity." If Manners is a member, he feels that he has been cheated and robbed by his brothers.

No favors, no dreams served up on silver platters with Christmas ribbon. Now . . . finally I get something for myself and hang onto it . . . something for all of us . . . but it's not enough for you . . . I'm prejudiced! Get wise, there's damned few of us interested in putting on a colored show at all, much less one that's going to say anything.

He can defend the script that he is directing not in terms of its being the truth—after all, who would invest in the unvarnished truth?—but by calling it an honest lie:

So, maybe it's a lie . . . but it's one of the finest, most honest of lies you'll come across for a damned long time! Here's some bitter news, since you're living off truth. . . . The American public is not ready to see you the way you want to be seen because, *one . . . they don't believe it, two . . . they don't want to be-lieve it . . . and three . . . they're convinced they're superior.*

He advises the actors to touch the American heart rather than try to change the American mind. If the audience feels sorry for the Negroes in the play, something good, he contends, will have been accomplished.

Manners is so involved in self-pity and sermonizing that he is caught off guard by Wiletta's next question: "Would you send your son out to be murdered?" He answers hastily without thinking:

Don't compare yourself to me! What goes for my son doesn't necessarily go for yours! Don't compare him (points to John), with three strikes against him, don't compare him with my son, they've got nothing in common, not a goddam thing!

His confusion and embarrassment are immediately evident; he had not intended to go this far. He has lost whatever sympathy or understanding that he had had, and so he makes a quick retreat to the dressing room.

The members of the cast are forced to discuss the new position they find themselves in. They are divided in their response to Wiletta's stand of "I want this script changed or else," but it is soon clear that most of them need the job so badly that they find it difficult to contemplate quitting even though they have little or no faith in the script.

When Manners returns to the stage, he addresses himself to Wiletta by speaking to the cast generally about the difficult times in which they are living and by recognizing anyone's right to leave if working conditions are not suitable. Not until he asks the cast to pick up the rehearsal at a certain page in the script does Wiletta announce, "I want the author, producer and director to see that this script gets some changes because I can't do it as it is." Again Manners suggests that she quit, but she stubbornly refuses, saying, "No, no. You gonna have to fire me." Since she insists, he fires her, giving her two weeks' pay.

Wiletta's next step is to ask everyone in the cast to walk out with her. Manners, shocked by her threat to notify all the newspapers, tries to persuade her that this is no way to help her people. He insists that he is their friend, that he does not deserve this treatment. He reminds her that he has given them jobs, opportunities in the theatre. Her answer is militant and forceful:

> If you have gifts to give, give 'em. I got nothin' else to give away. You say you can't do this, can't do that and can't afford to tell the truth. That's you, I'm sorry for you . . . but I'm gonna be free to tell it, and if not now, when?

Manners still cannot understand why she takes exception to Job's death. After all, he says, if the Negro characters in the play were to shoot it out with the lynch mob, that would be "sheer violence." She questions his logic with "Yeah, kill my child and call me violent, that's what comes of all this justifyin'."

Manners again accuses Wiletta of being ungrateful. He claims to have helped her in the past to get roles other than that of a "stereotyped mammy." She laughs at the idea of any Negro woman's character role being anything but a mammy. She does several parodies of such parts and then concludes:

> You stayin' up all night fixin' up character parts for me! Givin' 'em what you call . . . dignity! Dignity! You know what your dignity is? A old, black, straw hat with a flower stickin up in front, hands folded cross your stomach, sayin' the same dern foolishness nice and easy and proper!

Nor is it a question, she reminds Manners, of playing maids. The problem is that the maids are not people. (Lorraine Hansberry once said that the dialect in *Porgy and Bess* did not worry her, but it did bother her that "Porgy is not a man.")[35] Wiletta begins to warm to the subject of acting.[36] Next she tells Manners that when a film is made about a colored girl who is "passing," the part goes to a white actress. It seems inconsistent to Wiletta for a director to speak of truth and justifying when this kind of casting exists.

All these passin' folks supposed to be tore up inside and sufferin'; no sucha thing, they at the cocktail party with you, havin' a ball, without a care in the world! An don't dare be black . . . then you got to scratch your head (demonstrates) every time you start to think . . . plowin' up thoughts. Justify, ha! Oh, I'm holdin' class today, free of charge, the ten year course in ten minutes.

It is at this point that Manners begins to listen to Wiletta. No doubt Bill O'Wray listens, too, when she sympathizes with him about his stereotype as a white actor:

On that television yall shootin' down each other every night and all night long . . . shootin' and kissin', that's all you know . . . how big is your bust, who's drunk, who's on dope and murder, murder, murder . . . yes indeed, that's your stereotype. Suit yourself but I'm sicka mine.

Wiletta has worked herself up to the kind of excitement usually associated with prayer meetings, with what the author calls in one stage direction "the old-fashioned love feast." It is time for clasping of hands, embracing, and tears. The Negroes join her—even Sheldon, who is afraid to let the newspapers report that he did not—and Manners must shout her name to call Wiletta back and to halt the walkout. All eyes are on the two of them as Wiletta tells the director that she forgives him and loves him.

Touched by what has happened, not just this day but during the past four days, Manners confesses his prejudices, reminds them of theirs, and asks them to start all over again. His suggestion, in part:

I, a prejudiced man, ask you, a prejudiced cast, to wait until our prejudiced author arrives tomorrow. I propose that we sit down

*in mutual blindness and try to find a way to bring some splinter
of truth to a prejudiced audience.*

These are only two sentences out of a long speech, which is
amazingly well informed by a psychological awareness that
Manners has kept well hidden in earlier scenes.

To return to their rehearsal he asks Wiletta for a song, and this
time she chooses one that they can all sing together:

We are climbing Jacob's ladder
We are climbing Jacob's ladder
We are climbing Jacob's ladder, Soldiers of the cross.

The play ends on a note of optimism, although there is little
doubt that the soldiers have many battles ahead of them.

Trouble in Mind has interesting characters and dialogue, though
both tend to ring false whenever they are saturated with sermonizing. The setting, the stage of a theatre during rehearsals,
invites an audience to participate in a ritual usually forbidden
them and therefore tantalizing. The plot amounts to very little—
a group of actors rehearse a play, quarrel about interpretation, get
the director to agree to ask the playwright to make changes in the
script. What lends the play significance is that the cast is predominantly Negro. As attitudes in the company are modified,
people's lives are affected, and this play about a rehearsal makes
a comment on life itself.

And yet, too much of *Trouble in Mind* is willed—what the
French call *voulu*. A reader of the script is very much aware of the
author pulling strings, putting her own words into a number of
mouths. This is not, however, to deny the theatrical effectiveness
of the play in production. One critic's description of the audience
participation suggests a very direct involvement:

*The satirical scenes rocked and moved the audience until it be-
came part of the action on the stage. Many members of the
audience were so moved that they vocally expressed dislike or
approval of the actions and speeches of the characters on stage*

I have not seen anything like it since I was a boy and sat in the gallery with other kids watching Wild West melodramas.[37]

Brooks Atkinson found the play "well worth a trip downtown" and praised Miss Childress for writing a "fresh, lively and cutting satire" without sermonizing until the last ten or fifteen minutes.[38]

To read the play is to be much more aware than these critics were—they were under the spell of what was reportedly a good production—of the extent to which Miss Childress loaded the play with Negro problems. True, she makes us understand her need to write about her people when she says:

> *Many of us would rather be writers than Negro writers, and when I get that urge, I look about for the kind of white writer —which is what we mean when we say "just a writer"—that I would emulate. I come up with Sean O'Casey. Immediately, I am a problem writer. O'Casey writes about the people he knows best and I must.*[39]

It would be better if she did not assault race prejudice at every turn, for she sometimes sacrifices depth of character in the process.

What a critic once said of Mildred, the heroine of Miss Childress' collection of stories, *Like One of the Family*, could be said of characters in her play, especially of Wiletta:

> *One longs for the shock (so often encountered in life) of an unexpected taste or point of view. One longs also to penetrate beyond the "typical" view we are given . . . to the private agony and unique courage of such a woman.*[40]

The characters need a humanizing complexity to keep them from ever becoming the stereotypes featured in "Chaos in Belleville."

A Land Beyond the River

Street fights in his native Harlem with the children of immigrants and experiences in what he and others have characterized as a sadistic school system taught young Loften Mitchell to distrust whites and to develop a will to survive. In New York City he went to several public schools in the twenties, to Cooper Junior High in 1930, and to DeWitt Clinton High School, from which he received a "certificate" at graduation. He recalls that many Negroes who graduated during the Depression were unable financially and academically to attend college, but "Southern Negro colleges, offering athletic scholarships and grants-in-aid, rescued many from the despair into which they had been dumped."[41] He himself graduated from Talladega College, Talladega, Alabama, in 1943.

In the twenty-odd years since his graduation from college, Loften Mitchell has been a social worker and a writer. Always interested in theatre, he worked with the Rose McClendon Players and had plays (e.g., *The Cellar* and *Bancroft Dynasty*) produced at the Harlem Showcase. He studied playwriting briefly with John Gassner at Columbia University. He has written plays, radio scripts, screenplays, a children's book for a series edited by Langston Hughes, a portion of *The American Negro Writer and His Roots* (1960), plus articles on the theatre for magazines and newspapers. To both the Italian *Encyclopedia Della Spettacolo* and the British *Oxford Companion to the Theatre*, he has contributed articles about the American Negro in the theatre. In 1958–59 he had a Guggenheim fellowship for creative writing, and in 1961 a Rockefeller Foundation grant. A musical that he wrote with Irving Burgie, *Ballad for Bimshire*, was produced on Broadway in the 1963–64 season. His most recent book is *Black Drama* (1967), and soon to be produced is his musical about Florence Mills, *Ballad of a Blackbird*.

Mitchell's one published play, *A Land Beyond the River*, opened at the Greenwich Mews Theatre on March 28, 1957. Scheduled to run for ten weeks, it continued throughout the year. At the close of the New York run, the play was presented on tour in New Haven, Philadelphia, Great Neck, and Newark. In 1958

it was revived in Brooklyn. It has since been produced at Talladega College and in Chicago and Cincinnati.[42]

A major theme of A *Land Beyond the River* is desegregation.
The play is based on the experiences of the Reverend Joseph A.
DeLaine (Joseph Layne in the play), who brought a case to court
in 1949 in Clarendon County, South Carolina; he was seeking bus
transportation for Negro children in that rural area. The case developed into a suit for separate but equal schools, and the Negro
petitioners lost by a vote of two to one in a Charleston, South
Carolina, court. The judge's dissent formed the basis of an appeal
to the United States Supreme Court, making this one of the cases
that brought about the decision of May 17, 1954, to outlaw segregation in the public schools.

The suffering endured by DeLaine as a result of his fight for
desegregation is summarized in this tribute from his church, the
African Methodist Episcopal Church:

> In retaliation the enemies of Christian democracy burned De-
> Laine's house to the ground. His wife and relatives were de-
> prived of their positions as school teachers. Economic sanctions
> were forced upon them. For safety his Bishop transferred him
> to . . . Lake City. There his enemies burned his church and
> Bible. They fired shots at him and he left town making his
> home in New York City where he found asylum.[43]

Attempts were made to extradite the minister—"[he] was charged
in Lake City, S.C., with felonious assault for assertedly shooting
at a group of white persons"—but he was cleared by New York
Felony Court on January 16, 1956.[44]

Loften Mitchell learned of this story through Ossie Davis, who
has used some of it as background material for a concert reading,
and who urged his friend to develop it into a three-act play.[45]
Mitchell was able to consult with DeLaine, now the pastor of a
large Brooklyn church. He worked closely with the minister, whose
story he neither distorted nor simply duplicated in his play.

There are several scenes in each act of A *Land Beyond the*

River, but they are not labeled as such. A flexible set makes it possible for the play's action to move from place to place as different areas of the stage are lit and bits of scenery moved. The playwright describes the scene as "a cross section of a panoramic view of the entire county," a rural county in South Carolina.

Two little eight-year-old Negro boys, Willie Lee Waters and Glenn Raigen, open the play. They have been sent by their teacher, Laura Turnham, to find Mr. Layne and to tell him that the schoolroom floor has caved in. There will be no more school until it is fixed. Willie Lee is tempted not to deliver the message but to go fishing instead. Glenn vetoes that suggestion, because he remembers that his father, for lack of an education, carried boxes in the Navy when he wanted to fly airplanes. Then Glenn talks about his own plans for the future. He wants to live in a tall brick house by a paved road. Willie Lee starts a fight by reminding Glenn, "Boy, you colored! Houses with two stories, made outa brick. . . . That's for white folks!" The angry phrases that punctuate their fist fight show that Glenn's father has taught his boy to dream, while Willie Lee's has warned his of the folly of dreaming when one is black. In characterizing the boys, the playwright has begun to characterize their fathers.

When the minister appears, he is not a stereotype Negro preacher in black suit and steel-rimmed glasses. He wears a brown suit, a brown hat cocked on the back of his head, a white shirt and brown tie. He is neatly but not fastidiously dressed. There is a pipe in his breast pocket. He has prematurely gray hair and a youthful face that is "at times pleasant and humorous, then it becomes quite sober and serious." The playwright's description of Joseph Layne concludes with the observation that he is a man who moves "easily, rapidly, from the homespun to the intellectual, from the slow-talking, slow-moving country preacher to the sharp, stubborn, dogmatic individual that he often is."

Willie Lee and Glenn give the minister their news about the schoolhouse floor. He accepts it philosophically and sends the boys to tell their fathers to bring hammers and saws to the schoolhouse after supper. Layne starts off, singing "Nobody Knows the Trouble I See." He stops, catches his breath, and says:

> Lord, I'm not complaining, but it's mighty hard to be principal of a school, preacher, and general repairman. Fact is, if I wasn't a man of God, I'd say it's mighty damn hard!

This one speech establishes his pleasant, humorous side; the sober, serious one is soon to be revealed.

There is a brief transitional scene between the minister and a white doctor, George Willis, in front of Layne's home. Doc Willis is a good white man of a sort often featured in American fiction and films—a gruff old character who is really very kind and who embarrasses everyone with his salubrious frankness. "He has simply discovered through science," Loften Mitchell tells us, "that people are alike and he does not have time to waste treating them as though they were different." What is accomplished by this brief scene is a foreshadowing of Martha Layne's illness (a heart condition) and an indication of how readily two individualists, white and black, can communicate with one another.

In the little time that they have alone, Joseph and Martha Layne share talk of their work and their worries. When they speak of school matters, it is Martha who brings up the subject of reform. She asks her husband if he has considered carrying the fight beyond buses. His answer is that "a school bus fight is big enough." It is obvious that Martha hesitates to spell out exactly what she wants him to do. She speaks of the young Joe Layne whom she remembers in college, a fearless boy who was "on fire to set the world right." Now, she says, he is no longer leading a fight but just "dancing on the edges of one." His answer does not satisfy Martha, but it does help clarify his current hesitation to lead his people. He too recalls the boy that he was:

> A boy who led ten Negroes in a picket line against a Jim Crow movie house. A boy who cried out in horror as the police tore into the line, swinging clubs and fists. The sight of the blood they spilled still sickens me. And when we went to jail, our

wounds still bleeding, the others stared at me, not speaking, but their eyes judged me guilty. That's when I learned there's something wrong with a man who gets ahead of the people.

"That was years ago, Joe," his wife reminds him. "Those pages aren't on the calendar today."

Their discussion is interrupted by the arrival of two men, a white minister, John Cloud, and Laura's father, Philip Turnham. Cloud, who is superintendent of schools, accuses Layne of closing down his school in order to go off "agitating." He lets Layne know that he, Cloud, has kept the Negro in his job. "If any other white man in the country knew you were in back of this bus business," he says, "you wouldn't be allowed in the front door of a school, much less work in one!"

As a parting comment, the white man asks Layne why he calls him "Superintendent" and not "Mr. Cloud." Layne says that he is unaware of making such a distinction. Cloud suggests that "some folks think you do that just to keep from calling me 'Mister.'" Giving Turnham a significant look, Layne says deliberately, "Good night, Superintendent."

The next scene takes place at the home of Bill and Mary Raigen, an attractive Negro couple in their early thirties. It starts quietly, and then, like the previous scene, it builds in intensity to a purposeful climax. At the beginning, Bill, standing on the porch looking at his property, tells Mary of his dreams of improving the land, for his home gives his life meaning.

Dreaming about all this is what made them ammunition boxes I had to lift in the Navy seem light as feathers. Pay day used to come around and the other boys would run off and get drunk. Not me! Saved my money, Mary—'cause I knowed I wasn't gonna be a sharecropper all my life. Knowed someday I was gonna own my own land and—there it is! Just name one of our folks got land like this—'cepting Reverend Layne.

When the minister arrives and mentions the job that has to be done in fixing the schoolhouse floor, Bill bursts out angrily, "I done put in my last time! It's that School Board's job to fix up the place! Let 'em try it for a while and maybe they'll give us a new schoolhouse!" They are quick enough to take his tax money, he says, and quick enough to "integrate" it. Bill is so furious that even his land looks less pretty to him—"It's in the wrong part of the country!"

Layne concedes that "this repair work certainly isn't the answer," but he has no other at the moment. Bill accuses Layne of not being a real leader of his people. When asked what he wants, Bill replies bitterly:

> I want a new school! Listen, Rev—during the war I was with the Amphibs, delivering supplies to a bunch of Marines on a beachhead. When we got there, weren't no marines around. They was all shot up. . . . Delivering supplies to Marines who weren't even there. Like putting kids on buses to get to schools that ain't even there.

Layne is struck by the simile, but he cannot think of tomorrow's schools when today a floor needs mending.

Bill stands firm on his decision not to go with the minister until he is persuaded to do so by Mary:

> I don't want my child missing one single solitary day of school, you hear me? 'Cause it's real easy to miss one day, then another, and another! I ain't having him growing up, not knowing nothing, and having to work like a mule. . . . I ain't having him abused every single hour of the day 'cause he's ignorant! He's got to learn he's just as good as everybody else, and I want him to learn it good!

The next scene, the last one of Act I, is the first crowd scene and takes place at the school. Men's voices rise out of the darkness between the scenes. They are singing a spiritual that begins, "I'm going to tell God all my troubles when I get home." The lights reveal the men down on their knees mending the floor. In addition to Bill Raigen and Joseph Layne, there are Duff Waters, a minister named Shell, and J. C. Langston. They indulge in jokes and playful arguments while they work. Duff and J. C. begin to fight in earnest when Duff stops working because the boards are too rotten to hold nails.

What has become a kind of free-for-all is interrupted by the arrival of the women—Martha, Mary, and Duff's wife, Ruby. The women pass out coffee and food, and Layne starts to give thanks. He finds that he cannot pray. While the others watch him in amazement, he cries out, "Jesus, God! It's wrong—wrong!" Then turning to his neighbors he says:

> It is wrong, I tell you—to have you here at this hour of the night, away from your kids, freezing in this shack, working on floors that aren't floors. Spilling your blood over them for nothing! God knows it's a sin!

Bill agrees and declares that he would burn the school down if he had a match.

They are all beginning to realize that the school is beyond repair, but it takes Martha to articulate what their next step must be:

> We've got to do more! This bus fight isn't big enough. We've got to haul these folks into court and make them give us decent schools! The state laws say separate but equal schools shall be provided for both races.

"This school is separate, all right," Ruby observes, "but it sure ain't equal."

Layne, agreeing now to lead them, proposes that they get a lot of names on a petition and authorize Ben Ellis, a city lawyer interested in his people and their problems, to represent them in court. He warns them that this will not be an easy fight. Duff says that someone might get killed, and Ruby answers, "A body can die but once, and it might as well be for something like this." Layne prays to God that if "any soul has to die in this, let it be me!" The act ends with everyone singing courageously:

Oh Freedom over me!
And before I'll be a slave,
I'll be buried in my grave,
And go home to my Lord and be free!

Act II opens with a scene in Joseph Layne's study. It is evening. By now, two months after the Negroes' decision to sue for separate but equal schools, Layne is the object of threatening phone calls, and Martha reports that men have been shooting at the house from passing cars. With the Laynes are Doc Willis and Mrs. Simms, an elderly Negro woman who is as blunt of speech as the doctor. When Willis says that the men who are shooting at the minister's house are ignorant folks who have to learn, Mrs. Simms asks, "When they gonna start?" His answer is that we start learning at different times in our lives. He tells how he came to know about colored folks:

> When I first started practicing around here, I didn't like being around colored folks a bit. Well, one night old Sam Smith got sick up yonder in the hills. Well, no matter what I thought of folks, I couldn't let them die. So I drove all the way up in the hills and doctored on Old Sam. Wild storm come up and . . . was no way of getting out of there till morning. Sam told me I'd better stay all night. He didn't have but one bed, though, and I sure wasn't going to sleep with no colored man! I tried sitting up in a chair all night, but . . . pretty soon I got cold! Long about three a.m. I crawled on in that bed beside old Sam and covered up, nice and warm. Next morning I woke up the same man. Hadn't tarnished a bit! . . . If I'd started off knowing something about colored folks, I'd have gotten me a full night's sleep up at old Sam's.

Layne comments sadly, "The only trouble is, Doc . . . most folks never get up to old Sam's."

When a bullet shatters a window, Layne appears with a rifle. He is ready to shoot to protect his property, but John Cloud (accompanied by Turnham) arrives and sends the trespassers away. Even more upsetting to the Superintendent than Layne's stated reason for using a gun—"when the Good Book mentioned turning the other cheek, gunpowder wasn't invented"[46]—is the petition that Layne has circulated for signatures. Cloud has a copy in his hand and has come to ask Layne, who has already been dismissed from his job as principal, to stop the petition. In exchange for this favor, Cloud would give Layne a new position as principal of another school. Cloud tells the Negro minister that he owes it to his people to give them better leadership. "That's exactly what I'm trying to give them," Layne says, and adds deliberately, "You'd better learn—there are Negroes who can't be bought." Martha reinforces Layne's point by resigning when Cloud offers her a promotion.

Throughout the next scene, which takes place at the Raigens' home, a storm is brewing; at the end of the scene, it breaks. The symbolic significance of the storm is hard to miss when Bill says of the wind, "There's something heavy and powerful out yonder, pushing down against the trees—like something wants to tear them loose and there ain't nothing in the world can stop it." And when the Laynes arrive with Ben and Laura, Layne answers Ben's comment about "a storm blowing up for sure" with, "In more ways than one."

The Laynes share with their friends news of the shootings and also the threats from Cloud and Turnham. Laura decides to stay with Ben and the others even though she must fight her own father. Talk moves to the school issue, and Bill says of the whites' opposition, "You'd think we was trying to send our kids down to their schools!" His opinion of white folks—Doc Willis is obviously the exception—is epitomized in this outburst, "They make bombs and drop 'em on top of one another, don't they? What you expect 'em to do to us if they do that to theirselves?"

Duff arrives with the news that economic pressures are being put on Negroes to get them to remove their names from the petition. Layne decides that he must speak to those being threatened, and he orders the others to take refuge in the church.

The remainder of Act II takes place in the church. Forced to wait with women and children, Bill is restless, frustrated by his inability to strike back at his attackers. Martha reminds him that he is falling into a trap set by the enemy:

> *That's what they want—to rile us up so much we'll strike back. And when we do that, Bill, we've lost. Grow up, Bill! And get used to this—for there's more coming. More shooting and slander and spitting in faces. Lots more before the end.*

Hers is the nonviolent position preached by Martin Luther King, who warned that "the nonviolent approach does not immediately change the heart of the oppressor . . . but it does something to the hearts and souls of those committed to it."[47]

As the scene progresses, a debate between Bill's and Martha's ways poses the central issue of the drama—nonviolence versus violence as a way of meeting aggression. Bill wonders if a man can practice nonviolence and feel like a man before his children. When Layne arrives at the church, Bill shouts at him:

> *This is got to stop! We can't be having our kids seeing us running around in the night like this! I got to be able to look mine in the face, and I can't if this keeps on! I shot down men in the war for less than this!*

Duff agrees, saying that if he had been at home he would have "killed 'em dead." Reminded by Martha that their enemies have more bullets than they have, Bill answers, "Then they'll just kill us, and that way we won't hafta be shamed to show our faces!" Layne can no longer remain silent. He asks the two men if they would shoot Glenn or Willie if one of them were the Prodigal Son. When they protest that this is not a fair question, that they are proposing to shoot grown men, Layne answers his own question. "No, you wouldn't," he says. "You'd teach them. And that's what we've got to do to all these Prodigal Children." Not a simple concept, for the moment it escapes Bill and Duff.

They are not ready to think of teaching and loving their white brethren when all they hear outside is the harsh sound of gunfire.

Bill, in blind rage and frustration, is nearly out the door when Layne stops him with a speech that is the turning point of the scene. He begins by saying that he has no answer, that he aches, just as Bill does, to shoot at the enemy. But he adds:

> There's something else holding me back—telling me that even if a white man walked into this church and stuck a gun in my face, I'd have to pray for him . . . because he's sick deep down inside his soul! God Almighty, you're calling on me to have guts to let people kill me!

What he says next Bill is unprepared to hear: "So—you go on home if you want to, Bill. I don't know if I've got the right to ask you to turn the other cheek." Deeply moved, Bill finds that he cannot leave the church. He is beginning to see the bravery it takes to resist fighting.

When the shooting stops, there is an eerie silence of the sort that Bill remembers from wartime. He remembers, too, that shooting then seemed right because he and his buddies had sworn to fight for the United States Constitution. The irony of that patriotism causes him, as it caused the characters in A Medal for Willie, to remark on how little the Constitution means in the South. Layne quotes from the Constitution: "No state shall make or enforce any law which shall abridge the privileges and immunities of citizens of the United States." Martha's rephrasing— "they mean that South Carolina or no other Carolina can make a law cutting off our rights"—makes the irony clear to the whole group and leads to a discussion of the rights of Negroes as United States citizens.

Gradually it dawns on them that they have circulated a petition asking for separate but equal schools when constitutionally they have a right to ask for more. Their excitement grows as they realize that Jim Crow education is and always has been illegal. Simple, direct reactions to what their discussion has unearthed reflect both astonishment and a determination to see the issue clearly:

DUFF: *Going against the Constitution!*
RUBY: *For eighty odd years!*
MARY: *Eighty odd years of meanness and aggravation!*
DUFF: *And busting the law. The Constitution!*
BILL: *The thing I swore to fight for—they busting it!*
RUBY: *We caught particular hell tonight, and it was against the law! It's a downright shame!*
BILL: *Reckon that's the law we oughta be suing 'em about, not all this separate stuff!*

Now it is out. They want, though they do not as yet have the word for it, desegregated schools. They consider circulating a new petition, suing not for separate and equal schools but simply for schools. "We'll sue this state," Layne says, "because its Jim Crow laws are breaking the United States Constitution."

They are all so busy laughing and talking that they scarcely hear Laura when she arrives with the news that the Laynes' house is on fire. The women try with great difficulty to restrain Martha, who wants to go to her home. Word is brought by Doc Willis that the fire department has refused to put out the fire, claiming that the house is outside city limits. Martha is particularly disturbed by this report and breaks loose, running out onto the road to join her husband. A sudden pain stabs her, and she dies in Layne's arms, as he cries out wildly, "Almighty God, I said, let it be me! Didn't you hear me? I said—let it be me!" The fire in the distance is bright and then fades as the curtain falls on Act II.

The last act of *A Land Beyond the River* is a short one in two scenes, one in the church and the other at the Raigens' home. Two months have passed since the new petition was circulated, and this is the day of decision. The instigators of the court trial are gathered in the church, waiting to hear the verdict. Bill's voice is heard in the darkness singing a spiritual:

There's a land beyond the river
That we call the sweet forever,
And you only reach that shore by faith's decree—

His voice is joined by Mary's and then by the whole group singing stanzas that build to:

There we'll know no grief, no sorrow
In that haven of tomorrow
When they ring them golden bells for you and me!

When Ben and Layne arrive with news, Ben announces simply, "We lost." After a moment, Layne adds, "The judge said segregation is legal, but the state has to make the schools equal." Gradually it dawns on the group that they have won what they originally wanted. As Bill puts it, "We started off asking for ten bucks and got five. Which is five more'n we had." Duff, serious for a moment, says to his wife, "Ruby, my boy gonna be able to read and write better'n me." He and Bill and J. C. leave for the Raigens' to prepare a celebration.

Not everyone, however, is ready to settle for what has been gained by the Court's decision. Old Mrs. Simms wants to know if they are going to sue further. When Layne asks for what, Mary answers, "For what we want. For school for just children so they can grow up like they oughta." Both women are shocked to learn that Layne is willing to compromise, that he no longer wants "our kids going to school with their kids." Ben, who also finds it impossible to celebrate a decision in favor of segregation, asks the minister, "Do you think your wife would have settled for what the court said today?" Though disturbed by the question, Layne refuses to try to answer it.

The celebration in the Raigens' backyard is well attended and noisy. The festivities are soon interrupted, however, by the arrival of Doc Willis with Glenn in his arms. The child has been beaten by a group of white men who, he says, called him an "ugly ape." They threatened to beat him until he agreed with them. Glenn, rescued by the doctor, is proud not to have given in to the men. One remembers another child of whom Langston Hughes wrote:

> Concerning this
> Little frightened child
> One might make a story
> Charting tomorrow.[48]

Tomorrow is seen very differently by Bill and by Layne, who, under the influence of this incident, again become proponents of the two ways of meeting aggression. Bill wants to go out and find the men who harmed his son, to pay them back in kind. Layne wants to know what that will solve. Much against his will, Bill is forced by the others present to sit down and listen to the minister.

The balance of Act III, a sermon with interspersed comments from Layne's congregation, serves to make absolutely clear Mitchell's emphasis on Judaeo-Christian morality as the only basis for Negro freedom. Taking as his text "A Little Child Shall Lead Them," Layne proceeds to tell those present the lesson that can be learned from what has happened to Glenn. They are all, he says, being tested. His own house has been burned down, his wife crucified; like Job he most endure these trials, for they are part of God's plan. The children of Israel were tested as the Negroes are still being tested by a God who wants His work done on earth as it is in heaven. And again Layne speaks of the white Prodigal Children who must be redeemed by their black brothers. (Martin Luther King even went so far as to say, "If physical death is the price that a man must pay to free his children and his white brethren from a permanent death of the spirit, then nothing could be more redemptive.")[49]

Layne asks only that God make His people worthy of their duty, which, at this time, is to suffer:

> For, even when the Law has been read, and the signs that read:
> "This is for black" and "This is for white" have been burned—

*still shall there be fires! Still shall there be lynch mobs! Still shall
there be deaths!*

Negroes must not, he tells them, hide from this truth. Addressing
himself specifically to Bill, Layne says, "We cannot hide by
trying to kill the killers." Only through love, he maintains, will
all be saved, both black and white. And where will love be
taught? It will be taught in the homes, in the churches—in the
schools.

They started out, Layne reminds the group, asking for buses.
Now they have gained separate but equal schools. In order not to
be a traitor to Glenn—here is the climax of the sermon and an
answer to his dead wife—they must ask for even more, because
"the only thing a man learns by being separate is that he's not
equal."[50] Layne vows in the last moments of his sermon to take
their case to "the Highest Court in the World!" To which his
congregation says, "Amen."

It is significant that after the sermon, when Mary turns to Bill
with the comment that they are going to teach white folks that
there are better ways of fighting than with fists and guns, he
answers, "Well, they better start learning, 'cause I ain't gonna
keep on waiting." His anger will not be held in forever. Nor
should it be according to some critics of a policy of nonviolence.
It is well to remember what psychologist Kenneth Clark, for
example, has to say about the unrealistic basis of Martin Luther
King's doctrine:

> The natural reactions to injustice, oppression, and humiliation
> are bitterness and resentment. The form which such bitterness
> takes need not be overtly violent but the corrosion of the human
> spirit which is involved seems inevitable. It would seem, then,
> that any demand that the victims of oppression be required to
> love those who oppress them places an additional and prob-
> ably intolerable burden upon these victims.[51]

Loften Mitchell had the good sense at least to suggest that Bill's conversion to nonviolent techniques could be a temporary one, depending on its effectiveness as strategy in the Negroes' fight for human rights.

A *Land Beyond the River* is heavy with message, unashamedly didactic in purpose. The original idea, according to Loften Mitchell, was to present the play to raise money for DeLaine's rural parishioners, who were still suffering economic reprisals in South Carolina for their part in the struggle for desegregation. As a matter of fact, there were several benefit performances, notably one sponsored by the United Auto Workers which raised eleven hundred dollars for the purchase of a harvesting combine for the people of Clarendon County, South Carolina.[52]

The reviewers of the Greenwich Mews production were all pleased with the topicality of the play, and even those who found fault with its construction were delighted with the characters. Brooks Atkinson wrote of the play that "despite the seriousness of its theme, it flares into comedy repeatedly. Mr. Mitchell has not lost his sense of humor in the heat of a crusade."[53] Frances Herridge, too, commended Mitchell's use of humorous detail and his "accurate ear for language." She even found it important to state the play's message for her readers. Of the Negroes she wrote:

> They will win finally . . . not by gunfire or bitterness, but by love and understanding. The implication is that Negroes must set white people a good example, treating them as prodigal sons who will return to brotherhood.[54]

As awkward as the play is—with its speeches that stop the action to inform or persuade the audience, with its repetitious arguments and statements of faith—it makes good use of conflict among the Negroes themselves. Sometimes it is a temptation to think that on such an issue as desegregation all Negroes think alike or at least that they are consistent in their individual responses to it. Loften Mitchell has avoided a simplistic viewpoint and has explored two approaches to the fight for desegregation.

Nonviolence, at the moment in history with which this play is concerned, is the way that wins—and then only after a struggle between individuals and within the heart of the play's central character, Joseph Layne.

BROADWAY

Take a Giant Step

Louis Peterson's first produced play, *Take a Giant Step*, was a success both on and off Broadway, during the respective seasons of 1953–54 and 1956–57.[55] All the critics referred to it as an apparently autobiographical play, a suspicion that is confirmed by the author, who has stated:

> I was born in Hartford, Connecticut, and remained there until I went on to college. I attended the public schools in the south end of the city there, which is still predominantly a white community. I am not sure, however, whether it is because of prejudice completely. Of course some of it has to be, but some of it must be because Negroes have never really wanted to live in the south end of Hartford. There is nothing overly spectacular about it. It is neither terribly wealthy nor terribly poor. It is just very horribly middle-class, and it is a neighborhood that has seen many immigrant families of all nationalities, and my generation was largely the first generation of young people to have been born in this country.[56]

This is a good description of the milieu of *Take a Giant Step*, and it prepares us for the characters who inhabit the play.

Asked if he studied playwriting formally, Peterson replied that drama was considered an extracurricular activity at Morehouse College in Atlanta, Georgia, where he did his undergraduate work. He majored in English and participated in the Little Theatre at Morehouse. Though he was at the Yale School of Drama for a year, he did not study playwriting, as it was not offered in the first year of graduate study. While he was there, however, he did try his hand at a "first play," the name of which is forgotten. Peterson went on to receive a "Master's in Drama" at New York University. Other activities at this time must also have contributed to his development as a playwright. He has recorded some of them:

I also worked as an actor in and around New York during this period, and finally played in my first professional role in the theater. It was the lead in a play produced by the Shuberts called A Young American. It did not last long [January 17 to February 10, 1946]. During that period I studied with Sandy Meisner at the Neighborhood Playhouse as an actor. . . . I wrote another play which attracted an agent named Audrey Wood, which in turn led to me being accepted into a Playwriting Class which was just starting which Clifford Odets taught at the Actors Studio.[57]

Since Peterson must have attended these classes in the late forties, it can be assumed that Take a Giant Step was one of the plays to come out of this experience.

The frustrations, the perplexities, even the clichés of the adolescent hero of Take a Giant Step were familiar to New York audiences because the play takes place in a middle-class home. Basically Spencer Scott's problem is being a Negro, but his actions and speech are similar to those of any white boy of his class. Louis Kronenberger has suggested that "the middle-classness that adds piquancy in terms of a Negro adds familiarity in terms of adolescence itself."[58]

To write with sensitivity about adolescence is usually to record the confusions and frustrations of this period during which children are, with some difficulty, turning into adults. In adolescence sudden physical growth and new emotional urges make for awkwardness that may be painful, even tragic, for the young person, while often seeming comic or brash or both to the world at large. All teenagers share these apprentice years, this struggle for identity. Lillian Smith warned that a child needs self-esteem and feelings of security in order to reach maturity, needs "faith in the world's willingness to make room for him to live as a human being."[59] If most adolescents wonder whether or not the world has room for them, how much more the colored adolescent must wonder about his status in view of his parents' position in American society. It is hard for a boy to become a man when his father is called "boy" by men who seem to matter.

Take a Giant Step is a play in two acts, with three scenes in each act. The settings recommended by the playwright are simple and suggestive rather than elaborately realistic. The Scotts' home, in which all but two of the scenes take place, is described as a house in a middle-class street in a New England town. "If the house has any character at all," the author tells us, "it should resemble a fat old lady who has all the necessary equipment about her person." It is a comfortable, well-appointed house. The setting alone reminds us that the Scotts have managed to leave a ghetto, to move to a white neighborhood in order that their children may have a better life than they themselves have known. What the parents intend, the child may not easily experience. The dramatic action of the play is a clash between generations in a milieu that has different meanings for the various members of this Negro family.

The first scene, which takes place in late October, introduces Spencer Scott, a sensitive seventeen-year-old Negro boy. At this moment he is consumed with anger because he feels that he has been unjustly expelled from school. He has come home to his grandmother because—as often happens in newly middle-class American homes—both parents are at work. The boy walks about the house hitting his leg with a croquet stake that he has brought in from the yard. He criticizes his school, complains about never getting any mail from his brother who is away at college, and is generally disagreeable. Grandma persists in asking him what has happened, and he finally tells her about a clash he has had with his history teacher, Miss Crowley.

Up to this point, Spence could be an adolescent of any color.

To lash out at his school, to curse an absent brother who does not answer letters, to hit himself with a croquet stake—these actions are all part of recognizable adolescent behavior. Then Spence tells about the teacher who has distorted an account of the Civil War in a way that insults Negroes. Here he speaks not just as a confused boy but as a hurt Negro:

> Today they started talking about the Civil War and one of the smart little skirts at the back of the room wanted to know why the Negroes in the South didn't rebel against slavery. Why did they wait for the Northerners to come down and help them? And this Miss Crowley went on to explain how they were stupid and didn't have sense enough to help themselves. Well, anyway, Gram, when she got through talking they sounded like the worst morons that ever lived and I began to wonder how they'd managed to live a few thousands years all by themselves in Africa with nobody's help. I would have let it pass—see— except that the whole class was whispering and giggling and turning around and looking at me—so I got up and just stood next to my desk looking at her. She looked at me for a couple of minutes and asked me if perhaps I had something to say in the discussion. I said I might have a lot of things to say if I didn't have to say them in the company of such dumb jerks. Then I asked her frankly what college she went to.

Miss Crowley had called him impudent but had told him the name of her college. Then, surely confirming her opinion of his impudence, the boy had asked, "And they didn't teach you nothing about the *up*rising of the slaves during the Civil War— or Frederick Douglas [*sic*]?" She had answered that they did not, and Spence left the classroom, saying, "In that case, I don't want to be in your crummy history class." All this he tells his grandmother, adding that he then went to the men's room to smoke a cigar he had stolen from his father (with the intention of selling it for the price of a sundae.) The cigar was his undoing; he must stay out of school for two weeks (one of which is a vacation anyway), and then he may return, in the company of his father, to apologize.

When someone calls Spence from outside, he at first ignores it, but his grandmother forces him to answer and to invite Tony, a neighborhood boy, into the house. When Tony sympathizes with Spence about being thrown out of school, Spence thanks him sarcastically for being sorry now but not seeming to care when "Miss Crowley was bitching me out." The boys' initial dialogue consists of ordinary adolescent accusations and denials, but when Spence makes fun of Tony's girl friend, Marguerite Wandalowski, Tony's answer begins to get beneath the social surface:

> She likes you. She thinks you're a nice kid. It's her father—he —well he just doesn't like colored people. I'm sorry . . . that's the damn truth, Spence—he just doesn't like them.

Though Spence is hurt, he does not appreciate his grandmother's rejoinder:

> Well, I don't like Polish people either. Never have—never will. They come over here—haven't been over, mind you, long enough to know "and" from "but"—and that's the first thing they learn. Sometimes I think Hitler was right—

Spence interrupts her and, turning to Tony, asks him what the real purpose of his visit is. When Tony protests that he "didn't want nothing," Spence begins to press things on him, to offer him books, the chance to watch television or listen to Bach—and finally, in a burst of wild generosity, to give away his baseball equipment. The last offer brings from Tony the admission that he was sent to borrow a bat. Spence makes a gift of pitcher's glove, catcher's mitt, and bat, "because you've been such good friends to me—one and all." If Tony is stupid enough to miss the heavy sarcasm (and he seems to be), he cannot miss the anger in Spence's shouted farewell: "Now scram the hell out of my house before I beat you and your whole team over the head. Get out!"

Alone with his grandmother, Spencer observes, "Well I sure went and milked myself in public that time." He is sorry that he let Tony see how hurt he was. Grandma does not understand either the cause or the effect of his giving away cherished belongings to boys who have begun to shut him out of their group. And when Spence says, "They don't want me around any more, Gram. I cramp their style with the broads," she asks, "Why?" He answers simply, "Because I'm black—that's why." As hard as she tries, the old lady cannot do more than criticize his parents for moving into a neighborhood full of Wops and Germans and Polacks. Her grandson is forced to rebuke her again for this kind of talk, this inverted prejudice. Then he sums up his misery in one sentence: "We're here, Gram—right here—and I was born here—and they're all the friends I've got—and it makes me damned unhappy, Gram."

Grandmother and grandson have a need to talk to each other since they both feel like aliens in this neighborhood chosen by the generation between, by Spence's hard-working parents who knew only that they wanted to raise their children outside the ghetto. Grandma is old enough to be allowed to live in the past. Spence has to face the future, and his present seems bleak indeed when "all the friends I've got" have rejected him.

One boy, significantly a Jew, does come to see Spence just at the moment when the Negro boy has decided to run away from home. Iggie is a nice boy who usually manages to say the wrong thing because he does not take the trouble to dissemble. When Spence gives this boy his stamp album, it is not at all in the manner in which he gave the baseball equipment, for he really wants Iggie to have his beautiful album. Spence tells Iggie that he has no more use for such childish things because he is pretty certain that he will not be returning to school. He even invents a story about a girl friend. When asked to, Spence cannot name the girl, but he speaks of getting a job "and stuff like that" to show his serious intentions.

After striking defiant poses (probably to give himself the courage to leave) and bragging of no longer needing his stamp album, Spence asks if he may come to check on Iggie's progress with the album occasionally. The Jewish boy is pleased, and if he is puzzled by his friend's behavior, he has the good sense not to question it. The scene ends with Spence hastily packing a suitcase so that he can "get the hell out of here before I really do something desperate."

One critic referred to Spencer Scott's "tragicomic scuffle with adolescence."[60] Nowhere is the comic aspect of the scuffle more evident than in the next two scenes, the first of which is set in a bar in the Negro section of town, the second in a prostitute's room. More than once we are reminded of the young hero in Eugene O'Neill's *Ah, Wilderness!*, for he, too, went to a bar to try to prove his manliness.[61] But where Richard found one prostitute, Spence finds three of them—Violet, Poppy, and Rose—and a quiet girl named Carol to whom Spence introduces himself quite formally, treating her very differently from the casual way in which he has treated the other three. Soon he is telling Carol all about himself, assuming, as adolescents will, that everyone is as interested in him as he is in himself. No one is as lonely or as miserable as he is. "I know you wouldn't believe it to look at me," he tells her, "but you're looking at one of the most friendless persons in the whole United States." Encouraged by her sympathetic response, he blurts out the biggest problem in his young life:

You see, I live . . . down at the South End. There aren't many colored families down there; in fact, there are about two. So Mack and I grew up with the white kids who lived on our street. We had lots of good times together—and it wasn't until the kids started getting interested in sex that my troubles began.

Having said it, and to a friendly stranger who is also an attractive woman, Spence gains considerable courage. Finally he proposes to Carol. She thanks him but advises him to go home, telling him she has troubles of her own. Spence is hurt to learn that she is married to a poor laborer and that poverty has forced her into prostitution, but his adolescent self-centeredness prevents him from being affected by her desperation when she explains that, although her husband would kill her if he ever found out, she intends to pick up men. In response to his suggestion that she leave, Carol replies:

> It's funny how when you're young you can be so selfish about your feelings, isn't it? Thank you for the proposal.—Please don't be sore. I tried to help you, Spence. There's a nursery rhyme I used to know. It goes,
> "Merry have we met, and merry have we been,
> Merry let us part, and merry meet again."
> Let's not part angrily.
> (He doesn't answer.)
> Spence! (She walks over and kisses him squarely on the mouth) Good luck, kid.[62]

Violet, having some time on her hands, and discovering that he has a little money, invites Spence to leave with her. Her parting comment shares a certain vaudeville quality with other speeches in this scene and the one following. Her exit line, in reference to his having two dollars and thirty-nine cents, is, "That sounds like the price of something in a fire sale—doesn't it? Well, Hell—."

The third scene, in Violet's room, is little more than a series of obvious jokes, none of them much above the level of this exchange that follows the stage direction, "Radio plays Chopin Sonata in B-flat minor. Opus 35. Funeral March."

VIOLET: What's that they're playing?
SPENCE: It's Chopin.
VIOLET: Is he playing or being played?
SPENCE: He's being played. Chopin's dead.
VIOLET: Recently?
SPENCE: Not too recently. Over a hundred years ago.

VIOLET: *Isn't that sad.*
SPENCE: *I guess it was when it happened.*

Most of the scene reads like a sketch rather than a scene from a serious drama.

There are some particularly believable moments toward the end of the scene when Violet and Spence agree to keep each other's secret: he will never tell anyone that she accepted only "two thirty-nine" from him, and she well never let anyone know that he was "such a—bust." Before he leaves, he borrows a dime for bus fare. When he thanks her, Violet says, "Don't thank me. It hurts me to give it to you." Spence has the last word, however, when he tells her, "There's one thing I want you to know . . . I think that's one of the ugliest bath robes I've ever seen in my life!" The humor throughout the scene has been warmhearted, avoiding both sentimentality and moralizing.

All the scenes in Act I make us like Spencer Scott. Whether he is talking to his grandmother, his peers, a bartender, or a prostitute, Spence has winning ways, not the least of them being his directness, his refreshing honesty. He comes across as self-centered and self-pitying (both are endemic to youth), an adolescent who is filled with curiosity about himself and the world around him. More than anything else, he seems to be a boy who is determined despite the limitations white society imposes on even the middle-class Negro, to become a real man. Interestingly enough, the only scene in the entire play in which there is no reference to color and its attendant problems is the rather superficial scene in Violet's room.

In the first scene of Act II there occurs the confrontation of generations that has been postponed by Spence's running away from home. It is later the same evening, and we have a chance to witness the parents' anxiety, which is expressed mainly through bickering and accusations directed at each other and at Grandma. When Spence comes home, carrying his suitcase but saying only that he has been at the library, the dialogue between him and his father is of that painful sort that says more about their inability to communicate than about the problem at hand. There is no denying that Spence sounds like a "fresh kid." His speeches capture the irritating quality of the adolescent who must put on a brash front or be a little boy again:

LEM: *Do you think I'm crazy, Spence?*
SPENCE: *I honestly don't think you're crazy, Pop.*
LEM: *Well, you must think something like that. Don't you think I know what time the library closes?*
SPENCE: *What times does the library close, Pop?*

At this point Lem calls his wife from the kitchen, trying to elicit her help before he breaks "this little bastard's" neck.

May asks Spence where he has been, carefully avoiding accusations that lurk under the father's profanity, but she has no more success than her husband. What they do learn, when Spence is ready to tell them, is that he has been expelled from school. He tells them the same story that he told his grandmother earlier and repeats his feeling of justification in doing what he did. Lem is particularly shocked to learn of the stolen cigar, and May insists that Spence apologize to the teacher and be reinstated in school. Neither parent even begins to see the son's point of view. Their middle-class values prevent them from understanding that Spence needs their support in his search for identity rather than this censure for his break with the values they have tried to make his.

The parents' reasons for not being on his side are well expressed in two long speeches in answer to his bid for understanding. First Lem speaks:

We don't care how you feel. Now, what do you think of that? You talk about what you'll do and what you won't do. We do things we don't like to do every day of our lives. I hear those crumbs at the bank talking about niggers and making jokes about niggers every day—and I stay on—because I need the job —so that you can have the things that you need. And what do you do? You get your silly little behind kicked out of school. And you're too proud to go back.

Then, although Grandma tries to interfere, May tells Spence that she has worked hard to give "you boys everything you could possibly want."

> We've bent every effort to see that you were raised in a decent neighborhood and wouldn't have to live in slums because we always wanted the best for you. But now I'm not sure we haven't made a terrible mistake—because you seem not to realize what you are. You're a little colored boy—that's what you are—and you have no business talking back to white women, no matter what they say or what they do. If you were in the South you could be lynched for that and your father and I couldn't do anything about it. So from now on my advice to you is to try and remember your place.

Spence, not persuaded by his parents' words, says, "That's the biggest hunk of bull I've ever heard in my whole life." For this his father slaps him "full across the face," but Spence goes upstairs, saying that he is ashamed of them and wants them to know it.

What has taken place here is related to what Max Lerner has called a clash between the cultural image and the identity image:

> The cultural image is the one borrowed and imposed from without, and inevitably it tends toward conformity. The identity image is one that emerges from the quest for a distinctive selfhood and is the product of a continual interplay between the individual's need and whatever measure of cultural elements he is able to absorb in growing up. The clash is always there because there has been no culture in history in which the individual has been able to ignore the cultural demands and pressures.[63]

Lem and Mary speak in behalf of the cultural demands made of

Negroes by society and by themselves when they accept their role as prescribed by society. They uphold the status quo. Spence, still in process of defining his personality, must, of necessity, counter their arguments in terms of his own emerging identity image.

It takes the grandmother to state a synthesis of the partial truths expressed by Spence and his parents. She has the special bravery as well as the insight of the very old when she confronts Lem and May:

> When you moved down here, did you ever stop to take into consideration that something like this was bound to happen sooner or later, and that the most important thing might be just having your love and company? You did not. . . . Instead of your company, they got a book or a bicycle or an electric train. Mercy—the stuff that came in this house was ridiculous. . . . I don't agree with that kind of raising one bit—and allow me to be the first to tell you both. You got away with it with Mack because Mack had Spence. But do you know that that boy is absolutely alone? He hasn't a friend in the world. You didn't know, did you, that all his little pals around here have taken to the girls and the girls' mothers don't want their daughters going around with a colored boy. . . . Well, whether you know it or not, he's alone. And now you want to desert him completely by not backing him up. You moved him out of a slum and taught him to think of himself as something to be respected —and now you get mad when he does the things that you made it possible for him to do. That bull—as he called it about staying in his place. I'm shamed of you both and I want you to know it.

Spence comes downstairs, and there is a brief scene in which his father tries awkwardly to console him and to give him advice:

> Now you go on and forget these little bastards around here. Don't pay any attention to them. You've got bigger things to think about—and if they won't play with you—you just tell

them to go to hell—because you're better than any ten of them put together. All right. Now—you've got your books and you've got your music—and if there's anything you want—you just tell me about it and I'll get it for you.

Spence thanks him for trying to help. At that moment there is a cry from upstairs. Grandma's voice, "muffled and rather terrified," calls for Spence. Spence is with her when she dies of a heart attack.

This scene, with its waves of emotion, its remarkable climaxes, ends now—after the high point of the grandmother's speech, followed by her death—on a profound note that is both psychologically sound and dramatically satisfying. Spence gets his coat and announces that he is going out for a walk. He wants to be by himself. At first his father tells him, "I think you'd better stay here with your mother. She needs you." Spence answers, "I can't. She's got you anyway." In these few sentences, the author has caught that agonizing but necessary moment when a child knows that he is a person, that he is alone, and that his parents have each other in a special way that he cannot really share. Nor does the scene end on this truth alone. Spence's mother says to him, "You don't have to go outside to cry, Spence. You don't have to be ashamed before us." Spence, according to the stage directions, "begins to sob incoherently, his head on Lem's shoulder; breaks away from his father and runs out of the house." May stops Lem from following the boy, even though she suspects that he is running a temperature. She respects his need to mourn by himself, and the father, too, is persuaded to let him go. They can no longer postpone Spence's break with childhood.

The next to the last scene of the play, two weeks later, is an initiation scene in which Spence gets his wish to "sleep with a girl." The girl is a young woman named Christine, hired by Spence's mother to do housework and to look after Spence, who is just getting over pneumonia. It is afternoon, and the two are in the boy's semidarkened room. When the scene opens, they

are indulging in the same kind of humorous banter that Spence
and his grandmother used to enjoy. Their ease in conversation
is preparation for their "romance," which does not happen suddenly, but rather slowly, sweetly, and playfully. Sex grows out of
talk, out of shared grief, and out of a lonely time in the lives
of both.

The adolescent boy, at first, is making the most of this chance
to recite his woes. When Spence asks Christine if one can stop
thinking of the dead, she answers, "Yes, yes you can if you want
to. You just don't open the door and let yourself in, that's all."
She speaks of her childhood in Alabama, of her family, now all
dead except for brothers and sisters who have disappeared. Spence
listens to this woman (we know from his questions) as he did
not earlier to Carol. She tells of coming North, going into service
for a while, and then marrying a man who died two years later.
She states simply, "And about two months after he died, I had a
baby and he was born dead." Spence senses that she has brought
out painful memories long locked away in "those little rooms of
the mind." He apologizes for bothering her with his problems but
continues his recitation.

He confesses, all in a rush, the two things that, above all others,
trouble him: he hates being black, and he wants to sleep with
a girl. Perhaps the most humorous moment in their discussion of
sex is the moment when Spence, who has been bemoaning the
fact that he is nearly eighteen and has never been with a girl, says:

> Hell, I'm practically a virgin. And you know I was thinking
> when I was sick, supposing I died. Supposing I just passed out
> now and died. (Indicates imaginary body on floor) Why, I'd
> regret that I hadn't slept with anybody for the rest of my life
> practically.

The speech is short on logic but long on adolescent fervor.

Their talk is mainly playful banter until, when she is about
to leave, Spencer asks Christine to turn her back so that he can
put a question to her. She does so, and he asks, "Do you like me,

Christine?" "I certainly do," she answers. The turning point of the scene occurs in the following dialogue:

SPENCE: *Well, I know liking doesn't mean loving—but I kind of thought—that since—well—you're lonely, aren't you, Christine?*

CHRISTINE: *I've been lonely for a long time now, Boy.*

SPENCE: *Well—in case you didn't know, I'm lonely, too, Christine —and I know that you're older than I am and I know it makes a lot of difference.*

CHRISTINE: *I have to go, Spence.*

SPENCE: *But what I'm lacking in age, Christine, I sure do make up in loneliness, and so we do have that much in common. Don't we, Christine?*

She does not make her decision immediately. Instead, she gives herself time to think about what he is asking by going downstairs with the luncheon tray. Spence asks her to ring a bell that is down there if she decides to stay. Otherwise she should just leave. There is a moment of suspense as he waits alone in his room and then, at the sound of the bell, he crosses to the window and pulls down the shade as the lights fade.

Take a Giant Step does not end with Spence's sexual awakening. It goes on to another scene, because Louis Peterson was not content to suggest that Spence's growing up was wholly dependent on his "sleeping with a girl," any more than on his running away from home or learning about death. These are all steps toward maturity, the author seems to say, but there is one more important step to be taken before the sum of them can be called a giant step. In the final scene of the play, which takes place the following afternoon, a Saturday, Spence has to face everyday existence—unaided by the spectacular or the erotic. He has to come to terms with his family and friends.

We are back, then, with the difficulty of communication between the generations, back to prescribed responses and expected explosions. May announces to Spence that she has invited a few of his friends over for ice cream and cake. Spence is furious.

Nothing is more symbolic of childhood than its parties with ice cream and cake. "Why don't you make a little pink punch to go with it?" he asks her. "I did," she replies. In a rage, he tells her that her whole scheme strikes him as bribery, and he will not bribe anyone to be his friend. Spence is about to leave the house when his mother musters an eloquence that holds him there.

> Your father's right about you. You're too proud. You think you can go through life being proud, don't you? Well, you're wrong. You're a little black boy—and you don't seem to understand it. But that's what you are. You think this is bad; well, it'll be worse. You'll serve them pink punch and ice cream—and you'll do a lot worse. You'll smile when you feel like crying. (She begins to cry) You'll laugh at them when you could put knives right into their backs without giving it a second thought—and you'll never do what you've done and let them know that they've hurt you. They never forgive you for that. . . . You think it's easy for me to tell my son to crawl when I know he can walk and walk well? I'm sorry I ever had children. I'm sorry you didn't die when you were a baby. Do you hear that? I'm sorry you didn't die.

It is a strong speech, and it has a strong effect on Spence. He finds that he must admit even his mother into the sphere of his feelings. When he hears himself apologizing to her, he says, "For the past two weeks all I've done is apologize to people. I seem to be apologizing for trying to be a human being."

At this moment his "old buddies" arrive. They recall the excitement of a chase and the joys of eating. Only a couple of times is the social surface disturbed—once when, in Iggie's presence, a reference is made to a "fat Jew bastard" and once when Gussie innocently starts to include Spence in plans for a hayride. Tony changes the subject each time, showing that he has acquired a certain social astuteness that the others lack.

When the subject of school comes up, Spence takes the opportunity to state his position and to put his white friends at ease:

> You know, I've been doing a hell of a lot of fooling around and I've been neglecting my lessons, not practicing, and . . . if you're going to college you got to be a little more serious about things than I've been. So from now on I've got to buckle down to the old books and concentrate on things of the mind. . . . So I had all you guys over to kind of say goodbye and all 'cause I don't think I'm going to have much time for playin' around. 'Course, it's going to be a little hard at first 'cause I'm not used to it, so all you guys can help me if you just kind of let me alone and let me get my work done.

Such set speeches may seem too pat, but they ring true to Spence's determination to face growing up in a white world.

The boys leave, thanking Spence for the party and, by implication, for releasing them from future social embarrassment. Gussie speaks again of what a great time they had the previous summer. It was their last summer of childhood and childhood's irresponsibility. Only Iggie still has a place in the world Spence envisions for himself. He and Iggie will go on to college. "That is something, isn't it?" Spence says to the Jewish boy when they are alone.

The boys have all left by the time May returns from shopping. She accuses Spence of driving them away, and he explains, as best he can, that he has done what he must do. He closes the front door, shutting out the sounds of baseball, and begins to play the piano. His mother speaks the last line of the play: "Spence—I love you very much." It is as if she wants him to know that she has to trust him because she loves him—not because she understands him. He looks at her, surprised, and then resumes playing "Praeludium."

One critic expressed his opinion of the ending in these words:

> It is apparently the author's idea that this retreat from life, this counsel of despair, is the only solution open to his protagonist,

*and that his acceptance of it marks the first step in his emer-
gence as a man. I can say only that the step struck me as something less than a giant one and that its direction might easily
be regarded as mainly sidewise.*[64]

But this is to think too much of prolonged childhood or easy
acceptance by comrades of the moment and too little of Spence's
decision to arm himself with education so that he can compete
with white men in a white man's world. It is significant that he
does not take a step backward into the servitude originally prescribed by his parents.

The plot line of *Take a Giant Step* is clear, and the dialogue,
for the most part, rings true. The characterizations of Spence
and his grandmother are particularly convincing. Both Carol and
Christine have lines that are touching; although they are onstage
only briefly, they are memorable characters. The prostitutes are remembered more for jokes and situation comedy than for their characterizations, which are (perhaps deservedly) flimsy. Lem and
May are given long speeches containing arguments for Spence to
counter, and so they sound stilted at times. At other times there is
a painful honesty in their defense of the status quo. The boys
who visit Spencer are boring, repetitious, funny—believably adolescent. The dramaturgical weaknesses of the play show up mostly
in the amount of time given to trivia in Act I and to repetition
of arguments in Act II. But it remains true that the characters
are well drawn and their dialogue easy.

The giant step that is taken is from irresponsible childhood
through frustrated adolescence into maturity still undefined. One
has the feeling that Spencer Scott may someday echo LeRoi
Jones's words in *The System of Dante's Hell*:

Once, as a child, I would weep for compassion and understanding. And Hell was the inferno of my frustration. But the
world is clearer to me now, and many of its features, more
easily definable.[65]

A *Raisin in the Sun*

When Lorraine Hansberry was eight years old, her father bought a house in a middle-class white neighborhood just a few blocks away from the Negro Southside of Chicago. This move precipitated one of the NAACP's most celebrated housing cases: *Hansberry v. Lee* (311 U.S. 32). The Illinois Supreme Court had ruled that whites had the right to bar Negroes from their neighborhoods. Carl Hansberry, a wealthy real estate broker, challenged its decision. Among those who prepared the brief for the NAACP, when the Hansberry appeal was taken to the Supreme Court, were Louis C. Wirth of the University of Chicago and housing authority Robert C. Weaver. On November 12, 1940, the Supreme Court reversed the lower court's decision, and the Hansberrys were permitted to occupy their property.[66]

Lorraine Hansberry was born May 19, 1930, in Chicago. She attended Jim Crow grade schools, because, as she put it, "My parents were some peculiar democrats [who] could afford to send us to private schools, but they didn't believe in it." She recalled moving into the white neighborhood:

My mother . . . sat in that house for eight months with us . . . in what was, to put it mildly, a very hostile neighborhood. I was on the porch one day with my sister when a mob gathered. We went inside, and while we were in our living room, a brick came crashing through the window with such force it embedded itself in the opposite wall. I was the one the brick almost hit.[67]

Incidents of this kind contributed to her father's decision to leave the United States. Though he had been able to become a wealthy businessman and even a United States marshall, he never felt that he had true social freedom. When Carl Hansberry died in 1945, at the age of fifty-one, he was making preparations to move to Mexico. Though his daughter did not agree with "the leaving part," she did agree with her father's assessment of the

United States. Several years after his death, she was quoted as saying:

> Daddy really belonged to a different age, a different period. He didn't feel free. One of the reasons I feel so free is that I feel I belong to a world majority, and a very assertive one.[68]

This spirit led her to an early and lasting commitment to the struggle for civil rights.

Her choice of theatre as her medium came after she had moved from the Midwest to New York City, but it was influenced by earlier educational experiences. After graduating from Englewood High School, Lorraine Hansberry went to the University of Wisconsin for two years. At the university she saw plays by Strindberg and Ibsen for the first time, and later said that they influenced her. Earlier, on dates in Chicago, she had enjoyed productions of *Othello* and *The Tempest*. When she moved to New York in 1950, she began hanging around little theatre groups and discovered that "theatre embraces everything I like all at one time."[69]

It is not certain when she began trying to write for the theatre, but in an interview in 1959 she referred to *A Raisin in the Sun* as her fourth and only finished drama.

> I wrote it between my twenty-sixth and twenty-seventh birthdays. One night, after seeing a play I won't mention, I suddenly became disgusted with a whole body of material about Negroes. Cardboard characters. Cute dialect bits. Or hip-swinging musicals from exotic sources.[70]

Encouraged by her husband, Robert Nemiroff, a music publisher to whom she was married in 1953, Lorraine Hansberry wrote *A Raisin in the Sun* and saw it produced on Broadway.

Of producers she once scornfully said:

> Their receptivity to Negro work is horrible. Potential backers read my play and cried: "It's beautiful! Too bad it isn't a musical. White audiences aren't interested in a Negro play."

When she insisted that A Raisin in the Sun was not "a Negro play" but rather a play "about honest-to-God, believable, many-sided people who happened to be Negroes," producers were generally dubious. The two men who did present her play—Philip Rose and David J. Cogan—made their Broadway debut with this production.[71]

That A Raisin in the Sun won the New York Drama Critics Circle award for the 1958–59 season was more than a personal triumph for Lorraine Hansberry. The director, Lloyd Richards, was the first Negro to direct a Broadway play. Sidney Poitier had his first starring role on Broadway. Diana Sands had a chance to be seen by a wide audience (wider certainly than the one that had seen her two years before in Loften Mitchell's A Land Beyond the River). Claudia McNeil, too, moved from relative obscurity to stardom. And, perhaps most important, Lorraine Hansberry lived up to a promise she had made earlier to her husband: "I'm going to write a social drama about Negroes that will be good art."[72] Critics may still be divided on how good the art is, but most agree with Harold Clurman that A Raisin in the Sun is "an honestly felt response to a situation that has been lived through, clearly understood, and therefore simply and impressively stated."[73]

A Raisin in the Sun is the first play by a Negro of which one is tempted to say, "Everyone knows it." Thousands of Americans have seen it on the stage in New York, in other large cities, on college campuses, and in community theatres. Many more thousands have seen it on the screen. And, finally, millions of American who might not seek it out have seen the movie on their television screens. (It is fascinating to speculate that the majority of white Americans have had Negroes in their homes only via television.) Americans who read could have read A Raisin in the Sun in hardcover, in a very inexpensive paperback, printed alone or in anthologies. No other play considered in these chapters has had this kind of audience.

It hardly seems necessary, then, to analyze the play scene by scene in order to remind the reader/viewer of those elements that are reflections of American Negro existence. It will be sufficient to pull out moments in the play that demonstrate Lorraine Hansberry's use of Negro problems in creating a play that has become for many white people an introduction to the contemporary Negro.

Much has been written about A Raisin in the Sun, about Lorraine Hansberry (who died of cancer in 1965), and about the implications of her Broadway success, but neither the critics nor Miss Hansberry ever acknowledged her debt to Richard Wright's Native Son (novel or play), although surely one existed. Both plays are set in Chicago's Southside. Bigger Thomas and Walter Younger are both chauffeurs, black men who feel caged in a white society. And they both "explode" because of a "dream deferred." Walter's explosion, to be sure, is not so fatal as Bigger's, but it erupts from much the same frustration and confusion. Both plays even begin with the same sound—the ringing of an alarm clock. To press comparisons much further would not be fair; it is enough to say that the influences of Native Son on A Raisin in the Sun are striking. What the later play has that the earlier one lacked is warmth and humor as well as characters who never become categories.

The living room in which the action of A Raisin in the Sun takes place is scrupulously described by the playwright; she wants it to be known that the shabbiness comes from the fact that the room has had to accommodate "too many people for too many years." The Negroes who live here, like any other poor family, live with old furniture that reflects their own weariness and poverty. There is one window to light the living room and an area of that room that serves as a kitchen. One door leads to a bedroom shared by Walter Younger and his wife Ruth, another to one shared by Lena Younger (Mama) and her unmarried daughter Beneatha, and there is a third leading to the hall. Travis, Walter and Ruth's ten- or eleven-year-old son, sleeps on a "make-down bed" in the living room. And like the family in

Native Son, the Youngers must share a bathroom in an outside hall with other families.

Three generations in three rooms can lead to various complications. It is soon evident, for example, that the apartment has always been Mama's, with the result that Walter is no more the "head of a household" than a much younger Bigger Thomas was in a meaner apartment in the same part of Chicago. Not much is made of it by the playwright, but the little boy, Travis, has no single authority figure, and so he plays all three adults off against each other and is, as a result, "spoiled." This kind of domestic situation is common among the poor, black and white. There is, however, an added burden placed upon the Negro adult male; not only is he unmanned by the fact that frequently his wife and mother can more readily find work than he can,[74] but he is also subject to a dominant white society that would keep him a "boy," keep him harmless and "in his place."

A Raisin in the Sun is set up to demonstrate the clash of dreams, a clash between generations, between men and women, and even—because for all its commonality with domestic dramas about white people, and in spite of Miss Hansberry's statement to the contrary, it *is* a Negro play—the clash between black and white.

Walter wants to use his mother's insurance money ($10,000, her husband's life insurance) to invest in a liquor store. His frustration grows as first his sister and then Mama oppose his plans. Ruth, who often serves as a catalyst for other people's conversations, is torn between being supportive of her husband and preserving peace in the family.

Lena Younger is the old-fashioned Negro mother (we have already seen her in *Harlem,* in *Native Son,* and in *A Medal for Willie*) who has over the years worked hard, attended church, and made sacrifices for a family and a future in which she has always had faith. Early in the play Ruth tries to speak in favor of Walter's business plans: "Like Walter say—I spec people going to always be drinking themselves some liquor." (A Southern white character in Edward Sheldon's "*The Nigger*" says, "The wo'ld needs liquoh—an ev'ry bottle it drinks 's wo'th money in somebody's pocket!")[75] Mama tells Ruth that she will not be responsible for people drinking liquor; she has no desire to have that on her conscience at this late date.

What Mama wants to do with the insurance money is to put some of it away for Beneatha's schooling and then to make a down payment on a "little old two-story somewhere, with a yard where Travis could play in the summertime." Hers is a simple desire for a home that is the reward of her labors. And lest we think that she will capitulate easily to youth, there are two scenes that show Mama's strength as she stands up first to her daughter and then to her son.

Although Beneatha is a twenty-year-old medical student, she is quite adolescent in her behavior. She is fresh, full of talk about dates and "forms of expression." When she speaks of playing the guitar and riding horseback, one cannot help thinking more of the black bourgeoisie than of a lower-class family. Nor is it surprising to read that Lorraine Hansberry once said of Beneatha, "She's me eight years ago. I had a ball poking fun at myself through her."[76] Beneatha calls her rich boy friend, George Murchison, "shallow" and dismisses her own brother as an "elaborate neurotic."

At one point, when Mama says that her daughter will be a doctor, "God willing," Beneatha answers drily, "God hasn't got a thing to do with it." At first Mama tries gently to get Beneatha to retract her statement, but the girl persists in saying that she is sick of hearing about God. Mama warns her that she is about to get her "fresh little jaw slapped," but Beneatha feels compelled to state her modern position. She assures her mother that she will not go out and commit crimes or immoral acts simply because she no longer believes in God. But she is tired of having God get all the credit for everything the human race achieves. As far as Beneatha is concerned there is only man, and he is the maker of miracles.

Mama slaps her daughter across the face and after a moment of silence, forces her to repeat, "In my mother's house there is still a God." Beneatha does as told, but when her mother is out of earshot, she says quietly to Ruth, "All the tyranny in the world will never put God in the heavens!" Commenting further on her personal relationship to Beneatha, Lorraine Hansberry said, "I don't disagree with anything she says. I believe science will bring more rewards for our generation than mysticism and all that jazz."[77]

Beneatha takes her slap and goes her independent way. It is Walter who will inevitably clash with his mother. Medical school, after all, is more compatible with the Protestant ethic than Walter's highly suspect business adventure.

Some wonderfully warm, humorous scenes involve Beneatha and her African boy friend, Asagai. (Interestingly enough, much of the message of the play is embedded in the lighter speeches.) When she first tells her mother that an African student, an intellectual, will be coming by, Mama says that she has never met an African before. Beneatha is worried that Mama will ask ignorant questions because, like most Americans, she knows the dark continent only from seeing Tarzan movies. "Why should I know anything about Africa?" Mama asks indignantly. Beneatha reminds her not of her people's history but of the missionary work she has supported to save Africans from heathenism. Then, modern young woman that she is, she adds that they need salvation from colonialism, not from heathenism.

Asagai turns out to be a sophisticated young African who is delighted by Beneatha. He brings her a gift of colorful Nigerian robes and records of tribal music. Having draped the robes properly, he admires her, as he says, "mutilated hair and all." She tries to defend her straightened hair, but he reminds her that when they met she told him that she was looking for "her identity." To him she looks more like a queen of the Nile than like a Hollywood queen. She is both flattered and disturbed.

Beneatha protests when Asagai accuses her of being an as-

similationist, and yet she seems disturbed by what he is awakening in her. She does not want to be "someone's little episode
in America." He bursts into laughter, telling her that she is like
all American women; white or black, they are not so liberated
as they proclaim themselves to be.

Mama's introduction to the African is predictably humorous.
She recites her daughter's earlier comments about Tarzan and
colonialism in a way that seems inexplicably to relate these subjects. Fortunately, this speech past, she relaxes and invites Asagai
to come by from time to time for some "decent home-cooked
meals." A stereotyped response saves the day as far as the African
is concerned—but nothing can save the play from a confrontation
scene between Mama and Walter.

As soon as the check is an actuality, a check that can be
held in the hand, Walter is frantic to get his mother to agree to
his business plans. Mama is particularly adamant in her refusal
because she not only has her old convictions on her side, but
she also knows that Ruth has become desperate enough to plan
the abortion of a baby Walter has had no knowledge of. To
the old woman this is a sign of how ugly their life has become.
To her way of thinking liquor stores could only make it uglier.

Finally, in an effort to make her see his dissatisfaction with his
job—"Yes, sir; no, sir; very good, sir; shall I take the Drive, sir?"—
Walter speaks to her seriously, but with little hope, he says, of
being understood:

> Sometimes it's like I can see the future stretched out in front
> of me—just as plain as day. The future, Mama. Hanging over
> there at the edge of my days. Just waiting for me—a big, loom-
> ing blank space—full of nothing. Just waiting for me. (Pause)
> Mama—sometimes when I'm downtown and I pass them cool,
> quiet-looking restaurants where them white boys are sitting
> back and talking 'bout things . . . sitting there turning deals
> worth millions of dollars . . . sometimes I see guys don't look
> much older than me—

She interrupts him to ask why he talks so much about money.

"Because it is life, Mama!" he says passionately. To which she answers, almost to herself, "Once upon a time freedom used to be life—now it's money." Walter disagrees, saying that it was always money, but "we just didn't know about it." (Psychologists have described the basic Negro personality as "a caricature of the corresponding white personality, because the Negro must adapt to the same culture, must accept the same social goals, but without the ability to achieve them.")[78]

Although it accomplishes nothing, Mama tells Walter about the old days in the South when to stay alive was a goal. And for her it has been enough to work and save, to give her children the freedom allowed in the North. Walter cannot make her understand his frustration. Here, as in *Take a Giant Step*, the generations cannot communicate their different dreams. "The dream defferred is Walter's dream," Max Lerner once wrote, and then he observed:

> Examine it—the dream of getting away from his despised job, of setting up a business with a liquor license, of building it up big, of having pearls to hang around the neck of his wife, of enabling his young son to drive to school in a taxi—and you will see that it isn't particularly Walter's dream as a Negro, nor yet an intensely private one. It is a dream that comes out of the larger culture of the whites, in which Walter is caught up.[79]

Not their disagreement about money or even his refusal to say that he will accept the responsibility of another child, but rather the events that follow persuade Mama to look at Walter in a different light. He stops going to work. If he is at home, he is drinking beer. When he is out, he drives around Chicago in a borrowed car or walks all over the Southside, just looking at Negroes—unemployed ones like himself.

In the midst of a drunken scene in which Walter stands on the table, swaying to Beneatha's recording of African music and speaking to a tribe that he can see in fantasy, George Murchison arrives. ("The Murchisons are honest-to-God-real-*live*-rich colored people, and the only people who are more snobbish than rich white people are rich colored people.") A completely convinced assimilationist, he would be the last one to understand a wild parody of African ritual. George calls Beneatha eccentric, and when she accuses him of being ashamed of his heritage, he reminds her that her heritage is "nothing but a bunch of raggedy-assed spirituals and some grass huts." Although she counters with a proud reference to the Africans "who were the first to smelt iron on the face of the earth," she does agree to change from her Nigerian robes for their date.

Walter has drunk enough beer and had sufficient discouragement about his business prospects to welcome a chance to attack the privileged young Murchison. First he makes fun of the college boy's clothes. Then he goes into a sardonic appreciation of George's "old man," someone who "thinks big." When he suggests that he and George should sit down for a talk sometime, the boy's skepticism and boredom are very evident. Walter is offended to the point of belligerence. He attacks George for not learning anything important in college, not learning to run the world, only to read books, to speak properly, and to wear "fairyish-looking white shoes." George, who has remained aloof until this time, cannot resist saying to Walter, "You're all wacked up with bitterness, man." Walter replies, through clenched teeth:

And you—ain't you bitter, man? Ain't you just about had it yet? Don't you see no stars gleaming that you can't reach out and grab? . . . You contented son-of-a-bitch. . . . Bitter? Man, I'm a volcano. Bitter? Here I am a giant—surrounded by ants! Ants who can't even understand what it is the giant is talking about.

And soon after this scene Walter learns that his mother has made a down payment on a house in Clybourne Park, in what is a white, not a Negro, neighborhood. Walter turns on his mother then, accusing her of running her children's lives as she wishes. "So you butchered up a dream of mine," he says to her, "you— who always talking 'bout your children's dreams."

It is in response to his bitterness and the despair that she reads in her son's growing alienation from his family that Mama finally admits to Walter that she has been wrong. "I been doing to you," she tells him, "what the rest of the world been doing." Now she tries to make it up to him by giving him the $6500 left after the down payment on the house, for him to put in the bank—$3,000 for Beneatha's education and the rest for his own checking account. He is astonished to hear her say, "I'm telling you to be head of this family from now on like you supposed to be." This moment is a turning point in Walter's fortunes and in the play itself.

The crucial scene in Act II, a scene that begins with enthusiasm and ends in despair, introduces the one white character in the play, a middle-aged man named Karl Lindner. He interrupts a lighthearted scene in which the Youngers (all but Mama) are packing their things in anticipation of the move to their new home. As chairman of the New Neighbors Orientation Committee of the Clybourne Park Improvement Association, Lindner announces that he has come to see the Youngers in order to "give them the lowdown" on the way things are done in Clybourne Park. Commenting on the background of the members of the community, Lindner says that there is no question of racial prejudice. "It is a matter," he explains, "of the people of Clybourne Park believing, rightly or wrongly . . . that for the happiness of all concerned that our Negro families are happier when they live in their *own* communities." The welcoming committee turns out to be nothing more than an attempt to bribe the Youngers to stay out of a white neighborhood. Lindner lets them know that the association is prepared to buy the house at a price that would represent a financial gain to the Negro family. Walter, rising to his role as head of the family, orders him out of the apartment.

The young people are quite amused by the whole idea of the welcoming committee. When Mama is told of the white man's visit, she asks, "Did he threaten us?" Beneatha's answer serves to show youth's relaxed attitude toward what was and is very serious to their parents:

> Oh—Mama—they don't do it like that any more. He talked Brotherhood. He said everybody ought to learn how to sit down and hate each other with good Christian fellowship.

The relaxed atmosphere of the early part of the scene is easily recaptured, but it is interrupted once again by a doorbell. (The playwright has a sure sense of the dramatic value inherent in shattering moods in this fashion.) When Walter opens the door, it is to admit a frightened little man named Bobo, who confesses to Walter before his astonished family that another partner has disappeared with their money.

Walter cries out in sheer madness now, praying and cursing, begging an absent Willy to bring back the money that was "made out of my father's flesh." He falls to the floor sobbing, and he is there when his mother goes to him to ask if all the money is gone. Lifting his head slowly he says, "Mama . . . I never . . . went to the bank at all." His money and Beneatha's, all of it is gone. When Mama has taken in the enormity of his act, she tells her children about their father, who worked himself to death for the money that Walter has given away in a day. Standing over her son, she prays, "Oh, God . . . Look down here—and show me the strength."

On the page this climactic scene seems both melodramatic and sentimental, but it is doubtful that many members of the theatre audience could resist the performance of Claudia McNeil. As the critic for the *New Republic* wrote: "Her cries of anguish at the second-act curtain, when she discovers that her son has thrown away the family's money, rise to the distant corners of the theatre in a giant crescendo."[80]

Act III, in one scene, is short and still in a melodramatic vein.

It begins quietly with an episode that further defines Beneatha and Asagai. She tells her African friend about Walter's treachery, and Asagai expresses his concern for her future. Beneatha tells him that she may have stopped caring about being a doctor, about curing hurt bodies. He questions her original impulse if she can so easily give up helping the ailing human race because of her brother's childish mistake. He wants to know why she does not continue to struggle for the future. Disillusioned, she turns the questions back to him and to the Africa of which he dreams; she wants to know what he plans to do about all the crooks and stupid men "who will come into power and steal and plunder the same as before—only now they will be black and do it in the name of the new independence."

His reply is that he is living the answer to her question by getting an education for leadership. And he acknowledges the fact that there will be retrogression before there is progress. Like a good revolutionary, he knows that even his own death could represent an advance for his people. When Asagai asks Beneatha to go home to Nigeria as his bride, she asks for time to consider his proposal. Something about her hesitation implies that she will not go "home to Africa." The tug toward the exotic was present earlier in the play, and while even now she seems flattered by his attention, Asagai remains, for Beneatha, a symbol of the past, not a portent of the future.

The balance of Act III belongs to Walter. It depicts his temptation to accept compromise and then a reversal that leads him into real nobility. At first he announces that he is ready to make a deal with Lindner's welcoming committee. As he explains to Mama, life is divided up between "the takers and the 'tooken.'" He has been among the "tooken," but he has learned to keep his eye on what counts.

One of the most moving statements in the play is made by Mama when she says to Walter in response to his decision:

Son—I come from five generations of people who was slaves and sharecroppers—but ain't nobody in my family never let nobody *pay 'em no money that was a way of telling us we wasn't fit to walk the earth. We ain't never been that poor . . . that dead inside.*

Walter's only answer is that he did not make the world the way it is, and he does a heartbreaking imitation of a begging darky: "Yasssssuh! Great White Father, just gi' ussen de money, fo' God's sake, and we's ain't gwine come out deh and dirty up yo' white folks neighborhood."

And yet, by the time Lindner arrives, Walter has had time to consider his mother's words and his own humiliation, and he tells the astonished white man:

We have all thought about your offer and we have decided to move into our house because my father—my father—earned it. . . . We don't want to make no trouble for nobody or fight no causes—but we will try to be good neighbors. . . . We don't want your money.

When Lindner tries to appeal to Mama's good sense, she says that her son speaks for all of them.

The play ends with Walter's coming into his manhood and the family moving on to a future that promises to be bright only because it is predicated on the strength of the characters as we have come to know them. It is interesting to note Robert Nemiroff's contention that *A Raisin in the Sun* does not have a happy ending, "only a commitment to new levels of struggle,"[81] an idea that he says escaped most of the play's critics in 1959. Such an oversight is understandable in view of the fact that critics had nothing but the play before them, not Miss Hansberry's political statements or social proclamations.

John Davis, executive director of the American Society of African Culture, has said that the Negro writer's basic problem has been that "he must write for a non-Negro market which often is also the object of his protest." It would be difficult to disagree with this general statement. He went on, however, to call *A Raisin in the Sun* "social protest" that is "such consummate art" that audiences applaud the very protest that is directed against them.[82] A few observations should be made about both the art and the protest in Lorraine Hansberry's play.

In the first place, members of the Negro community supported this Broadway production of a Negro play as they had supported no other; there were nights, even in New York, when the audience was almost half Negro. This particular Broadway play, then, was not performed for the usual white middle-class audience. Also, the play is not what is generally termed a protest play. The values of white society may have warped Walter Younger (Max Lerner felt this very strongly), but it is not a play overtly protesting those values. Members of the audience, both white and black, could appreciate the play because Walter's rebellion is meliorated by the conservative values of Mama. In fact, he is shamed into maturity by his mother, which is to say that he is persuaded to accept her version of middle-class values.

Henry Hewes felt that the nearest thing to a message in *A Raisin in the Sun* was spoken by Asagai, the Nigerian revolutionist: "I know that we cannot allow life to depend on accidents." But few Americans would hear in this statement, as the critic did, a condemnation of sudden success and overnight acquisition of wealth in our society. Hewes concluded that Negroes are becoming a part of the illusion sometimes called the American myth of success. "Like the rest of us," he predicted, "some will be destroyed by it. But *A Raisin in the Sun* would seem to suggest that when the bubble bursts the families with the most courageous pasts will be best equipped to pick up the pieces."[83]

Other critics were less concerned with social commentary and more concerned with art. Brooks Atkinson wrote that *A Raisin in the Sun* could be regarded as a Negro *Cherry Orchard*. No matter how different the social scale of the characters, he observed, "the knowledge of how character is controlled by environment is much the same, and the alternation of humor and pathos is similar."[84] Kenneth Tynan's main reservation about the Hansberry play was in connection with its sentimentality, "particularly in its reverent treatment of Walter Lee's mother; brilliantly though Claudia McNeil plays the part. . . . I wish the dramatist had refrained from idealizing such a stolid old conservative."[85] But, like Max Lerner, he could compare the play favorably with those of Clifford Odets.

Some critics—Miss Hansberry agreed with them, according to a stage manager who knew her a few years after the original production of A Raisin in the Sun[86]—called the play a soap opera. It abounds in types: Mama is a tyrannical but good-natured matriarch; Walter, a frustrated young man surrounded by too many women; Beneatha, a free-thinking college student; the African Asagai, a poetic revolutionary; and the one white man, a cliché-ridden suburbanite. The interest in them lies chiefly in the fact that the central characters are Negroes, which is something new to soap opera. Tom Driver went so far as to say that this play would have done well to recover its investment if it had been written by a white woman about a white family. Of the play he concluded:

> As a piece of dramatic writing it is old-fashioned. As something near to the conscience of a nation troubled by injustice to Negroes, it is emotionally powerful. Much of its success is due to our sentimentality over the "Negro question."[87]

After everything is said that can be said about the form and content of the play, one must agree with Harold Clurman about the importance of the Broadway production of A Raisin in the Sun. As he put it, "The play is organic theatre: cast, text, direction are homogeneous in social orientation and in sentiment, in technique and in quality of talent."[88]

A look at the plays written by Negroes and produced in New York during the fifties has indicated that, while they have been few in number, they have reflected the Negro revolution in interesting and often powerful ways. Not one of these plays needs an apology. Each, in its own way, says something about current and persistent Negro problems; and each shows some dramaturgical advance over most plays of Negro authorship in past decades. But predictably the authors have not to date had a fair hearing. It remains for the future to decide if, when the theatre speaks to the American public of the Negro revolution, the plays of the fifties will be among those presented for consideration and debate.

The least known of these plays, William Branch's *A Medal for Willie*, is a simply stated play about the effect on his family of an American Negro soldier's death. By introducing Willie through those who mourn him, either sincerely or hypocritically, Branch found it possible to say a great deal about the paradox of a black man fighting and dying for democratic ideals that had so little meaning for him at home. As timely as the subject continues to be, no other Negro playwright has attempted to write about the Negro in wartime. Nor have plays on this subject by white playwrights had more than a short-lived appeal. *South Pacific* by Howard Rigsby and Dorothy Heyward, a play about a Negro soldier who is faced with deserting to the Japanese or continuing to fight for America in spite of Jim Crow treatment, ran for five performances in 1943. *Jeb*, a play by Robert Ardrey about a Negro war hero who comes home to a prejudiced community, ran for nine performances in 1946. *Forward the Heart* by Bernard Reines, the story of a blind veteran, a white man who falls in love with his mother's Negro maid, had a run of nineteen performances in 1949. The one exception to this pattern was *Deep Are the Roots* by Arnaud D'Usseau and James Gow, another wartime Negro-white love story, which ran for nearly a year during the 1945–46 season. Most of these plays are guilty of exploiting a situation without paying sufficient attention to characterization.

A *Medal for Willie* excels where these plays fail; the pity is that it was presented for a short time in Harlem and has been revived only infrequently since then.[89] The timeliness of the play is suggested by Loften Mitchell's statement that it "posed in strong dramatic terms the question: should the Negro soldier fight and die abroad or should he take up arms against the prejudiced southland."[90]

William Branch's second play, *In Splendid Error*, was certainly a more ambitious undertaking than *A Medal for Willie*. *In Splendid Error* is only the second historical play considered in this study, the first being Theodore Ward's *Our Lan'*. The characters in Ward's play seem more fully developed, more human than those in *In Splendid Error*. Perhaps it was easier to believe in a Joshuah Tain, who was born in the work of art, than to accept Frederick Douglass and John Brown, about whom we all have preconceptions before the characters appear in the play. When Ward came to write a play about John Brown, he met the same problem faced by Branch: historical figures can lack the credibility of men if they are not sufficiently transmuted by art.

On April 28, 1950, Theodore Ward's *John Brown* was presented on the Lower East Side. The theatre was, in fact, a garage leased by a group called People's Drama. The play had been written while Ward was on a Guggenheim fellowship, doing most of his research at Dartmouth College. *John Brown* ran for a few weeks, received little critical attention, and seems in retrospect to have been a work-in-progress, something not ready to be shown to the public.[91]

The subject of John Brown has occupied Theodore Ward's attention for eighteen or more years. He may never finish writing the play which now, in its latest version, is entitled *Of Human Grandeur*. He seems to have become obsessed with "the dramatic life of the old hero."[92] Though he admits that John Brown may be a better subject for a novel than for a play, he keeps reworking what has grown to be a sprawling historical drama. "I won't

give up John Brown," Ward said in 1963, pointing to piles of
material on the floor of his study. Then he added:

> To me he is the first real American, and not just because he
> was interested in the Negro problem. He was a rounded man,
> lost to our society. He saw values in American democracy.
> John Brown is too important to me to scrap, but it's almost
> impossible to get an image powerful enough, because of the his-
> torian's view of him.[93]

And so the author of *Big White Fog* and *Our Lan'*, plus several
shorter plays and a new full-length play called *Candle in the
Wind* (1967), goes on writing "the play that may some day be
regarded as my finest achievement."[94] Whether or not William
Branch knew the Ward play, his approach to the subject was so
different that the only evident similarity is their use of the same
primary sources.

What have these historical plays to do with the current Negro
revolution? A great deal. There continues to be a split between
the revolutionary or violent approach and the reasoned reform
or nonviolent approach to gaining civil rights for Negroes. When
William Branch argued with Communist friends in the early
fifties, he was not persuaded by them to their way of thinking
even though he was dissatisfied with and disillusioned by American practices here and abroad. He worked within the framework
of American democracy, and Frederick Douglass is the hero of
his play. Ward, on the other hand, was persuaded by left-wing
arguments, and John Brown is his hero.

Anyone, however, who thinks that *In Splendid Error* is a
plea for moderation should be reminded that Branch's Douglass
retains his rational nonviolent stand but is torn by a desire to
commit such error as Brown's. Indeed, one must admit it is
impossible to know whose stand history will mark as error—
splendid or cowardly. William Branch refused to let a Hollywood
producer have the rights to the play in the late 1950s because
the producer wanted to make of it a film about the need for

moderation in the struggle for civil rights. Branch strenuously opposed this misuse of his material.[95]

About stage productions of *In Splendid Error*, the author has had this to say:

> Regarding college productions, I've found that "white" colleges aren't interested in plays with Negroes as leading characters (casting problems are usually given as the excuse, though this certainly is not insurmountable), and by and large, Negro colleges are so busy trying to keep up with white ones, by doing the classics and Broadway hits, that they avoid plays involving Negroes also—except for the Broadway hit, "A Raisin in the Sun." As for community theatres, there are few Negro or integrated ones, and the white ones again are not interested in plays with Negro characters, despite Ford Foundation and public funds support.[96]

At a writers' conference at Fisk University in 1966, Alice Childress announced that she was proud to be from Harlem and to be a Negro writer. Then she added:

> All I know of generosity and kindness and love I learned in Harlem. Imagine a rose saying "I'm not a rose, I'm a flower." Well, I am a rose and a flower; I am a Negro writer, and also part of universal man.[97]

The spirit that permeated this statement is evident in her play *Trouble in Mind*. Even though the play has faults—not since *Big White Fog* has a play been burdened with the mention of so many Negro problems—it succeeds in dealing very perceptively with Negro-white relationships. And its concern with an integrated theatre company gives the audience a very special sort of perspective.

It is perhaps time to observe that all the Negro playwrights of the fifties were and continue to be professional writers. Alice Childress, the only one without a college education, came to playwriting through acting and directing, bringing with her a highly motivating social conscience. In the forties that conscience swung her (like Langston Hughes and Theodore Ward earlier) to the left. Today she meets with young people one day to discuss a new theatre for Harlem, and the next talks to the organizers of the Free Southern Theatre about fund-raising for another year on the road. *Trouble in Mind* was twice produced by the B.B.C., in October and November, 1964. In 1965 she was on a discussion program on the B.B.C.—with LeRoi Jones, Langston Hughes, and James Baldwin—entitled "The Negro Playwright." Yet in her own country she is little known, which contributes to her writing in a letter:

> *Am working on two new plays. Why? Why! Why!—I can't stop and the market being what it is—I should—How I wish I could stop. But there's an inner clock that keeps ticking away and running the works in one direction.*[98]

At least one of these plays is based on African materials.

Whether or not the American theatregoing public is soon to become aware of Alice Childress depends somewhat on what happens to her play *Wedding Band*. Written in 1963, it was optioned for Broadway shortly thereafter but has changed hands several times since then. Having had a trial run at the University of Michigan in 1966, it is scheduled to be produced by Ossie Davis on Broadway in the near future.

In *A Land Beyond the River* Loften Mitchell wrote about history in the making. With the exception of William Wells Brown in the nineteenth century and Joseph Cotter in 1903, none of the Negro playwrights have dealt so directly with events of the day. Sensing the drama inherent in early stages of the struggle for desegregated schools, Mitchell focused, in his play, on the experiences of one man who was at the center of that struggle. He did not, however, write a documentary or agitprop play about Joseph DeLaine. Instead, he wrote a fairly conventional play filled with conflict, not just between good Negroes and wicked whites, but between two ways of fighting for a cause. In this respect, the play is like *In Splendid Error*. Bill Raigen and Joseph Layne represent violent and nonviolent positions closely paralleling those of John Brown and Frederick Douglass.

There are several theatrical devices used in *A Land Beyond the River* that are recognizable from plays of the past. For example, spirituals are sung to show the goal of the group's struggle—in this case, integrated education. In earlier plays, from Hall Johnson's *Run, Little Chillun* to Alice Childress' *Trouble in Mind*, spirituals were used in the same way, usually as part of the action and always as a reminder of the play's theme. The most organic use of spirituals in a play has been observed in Theodore Ward's *Our Lan'*; the least, in Frank Wilson's *Brother Mose*. The storm imagery that pervades *A Land Beyond the River* is reminiscent of that in *Run, Little Chillun*, although by 1957 the images had become more subtle.

Lorraine Hansberry once said that most Negro playwrights are retarded in comparison with Negro poets who have transcended the color question. (If, as W. E. B. DuBois contended, the color question—or as he put it, the "color line"—is *the* problem of the twentieth century, one wonders about the virtue of such a transcendence.) Only Louis Peterson in *Take a Giant Step*, she felt, had come anywhere near presenting his subject matter in sophisticated terms. For the most part, Negro playwrights remained unproduced, she claimed, because "they show the Negro as all good and the white man as all bad."[99] It is impossible to argue about these unproduced, unnamed plays, but the ones mentioned here, the produced and/or published ones, certainly do not exhibit Negro chauvinism to an excessive degree. Where white men appear at all—as in Branch's plays or Ward's or Mitchell's—they are good *and* bad. Interestingly enough, the most stereotyped white man in recent plays is the "milquetoast" character in *A Raisin in the Sun* who comes to try to keep the Youngers out of a white neighborhood. And even he is not all bad, just one-dimensional and too predictable.

When Lorraine Hansberry praised the "sophistication" of *Take a Giant Step*, she was probably showing her personal predilection for what Negro critic Harold Cruse has called a "leftwing accommodation to middle-class ideology."[100] Peterson himself wrote honestly out of his middle-class experience. If he achieved a universality by writing a play that seems to be more about adolescence than about Negroes—something that cannot be said about *Harlem* or *Big White Fog* although they are also about adolescents and their parents—it is because, with the exception of the very important difference that provides the play with its conflict, there are many similarities between black and white middle-class experience. To put it another way, Peterson wrote about himself, a middle-class American boy, and middle-class audiences (white and black) were pleased to find themselves, according to Loften Mitchell, "identifying horizontally with a central character who happens to be a Negro."[101] By horizontal identification Mitchell seems to mean a kind of empathy that cannot take place if an audience is either siding with a sympathetic white character who is assisting "those poor Negroes," as in *Deep Are the Roots*, or patronizing the "simple souls," as in *Green Pastures*. If an artist's aim is integration, this sense of relatedness is one step toward it.

There is little profit in comparing *Take a Giant Step* and *Big White Fog* except to call attention to the fact that the Jewish boy in the earlier play is simply a mouthpiece for a revolutionary message, whereas Iggie in the Peterson play is more personalized, even though, like the young Negro hero, he does represent a minority group. The Ward play ends with black and white comrades ready to join hands in staging a revolution. The Peterson play ends with two boys—one Jewish, one Negro—ready to get as much education as possible so that they can succeed in American society.

It is perhaps more to the point to compare *Take a Giant Step* with *Tea and Sympathy*, a play by white playwright Robert Anderson. George Jean Nathan reviewed the two plays together, calling the Anderson play a "considerably smoother but considerably lesser play."[102] The young heroes, Tom and Spence, need to prove their manhood—one because he fears that he is homosexual, the other because he knows that he is black—and both are initiated sexually by mature women. (Spence, however, makes the overtures, whereas Tom is chosen.) Laura's poetic speech at the end of *Tea and Sympathy*—"Years from now . . . when you talk about this . . . and you will . . . be kind"—and the stage direction that follows—"Gently she brings the boy's hands toward her open blouse, as the lights slowly dim out . . . and . . ."[103]—seem right for her and Tom. The quality of their language earlier, the reticence of their actions, prepare us for this conclusion. Spence's last line in scene two of *Take a Giant Step* is, "Why in hell is she taking so long?" Then, at the sound of the bell, he pulls down the shades. Line and action match the matter-of-fact mood of the entire scene. The sexual initiations of these two boys differ, as their environments do, but they are similar in their expression of an adolescent need to know sex in order to begin to know other things about the self.

Take a Giant Step, then, is a psychologically sound play about an adolescent boy who is a Negro. Its reception by audiences and critics prophesied a bright career in the theatre for Louis Peterson. And yet, since he co-authored the screenplay for a film of *Take a Giant Step* in 1959, little has been heard from the playwright. One might think that this play was his single, highly autobiographical contribution to the theatre. In fact, he wrote a play called *Count Me for a Stranger* which was optioned but never produced; and in April, 1962, he had a play called *Entertain a Ghost* produced off-Broadway. Of the latter he reports, "It was a complete and utter failure."[104]

Louis Peterson was writing for television until 1962–63. In June, 1963, he suffered a heart attack and had to rest for six months. His account of what happened after that time is worth recording for what it says about this integrated Negro playwright:

> I was very unhappy with the television I was writing, but was forced into doing it to support a rather large apartment. I

*decided to put a stop to that. I moved out into smaller quarters
so that I could concentrate as much time as possible in writing
for the theater. I am a theater writer. There is no question of
that in my mind now. I have a rather respectable job now,
working for an insurance concern. . . . I prepare magnetic tapes
and operate an electronic computer. I spend the rest of my time
finishing my play. If someone asked me now whether if the play
were a tremendous success, I would stop working, I would say
"No." One of the things I loathed most in the period when I
was writing successfully were the times spent away from the
original sources of your productivity, namely everyday, honest
people.*[105]

When Lorraine Hansberry (also a member of the middle
class) arrived on the American theatre scene, she was considered
by many to be a new force in the theatre. One of the saddest
aspects of her career is that she died still serving her apprenticeship as a playwright—having written *A Raisin in the Sun,* a
naturalistic play *ne plus ultra,* and *The Sign in Sidney Brustein's
Window* (1964), a brave step toward the future in spite of a
social commitment reminiscent of the thirties. Unfortunately, she
did not live to achieve a synthesis of these two strands of her
promising talent, the domestic and the didactic.

Perhaps the strongest criticism leveled against Lorraine Hansberry to date is that of Harold Cruse, who calls attention to a
very delicate issue when he accuses the playwright of putting
middle-class sentiments into the mouths of her supposedly lower-
class Negroes in order to make them fit for integration. He wonders how a poor family of Southern origin has a $10,000 insurance
policy, or how the daughter attends medical school, or how a
chauffeur has the connections and the political pull to get credit
to buy into a business.

*All three of these circumstances in Negro life derive not from
a working class status, but a lower-middle or middle-class family background. They represent the class advantages that are*

economic keys, guarding the very limited world of social privilege and advancement of the Negro petite bourgeoisie and bourgeoisie, a world jealously closed against black working-class pene-
tration.[106]

Lorraine Hansberry's left-wing pose was somewhat of an embarrassment in view of her obvious lack of knowledge about the
Negro working class. Her play suffered from this dichotomy, suffered both in substance and in language, though Harold Cruse
does well to explain its success in this fashion:

> The phenomenal success of A Raisin in the Sun has to be seen
> against the background of the temper of the racial situation in
> America and its cultural implications for American art forms.
> Broadway and the rest of the American theater has not been at
> all kind to the Negro playwright or performer. Miss Hansberry's
> play provided the perfect opportunity to make it all up, or at
> least assuage the commercial theater's liberal guilt. . . . What
> obviously elated the drama critics was the very relieving dis-
> covery that, what the publicity buildup actually heralded was
> not the arrival of belligerent forces from across the color line
> to settle some long-standing racial accounts on stage, but a good
> old-fashioned, home-spun saga of some good working-class folk
> in pursuit of the American Dream . . . in their fashion.[107]

When A Raisin in the Sun opened at the Ethel Barrymore
Theatre on March 11, 1959, several critics called the play old-
fashioned and regretted Miss Hansberry's choice of naturalism as
a theatrical mode. Gerald Weales, for example, expressed the
opinion that naturalism had been, since World War II, the mode
of semidocumentaries and television and, therefore, no longer
belonged in the theatre, where the imagination has been conditioned to accept a highly stylized tree but not "a real room with
real doors and real furniture."[108] Tom Driver felt that Lorraine
Hansberry, in choosing to write a naturalistic play, was as anach-
ronistic as a composer of today choosing to write a concerto in
the manner of Tchaikovsky.[109] Harold Clurman, while agreeing

that the play is old-fashioned, defended the playwright's use of naturalism:

> While the drift away from naturalism in the American theatre is healthy, it is entirely false to assume that we have no further use for the old realism. America is still but little explored as far as a significant stage realism goes. . . . The traditional realistic play needs genuine identification with its subject matter . . . in addition to objectivity and heart.[110]

He felt that the authenticity of A Raisin in the Sun was both admirable and desirable in view of Lorraine Hansberry's determination to say "what she has seen and experienced."[111]

Robert Nemiroff has called attention to the nonnaturalistic levels of A Raisin in the Sun, claiming, for example, that Walter Younger's African soliloquy could not literally be his own:

> The liquor that loosens Walter Lee's tongue releases a language and imagery he could not have derived from the books he has never read, nor certainly from the movies that he has seen; and language is not a quality of the blood. It is the potential talking in him, not the actual.[112]

However, anyone who has heard Black Nationalists on the street corners of Harlem could tell Nemiroff that ordinary men can talk in "poetic compression, larger than life," and Walter Lee might well have their speeches in his experience, ready to be released by liquor. This is not to deny the existence of poetic language in A Raisin in the Sun, but rather to suggest that too much can be made of this playful episode in the play. It is possible to be grateful for being lifted momentarily "out of the circle of description and reflection"[113] by the African chant, but Nemiroff tries to claim poetic depths for the play that it just does not possess.

No single play considered in this study is dramaturgically sounder than A Raisin in the Sun. Whether or not it is soap opera, it is a well-made play. The characters are clearly defined, the plot moves forward with adequate motivation, the dialogue is both entertaining and revealing. There are echoes from other plays by Negro playwrights—plays that Lorraine Hansberry may not have known. When Walter cries out, "Here I am a giant— surrounded by ants!" one remembers John Henry in Theodore Browne's *Natural Man* saying, "Like a giant in a straight jacket! . . . Like a great king without a throne to sit on!" And when Walter dreams of success in terms of money, of the white man's values, one thinks of Bigger Thomas.

So, in a very real sense, *A Raisin in the Sun* is both a synthesis of the major problems and attitudes seen in Negro drama since its inception and a proof of the dramaturgical and literary advances made by American Negro playwrights—a summary, a proof, and the end of an era. An observation made by Henrik Ibsen could be applied to Lorraine Hansberry:

> It has been said that I . . . have contributed to create a new era. . . . I, on the contrary, believe that the time in which we now live might with quite as much reason be characterized as a conclusion and that something new is about to be born.[114]

EPILOGUE

Tomorrow is another day

MY INTENTION in writing this book has been fulfilled: Negro plays and playwrights have been placed in a social and artistic context that has allowed us to observe both the playwrights' continuing social concerns reflected in their plays and their artistic development as writers during the four decades under consideration. And yet so much (and so little) has happened since *A Raisin in the Sun* first appeared almost ten years ago that something must be said about the sixties, this decade that suffers a social revolution but lacks a cultural one, this decade that slays both Malcolm X and Martin Luther King—but leaves only a handful of plays that even hint at the change and violence of our time.

In 1965 Loften Mitchell complained:

Today—with the Negro making headlines in a great revolution —our widely acclaimed writers are not fully represented on Broadway, in Hollywood, nor on television. Since the artist must seek the truth, communicate, educate and entertain, I know that art is being distorted in these times. I know, too, that unless there is a sharp reversal, modern history will not be recorded in our plays and movies. It is unprecedented for a great revolution to be so completely ignored by cultural forms.[1]

And more recently a white critic, Renata Adler, writing about movies what could just as well be said about plays, stated:

You wouldn't know . . . that there have been black men of great intelligence and gentleness working in the south. You wouldn't know there has been a Watts, or ghetto life, or a Negro family, or a love affair, or a musical world, or an intellectual community, or dealings of most kinds between Negroes and whites. It is all a blank where the richest fiction and documentary material should be.[2]

Tomorrow is here, and it is not different enough from yesterday where Negroes are concerned. This is true in art as well as in life. As we near the end of the sixties in America, we are deeply involved in a social revolution, but the matching cultural revolution is lagging, and theatre in particular is out of step and often out of tune.

Standing at the edge of the sixties, critics were, for the most part, hopeful in their assessment of and predictions for American Negro playwrights. These playwrights were, it was proclaimed with a mixture of chauvinism and liberal paternalism, ready to be integrated into the main line of American dramatic tradition as they could never have been prior to this decade. It might, of course, take the appearance of one great Negro playwright— assuming that such an ethnic distinction continued to be made —to force critics to say that Negro playwrights had come of age. But their record was pretty good, everything considered, from Garland Anderson to Lorraine Hansberry. Let me try to suggest in the next few paragraphs the way in which Negro playwrights have been evaluated in recent decades.

In the 1920s, writers of various persuasions—Eugene O'Neill, Maxwell Anderson, Paul Green, George Kelly, John Howard Lawson—began using the theatre for serious experimentation. "Since they were simmering with ideas and thought they knew what was wrong with the world," Brooks Atkinson remembers that these men made the 1920s "the most dynamic decade the American theatre ever had."[3] Negro playwrights of the same period, Garland Anderson and Wallace Thurman, were not ready artistically or intellectually for such experimentation. They were scarcely free of melodrama and the minstrel tradition. It was a white playwright, Paul Green, who wrote about Negroes without resorting to sentimentality or generalized symbolism when he wrote *In Abraham's Bosom* (1926).

The Group Theatre and the Federal Theatre have been justly praised for their innovations, but they did not dominate the fourth decade of this century, which is best known for plays by Maxwell Anderson, S. N. Behrman, Philip Barry, Robert Sherwood, and Clifford Odets. The work of most of these playwrights illustrates a narrowing of the serious subject matter and technical experimentation of the twenties to preoccupation with the social and sociological aspects of existence. All of their plays showed a consolidation of gains made in the preceding decade. Negro playwrights, though still not very sophisticated at their craft, were making advances. Kenneth Burke could, for example, call Hall Johnson's *Run, Little Chillun* (1933) a better play than Marc Connelly's *Green Pastures* (1930), but his evaluation of the play was from a social and a theatrical point of view, not from a literary one. Most Negro playwrights of the thirties lacked both the maturity of dramatic technique and the roundedness of character portrayal that was evident in plays by white playwrights of the same period. Langston Hughes's *Mulatto* (1935), surely the best play written to that date by a Negro, reads more like a nineteenth- than a twentieth-century work.

Quiescent during the war years, the American theatre in the late forties produced two major talents, Tennessee Williams and Arthur Miller, who between them synthesized the psychological emphasis of the twenties and the social emphasis of the thirties. Again Negro drama seemed a decade behind the times. Theodore Ward's *Big White Fog*, produced in New York in 1940, was really a Federal Theatre play of the late thirties and comparable to Clifford Odets' early plays. Ward's later historical play, *Our Lan'* (1947), resembles historical plays by white playwrights— Sidney Kingsley's *The Patriots* (1942), Robert Sherwood's *Abe Lincoln in Illinois* (1938). The other outstanding Negro playwright of the forties, Richard Wright, did root his *Native Son* (1941) in both society and individual psychology, but it fails to achieve either the degree of symbolic sophistication or the dramatic strength of *Death of a Salesman* or *A Streetcar Named Desire*.

In the 1950s, while Miller continued to write social plays, Williams began to explore the sordid and the bizarre. The outstanding Negro dramatists of the period were, like Miller, still writing in the tradition of O'Neill and Odets. Louis Peterson's *Take a Giant Step*, as we have observed, is a Negro *Ah, Wilderness!*, and Lorraine Hansberry's *A Raisin in the Sun*, a Negro *Awake and Sing!* Both of these Negro playwrights created white characters who—like the Negro characters created by white playwrights (and Negro playwrights, too, when they work from models)—were by and large stereotypes. Still the introduction of white characters was important, because it paved the way for plays of the sixties in which white characters appear more frequently (they dominate Lorraine Hansberry's *The Sign in Sidney Brustein's Window*), are more humanly complex and more sophisticatedly symbolic.

Without the knowledge that we now have of the sixties, it was easy to assume in the late fifties that Negro playwrights were about to be assimilated artistically. After all, it was assumed that Negroes generally were moving into social integration. In 1959 Arthur P. Davis went so far as to call Negro protest writing the "first casualty of the new racial climate" that had existed in America since 1950. The possibility of *imminent integration*, he told a group of Negro writers, had killed the element of protest. Negro writers, he said, had retained Negro characters and background but had "shifted [their] emphasis from the protest aspect of Negro living and placed it on the problems and conflicts

within the group itself."⁴ This may be an accurate description of
A Raisin in the Sun, but that play was neither the literary nor
the theatrical watershed that Davis and others (black and white)
dreamed of its being. Nor have we witnessed the social integration
promised in his comments or in Miss Hansberry's play. The year
1959 was indeed a turning point, but few realized where the turn
was taking us.

Out of the turmoil of the sixties, out of insurrections and
marches, may come black playwrights who can help us to understand, not the New Negro of the twenties or the fifties, but what
Claude Brown has called "this new nigger . . . something that
nobody understood and that nobody was ready for."⁵ These playwrights are not with us yet. They are writing in and out of
workshops in Watts and Chicago and Harlem. Some of their
plays have been produced, but few have been published or reviewed. What is happening in the streets needs to be translated
into a kind of Living Newspaper; whether or not it will be
depends on whether or not our attitude toward theatre in this
country changes.

At the moment we have the strange accommodation of the revolutionary plays of LeRoi Jones to the commercial (white) theatre.
Even he, the most promising Negro playwright of this period,
could not find a black audience when he founded the Black Arts
Repertory Theatre and School in Harlem in 1965. The institution
lasted for seven months.⁶ It is doubtful, too, that he reached
many of the black bourgeoisie with ideas like these:

> *America has become a place where integration means not just
> dollars and cents—although that's what it is about, dollars and
> cents—it also means Radio City Music Hall. It means the in-
> sipidities of television, it means the impossibility of becoming
> a man in a place that doesn't demand manhood any more—in
> fact, a place where manhood has become a kind of alien grace.*⁷

He was asking his fellow Negroes to resist moving into a polluted
mainstream, to remain separate in their blackness and thereby to

create a satisfactory sense of self, not just one imposed upon them by a dominant white society. The reason that Jones's audiences are young may simply be that they have not yet "made it"; those who have, black *and* white, are repelled and frightened by Jones's words, not stirred to the murderous rage he proposes.

We are reminded by Harold Cruse that the dilemma in which Jones and other Negro playwrights find themselves is not only that of the American artist who must write for a theatre in which questions of finance generally supersede those of taste; it is also that of the American *black* artist who lacks a cultural home.

> *What lurks behind the disabilities and inhibitions of the Negro creative intellectuals is the handicap of the black bourgeoisie. Unless this class is brought into the cultural situation and forced to carry out its responsibilities on a community, organizational, and financial level, the cultural side of the black revolution will be retarded.*[8]

When an artist is shut out of one world and unrecognized by another, he becomes, as Cruse put it, "tongue-tied about the social implications of middle-class values in Negro life and his own relation to such values." The lack of a theatre and a cultured black middle-class audience to support it seems to Cruse (and I must agree) "the bitter fruits of racial integration on the cultural plane."[9] Negro playwrights of the past have made (were forced to make?) compromises with white middle-class society that have cost them their ethnicity.

Broadway and off-Broadway cannot be truly differentiated these days; they represent *the* theatre in New York. Critics regularly wander down or over to off-off-Broadway, but for the most part even plays by Negro playwrights become known and published on the strength of a Broadway or off-Broadway production. The best-known Broadway plays of Negro authorship in the past decade have been *Purlie Victorious* by Ossie Davis (1961), *Blues for Mister Charlie* and *The Amen Corner* by James Baldwin (1963), and *The Sign in Sidney Brustein's Window* by Lorraine Hansberry (1965). (The last became a *succès d'estime* partly because of the public's admiration for Miss Hansberry's gallant battle with cancer and partly because there was a large liberal audience for a play that hyphenated Jewish and Negro problems. The play itself seems, to me at least, more pretentious than profound.) Significant off-Broadway plays were LeRoi Jones's one-acters— *Dutchman, The Toilet, The Slave,* all produced in 1964—and Douglas Turner Ward's *Day of Absence* and *Happy Ending* (1965). All of these plays have been widely reviewed and published. For the most part, the playwrights have become more conscious than earlier Negro playwrights were of symbolism, of satire, of new ways of talking about old problems. That is to say, they have made dramaturgical advances, but they have failed as true social commentators in a decade that badly needs such commentators.

Negro playwrights are in the same position today that they were in yesterday. They must find patronage where they can and, having found it, present plays about Negroes to a predominantly white audience whose values their plays frequently attack. The result has been either a play of compromise or easy message *(Purlie Victorious, The Amen Corner)* or one that is a brutal attack that reaches the conscience of whites only through a sado-masochistic exchange *(Blues for Mister Charlie, Dutchman).*

Almost all the critics had a kind word to say about *Purlie Victorious,* Ossie Davis' comedy of racial stereotypes. Audiences, black and white together, enjoyed laughing at the playwright's mockery of fake Negro humility and pompous Southern white pride. Marya Mannes was an exception when she admitted that she was made uncomfortable by the production. As she put it, "Whites now know that they cannot laugh at Negroes, but they cannot laugh *with* them either."[10] There was something strangely out of date about the opening of Howard Taubman's review of *Purlie Victorious.* "It is marvelously exhilarating to hear the Negro speak for himself," wrote this critic thirty-five years after the same thing was said about Garland Anderson, "especially when he does so in the fullness of his native gusto and the enveloping heartiness of his overflowing laughter." And later in the same review, he wrote with transparently good intentions: "While *Purlie Victorious* keeps you chuckling and guffawing, it unrelentingly forces you to feel how it is to inhabit a dark skin in a hostile or, at best, begrudgingly benevolent world."[11]

The play was no more than a sketch of the one most critics benevolently praised—but that sketch was good theatre. In spite of its popularity and the support of the Negro community (the NAACP sent out letters endorsing it), producer Philip Rose later claimed to have lost an investment of $100,000 on *Purlie Victorious*. The more successful *A Raisin in the Sun* had made a $700,000 profit in nineteen months on an original investment of $100,000.[12]

As for Baldwin's *The Amen Corner*, a play originally written in 1953–54 and produced at Howard University in 1955, it is not a bad play so much as a sentimental, old-fashioned one. But to see Beah Richards in the role of the lady minister of a storefront church who has to learn about false piety was to witness a performance that gave the play special stature. As a play about religious disillusion, it did pave the way for Baldwin's outright rejection of the religious in favor of physical force in *Blues for Mister Charlie*.

"The play . . . takes place in Plaguetown, U.S.A., now," Baldwin wrote in the introduction to *Blues for Mister Charlie*. "The plague is race, the plague is our concept of Christianity."[13] In the course of an evening, audiences watched the murder of a young Negro, the acquittal of a white murderer, the arming of camps that had always been hostile but were now awakened to violence— fear winning out inevitably over justice in Plaguetown, U.S.A. Some critics called the play a sermon; others, agitprop; and still others, melodrama.

Tom Driver wrote that *Blues for Mister Charlie* failed on Broadway for the same reason that Brecht fails on Broadway: "It frightens people by challenging the status quo, while at the same time it challenges their way of seeing the status quo."[14] On the other hand, Philip Roth called the play "a soap opera designed to illustrate the superiority of blacks over whites," the kind of thing that would be shown on television in a Black Muslim nation.[15]

More to the point, Susan Sontag commented on the strange experience of being in the audience seeing *Blues for Mister Charlie:*

> It is eerie to sit in the ANTA Theatre on 52nd Street and hear that audience—sizably Negro, but still preponderantly white— cheer and laugh and break into applause at every line cursing white America. After all, it's not some exotic Other from across the seas who is being abused—like the rapacious Jew or the treacherous Italian of the Elizabethan drama. It is the majority of the members of the audience themselves.

Miss Sontag did not think that social guilt was enough to explain the docility with which white audiences accepted Baldwin's condemnation. "Only by tapping the sexual insecurity that grips most educated white Americans," she observed, "could Baldwin's virulent rhetoric have seemed so reasonable."[16] The same might be said about LeRoi Jones's *Dutchman,* a shocking play, full of sexual symbolism, in which a demented white woman ritualistically kills a young Negro male on a subway.

Several critics compared *Dutchman* to Edward Albee's *The Zoo Story,* finding similarities in their violence and their criticism of America—but finding Jones's play less controlled, more contrived than Albee's. Susan Sontag admired some of the early exchanges between the two characters but then tired of later verbosity.[17] Philip Roth found the Negro, Clay, too innocent and the woman, Lula, too viciously secretive in her madness.[18] Negro scholar Saunders Redding called *Dutchman* a fantasy "in which the allegory, whether intentionally or not, veils more than it reveals, and in which the symbolic devices are exactly those that whites have created for their defense against the Negro."[19]

Responding to the critics' reactions to his play, Jones made it clear that he did not want the boy or the girl (the black or the white) to "represent" anything. They are not, to his way of thinking, symbolic. They are real persons in a real world .

> [Lula] does not represent any thing—she is one. And perhaps that thing is America, or at least its spirit. You remember America, don't you, where they have unsolved murders happening before your eyes on television? How crazy, extreme, neurotic does that sound? Lula, for all her alleged insanity, just barely reflects the insanity of this hideous place. And Clay is a young boy trying desperately to become a man. Dutchman is about the difficulty of becoming a man in America.[20]

It is difficult, he warned, for a Negro—and even more so for a white man—to become a man in America.

This same theme—the difficulty of becoming a man in America —occurs in two other plays by LeRoi Jones, *The Slave* and *The Toilet*. In *The Slave* a Negro military leader, in a future war between the races, visits the home of his former white wife and her impotent white husband. Their talk is wild and their actions wilder still, but the playwright's raging against an American slave society sustains in the theatre better than it does on the page. (A production at the Act IV theatre in Provincetown in the summer of 1967, complete with projections of the recent revolt in Newark, was extremely harrowing.) *The Toilet*, too, has a theatrical quality that audiences found difficult to resist even as they were repelled by the sado-masochistic fantasies being acted out on the stage. In this instance they were treated to brutal fights between boys in a school toilet. A Puerto Rican boy who has sent a homosexual love letter to one of the Negro boys is beaten and bloody at the end of the play, though he is cradled in the arms of his Negro love object. Neither *The Slave* nor *The Toilet* has the symbolic sophistication of *Dutchman*, but all of these plays provided what Langston Hughes called "bloody kicks" for the audience.[21]

When he was asked in an interview in 1967 what his attitude was toward Broadway and whether or not he anticipated having any of his plays performed there (to date his plays have had well-directed, well-attended off-Broadway productions), LeRoi Jones replied:

> Broadway is stupid, filthy, meaningless, boring, vacuous—what can I say? But it reflects the American mind, because the American mind is exactly that. Would I mind having a play done on Broadway? I don't care where my plays are done as long as somebody sees them. I would like to have a huge, mobile unit to tour America with plays, so that I could play one night in one ghetto, the next night in another ghetto, and take 'em all over the country.[22]

When he had tried, a year prior to this interview, to establish a ghetto theatre in Harlem, it had failed. Some say that it failed because he compromised with the Establishment. According to the New York *Times*, his Black Arts theatre-school got "its biggest push . . . when it joined the Haryou summer program, Project Uplift, and gave nightly performances throughout Harlem and later in Central Park." The group was highly praised for a short time, but soon there were complaints about antiwhite themes and the use of profanity. Also, "police raided the organization's offices . . . and said they found several guns and knives."[23]

Harold Cruse is critical of LeRoi Jones—as much as he admires his creative ability—for not understanding how inappropriate it was for the Black Arts project to accept funds from federal sources. Cruse suggests that with Negro middle-class backing the Black Arts theatre-school would not have "come under the domination of activists and politicians who do not favor cultural front activities."[24] It is as difficult, however, to imagine the black bourgeoisie supporting anything resembling a revolutionary theatre as it is to imagine the federal government doing so. Of course, as this book demonstrates, it is no new cultural phenomenon for a Negro playwright to be caught between white support and black indifference.

The year before his Harlem venture, LeRoi Jones, speaking about *Dutchman*, made the following profound observation:

> The Negro writer is in a peculiar position because, if he is honest, most of what he has seen and experienced in America will not flatter it. His vision and experience cannot be translated honestly into art by euphemism. And while this is true of any good writer in America, black or white, it is a little weirder for the Negro since, if that Negro is writing about his own life and his own experience, his writing must be separate from what the owners and the estimators think of as reality . . . not only because of the intellectual gulf that causes any serious man to be estranged from the mainstream of American life, but because of the social and cultural estrangement from that mainstream that has characterized Negro life in America.[25]

At this point in his career LeRoi Jones was carrying the weight of "white America's social and cultural stupidity"; only later did he turn to Harlem—and still later to his home city of Newark, long enough to be a part of the revolt there in the summer of 1967. He was sentenced on January 4, 1968, for allegedly possessing a gun during the revolt and was subsequently released on $25,000 bail pending an appeal. Of course, all of these events are interrelated, and all of them reflect the frenzy of the sixties.

History is not neat, and so it is impossible, as we have seen time and again in these chapters, to characterize periods or their art forms definitively. Angry playwrights—especially when one's concern is with black playwrights—do seem to be the dominant voice of the present decade. We tend to hear LeRoi Jones and James Baldwin and to miss the softer voices, the more conventional words.

For convenience, it is possible to divide the Negro playwrights whose plays have appeared on or off Broadway in the sixties into three camps: angry, comic, and absurdist. To the names of Jones and Baldwin in the first category can be added Ronald Milner and Ed Bullins, both of whom have had plays produced at the American Place Theatre, which is housed at St. Clement's Church of the Episcopal Diocese of New York. Joining Ossie Davis in the comic category is Douglas Turner Ward. And the closest to absurdists among black playwrights are Adrienne Kennedy and Archie Shepp.

Ronald Milner's play *Who's Got His Own* (1966) is a fairly conventional one suffused with black anger against white exploitation. In it Tim Junior, whose father has been killed by whites, vows that he will kill in return in order to find peace. "The killing," as Walter Kerr remarked, "is meant to atone for yesterday. But, a resigned mother sighs at evening's end, no one can wait in ambush for yesterday."[26] This is, of course, to deny the validity of vengeance. The angry playwrights, heirs of Richard Wright, are advocates of retaliative violence, the purgative power of revenge. *Who's Got His Own* had a limited run at the downtown theatre and was revived a year later at the New Lafayette Theatre in Harlem. Milner, currently author-in-residence at Lincoln University in Pennsylvania, had a note in the program to the effect that his play takes place in "the continuing past," an indication that he has seen nothing to encourage him to believe in the improvement of the black man's condition in America.

Ed Bullins has written *The Electronic Nigger and Others*, three short plays that proved popular enough during the 1967–68 season to move from the American Place Theatre to the midtown Martinique. Although two of the plays are rather sophomoric exercises that belong in theatre workshops, the one called "Clara's Ole Man" has the kind of seething rage and disgust that inform *Dutchman* and *The Toilet*. Characters, setting, situation, everything is out of Negro existence. Whites who pay for the privilege of looking in on this world that has as much vitality as it has viciousness should be alarmed, should feel that uneasiness that comes from eavesdropping when someone is talking indirectly about you. For it is evident that whatever is sick about this segment of society has become that way in large part through white neglect. Whatever is strong excludes whites and indeed could destroy them.

It is worth noting—not only for the sentimental reason of observing the longevity of his career, but also for a reminder of his influence on writers of comedy—that Langston Hughes was represented early in this decade by *Tambourines to Glory* (1963), a play accurately described by him as "a fable, a folk ballad in stage form, told in broad and very simple terms—if you will, a comic strip, a cartoon."[27] In the play, good cooperates with evil to the glory of God, as two women convert an old movie house into Tambourine Temple. Like other plays of his last years, this one was highly dependent on music and filled with very amusing characters who speak humorously of serious matters.

Douglas Turner Ward (and fellow actor-playwright Ossie Davis before him) is a direct descendant of Langston Hughes. How delighted the older writer must have been with the situations in Ward's two plays, *Happy Ending* and *Day of Absence* (1965). They are as bizarre and as telling as situations dreamed up by Hughes for his newspaper column and his short stories. In *Happy Ending* two domestics (Negro women) give their militant nephew a lesson in American economics and the interdependence of the races. The boy has to learn the game that his aunts are playing when they seem to be bowing and scraping to their white employers. The women are in reality providing themselves with necessities and luxuries "salvaged" from the unsuspecting, affluent whites. The play is a joke, a slight one, and the joke is on a society that allows such socioeconomic hypocrisies to continue.

Day of Absence, the more substantial of the two plays, although it too is an extended joke, is about a time when the entire Negro population of a somnolent Southern city vanishes, leaving the whites without the vital services that they have always taken for granted. A television speech, in which the white mayor (played by a Negro actor in white-face) begs the "Nigras" to return, moves from sentimental kindliness to threats of violence and then back to sweetness and light as he holds up a rag and a brush as nostalgic reminders of former days!

I should preface my remarks about Adrienne Kennedy's *The Funnyhouse of a Negro* (1963) and Archie Shepp's *June Bug Graduates Tonight* (1967) by saying that I have neither read them nor seen productions of them. Reviews lead me to believe that these two plays could be called absurdist. They seem to belong in the Theatre of the Absurd as described by Martin Esslin when he says that "the Theatre of the Absurd concentrates on the power of stage imagery, on the projection of visions of the world dredged up from the depth of the subconscious; . . . neglects the rationally measurable ingredients of the theatre."[28]

The Funnyhouse of a Negro came out of a workshop at Circle in the Square and was presented off-Broadway during the 1963–64 season. Adrienne Kennedy was credited by most reviewers with having written an original, imaginative play. It lasted for less than an hour on stage and consisted of a series of mad fantasies during which a dying Negro girl has visions of Jesus, Queen Victoria, Patrice Lumumba, and others. In his review Howard Taubman commented on the girl's "secret resentments and guilt." According to him, "Miss Kennedy . . . digs unsparingly into . . . the tortured mind of a Negro who cannot bear the burden of being a Negro."[29]

Loften Mitchell concluded that *"The Funnyhouse of a Negro* reveals Miss Kennedy as a writer of considerable depth, quite introspective and quite knowledgeable of theatrical terms."[30] He predicted future theatrical success for her on the basis of her ability to create strong characters and to write good dialogue. Adrienne Kennedy most assuredly made the move from outer to inner reality, working in a genre very new to Negro playwrights, that of fantasy, and a somber, interior fantasy at that.

Archie Shepp, jazz saxophonist and author of the play *June Bug Graduates Tonight*, has seen in both the "black aesthetic revolution" and its political counterpart, the Black Power movement, not only justifiable anger but also an honesty that might begin to counteract the hypocrisy of America's past. "The image of Buckwheat and Aunt Jemima which had persisted in the American mythology as stock types," he wrote, "were exposed for what they were: the absurd projection of an elaborate white fantasy."[31]

A friend and admirer of LeRoi Jones (whom he has joined on occasion in angry diatribes at the Village Vanguard, a nightclub in Greenwich Village), Shepp would no doubt have been active in Jones's Black Arts Theatre if it had lasted long enough. As it was, *June Bug Graduates Tonight* was produced before the altar, on a small raked stage, in the Church of the Holy Apostles on Ninth Avenue at 28th Street, for the limited run of February 20 to March 3, 1967. The Chelsea Theatre Center is dedicated to finding and sponsoring new playwrights and to bringing free theatre to the community. *June Bug Graduates Tonight* was the first full-length Equity production of this off-Broadway group. Billed as a jazz allegory with music and lyrics by Archie Shepp, the play seems to have been given a production that would call to mind Brechtian cabaret.

The June Bug of the title is a sensitive young Negro who is plagued by questions on the eve of his graduation from high school as valedictorian of his class. The audience is asked to consider what goes on in his mind at this transitional moment in his life. One critic summarized June Bug's questions:

> If I play the white liberal game (integration, moderation, hot lunches in the schools), am I copping out on the black race? If I play the Black Muslim game (separation, action, blood—if need be—in the streets), am I copping out on the human race? Do I defend myself with my fists, or with my words? Or, do I forget about defense and start attacking?[32]

The questions are not surprising. William Branch's "Willie" might have asked something like them if he had stayed in school instead of enlisting in the army; Louis Peterson's "Spence" did not ask them only because he was so brainwashed by the American middle-class dream of success.

Like Adrienne Kennedy, Archie Shepp deserted the realistic tradition and had allegorical figures represent the alternatives in his arguments with himself. America is represented by a sexy young white girl in stars-and-stripes underwear, who tries to seduce June Bug. Uncle Sam makes promises and more promises. And Muslim, a character resplendent in white gown and red fez, asks June Bug to join him in shedding blood. "Are you with me?" Muslim asks the boy. June Bug, after a pause, answers significantly, "Sometimes I am."[33]

Critic Dan Sullivan expressed the worry that Shepp's allegorical terms would not help an audience to consider problems that they already think about too much in the abstract. (One wonders how much consideration they had given those problems when they were presented in the realistic plays of the past four decades.)

Without having seen the play or heard the accompanying jazz, it is impossible to know how successful it was as protest. As theatre it seems to have been exciting and might well be revived today, for even a year later American audiences could be more receptive to a play that asks, "Can America prevent June Bug from murdering her?"[34]

In the next few years we shall undoubtedly see some Negro playwrights joining "the prevailing cultural superstructure of America while protesting its standards and values,"[35] and others trying, in the face of traditional obstacles, to establish ethnic theatres in which they may do things their way for their people. Which route he takes will depend somewhat on the playwright's purpose. If he wants to attack white society, and white society for reasons of guilt or curiosity wants to pay to be attacked in the theatre, then he should get a foot in off-Broadway's door. (For the moment I am assuming that Broadway audiences want to be entertained, not attacked.) If, on the other hand, he wants to remind black theatre audiences that they are men and that they deserve respect, then Harlem is the answer.

Of course, it is not all that simple. Alice Childress, one of the most discerning of playwrights (of any color), believes that black writers should direct their work toward black audiences, and yet she aims for both Broadway and ethnic theatre productions. She has things to say to white and black audiences, and it is interesting to read her impressions of the latter:

> Black audiences are not always waiting with open arms for every word we have to say. Many of them listen with a "white" ear . . . they want us to say just enough but not too much. . . . It is not the simplest thing in the world to write for a black audience.[36]

William Branch shares her concern that black audiences are unaccustomed to the theatre and unused to the idea of thinking about it for themselves in terms of themselves. He wrestles with the black-white audience dilemma, he says, each time he writes. "Sometimes I lean more heavily in one direction, sometimes in another, hopeful that both black and white audiences will gain some (though differing) insight from what results."[37]

Who will the Negro playwrights be who will write for whatever theatre exists in the near future? By mentioning them I mean to suggest that Alice Childress and William Branch will be on the scene. Perhaps Louis Peterson will make a comeback. Theodore Ward, never entirely discouraged, writes from Chicago about a production of *Our Lan'* that has been kept alive for several months in spite of the fact that "critics have ignored it . . . including the Negro press."[38] He will certainly go on writing for the theatre. And so will Loften Mitchell, although if he writes a play again he will probably write about a Bill Raigen who has picked up the gun he was persuaded to put aside at least temporarily in *A Land Beyond the River*. (At a symposium at Fisk University a few years ago, the usually mild Mitchell called out, "We haven't gotten free yet, we got *integrated*—the double double cross!")[39]

It seems very likely that these middle-aged authors will write in the realistic mode to which they have become accustomed. Jones and Baldwin, if they have not been lost to the theatre, may yet write good dramatic literature as well as startling or shocking theatre. The younger playwrights—and here we can include Ossie Davis and Douglas Turner Ward, who are younger as playwrights than they are as actors—will hopefully continue their theatrical experimentation. The Negro Ensemble Company, the New Heritage Players, the Gossett Academy of Dramatic Arts, just to mention a few New York ventures, should turn up new plays in their workshops. Until February, 1967, when a fire gutted the New Lafayette Theatre in Harlem, there was hope that it would foster new playwriting talent. Now the future of the theatre is uncertain and a production of Ed Bullins' play *In the Wine of Time* has been postponed.[40]

There is also the possibility that drama will be "refreshed from non-dramatic sources." Robert Brustein once welcomed such a move and expressed approval of Lillian Hellman's encouraging novelists Saul Bellow, Herbert Gold, and James Purdy to write plays.[41] We have already seen LeRoi Jones go from poetry and essays to plays, James Baldwin from novels and essays, and Archie Shepp from jazz. A novelist-essayist who should be urged to write for the theatre is Ralph Ellison. Irving Howe has said of him: "He is richly, wildly inventive; his scenes rise and dip with tension, his people bleed, his language sings.[42] The dialogue in his work-in-progress, *Juneteenth*, begs to be spoken from a stage. William Kelley, in his novels *A Different Drummer* and *dem*, seems to have a remarkable ear for dialogue and a feeling for dramatic situations. John A. Williams, whose novel *Sissie* is about a playwright and whose latest novel, *The Man Who Cried I Am*, has scenes that one can visualize on a stage or, even better, on a screen, is another possible candidate for playwriting. If they are not too discouraged by Baldwin's experience in the theatre, these novelists may give it a try.

Negro playwrights have had rather special treatment from critics who, until very recently, were either sympathetically tolerant or guardedly insulting in reviews that seemed to promote cultural integration while at the same time not encouraging artistic growth. It should be said, too, that flattery or praise (sometimes for subject matter alone) in the Negro press has been as useless to Negro playwrights as patronizing white criticism.

Hoyt W. Fuller, editor of *Negro Digest*, asks for informed black critics in the future, critics who are not ignorant, as white critics must be, of "the intricacies of black style and black life." Young ghetto writers are in search of a black aesthetic, Fuller says, "a system of isolating and evaluating the artistic works of black people which reflects the special character and imperatives of black experience."[43] From such a discovery could come fruitful criticism.

A black aesthetic, however, will be viable among playwrights only when artists and audience alike feel the need for a separate Negro theatre. At the present time, according to Harold Cruse, "the Negro does not own, operate or sustain a single theatre institution of any critical importance in the United States."[44] James Baldwin has said that the trouble is that America *is* integrated but will not admit it. "There is no longer a white world or a black world," he once told his biographer, adding, "I'm not sure I've learned it yet."[45] The young black writers do not want to learn it; they dream of a black aesthetic and the chance to rebut white critics.

A few years ago at a writers' conference at the New School for Social Research in New York City, William Branch turned to white critics Richard Gilman and Gordon Rogoff and asked them how they had the nerve to criticize Negro plays without seeing them.[46] There is no doubt that over the years white critics have attended plays by Negroes without really seeing them. Brooks Atkinson, often generous to a fault, would sometimes review the audience when he went to a Harlem theatre, commenting on their childish delight or their appreciation of lines beyond his comprehension. In the twenties, George Jean Nathan used such words as "coon" and "darky" in reviews of serious Negro plays.

Today Walter Kerr has the good sense to admit that times have

changed, that "paternalism [is] dead . . . killed inside us while
we were scarcely looking."[47] And Richard Gilman, so recently the
recipient of William Branch's scorn, has shown in a review of
Eldridge Cleaver's *Soul on Ice* that he recognizes the impossibility
of applying white standards to Negro writing.

> *Negro suffering is not of the same kind as ours. Under the great
> flawless arc of the Graeco-Roman and Judeo-Christian tradi-
> tions we have implicitly believed that all men experience essen-
> tially the same things, that birth, love, pain, self, death are
> universals; they are in fact what we mean by universal values in
> literature and consciousness. But the Negro has found it almost
> impossible in America to experience the universal as such: the
> power, after all, is conferred upon the individual, or rather con-
> firmed for him by his membership in the community of men.*[48]

Gilman, and others who are trying to understand the varieties of
experience, are beginning to realize what the exclusion of Negroes
from "the community of men" has done to them as human beings
and as artists.

NOTES

Abbreviations

NYPL   New York Public Library   YUL   Yale University Library

PREFACE

1. Krigwa Players Program, "Little Theatre," 1926 (NYPL, Schomburg Collection, Theatre-Harlem Folder).
2. Langston Hughes, "Notes on Commercial Theatre," *Selected Poems* (New York, 1959), p. 190.
3. Colin MacInnes, "Dark Angel: The Writings of James Baldwin," *Encounter*, XXI (August, 1963), 22.
4. Edith J. R. Isaacs, *The Negro in the American Theatre* (New York, 1947), p. 15.

PROLOGUE

1. Sidney Kaplan, "Notes on the Exhibition," *The Portrayal of the Negro in American Painting* (Brunswick, Me., 1964). See also Cedric Dover, *American Negro Art* (Greenwich, Conn., 1960).

2. See Seymour L. Gross and John Hardy, eds., *Images of the Negro in American Literature* (Chicago, 1967).

3. James Baldwin, in a lecture, "The Novelist as Playwright," at the New York City YMHA, January 6, 1963.

4. Robert Bone, *The Negro Novel in America* (New Haven, 1958), p. 212.

5. Elizabeth Drew, *Discovering Drama* (London, 1937), p. 137.

6. Francis L. Broderick and August Meier, eds., *Negro Protest Thought in the Twentieth Century* (New York, 1965), p. xviii.

7. Richard Wright, *White Man, Listen!* (New York, 1957), p. 105.

CHAPTER I. BEGINNINGS

1. Laurence Hutton, *Curiosities of the American Stage* (New York, 1891), p. 94.

2. *Ibid.*, p. 104.

3. John Murdock, *The Triumph of Love* (Philadelphia, 1795), pp. 51–52.

4. Gerald Bradley, "Goodbye, Mister Bones: The Emergence of Negro Themes & Characters in American Drama," *Drama Critique*, II (Spring, 1964), 79.

5. Edith J. R. Isaacs, *The Negro in the American Theatre* (New York, 1947), p. 27.

6. *The Liberator* (Boston), August 1, 1856, p. 124. There is no extant script for *Experience; or How to Give a Northern Man a Backbone*.

7. Sterling A. Brown, *Negro Poetry and Drama* (Washington, D.C., 1937), p. 109.

8. William Wells Brown, *The Escape; or, A Leap for Freedom* (Boston, 1858), p. 4.

9. Abram Kardiner and Lionel Ovesey, *The Mark of Oppression* (New York, 1951), p. 43.

10. Brown, *The Escape*, p. 52.

11. Booker T. Washington, quoted in Rayford W. Logan, *The Negro in the United States* (Princeton, N.J., 1957), pp. 128–29.

12. Joseph S. Cotter, *Caleb, the Degenerate* (Louisville, Ky., 1903), not paged. Only the play itself is paged.

13. Hugh Gloster, *Negro Voices in American Fiction* (Chapel Hill, N.C., 1948), p. 98.

CHAPTER II. THE TWENTIES

1. James Weldon Johnson, *Black Manhattan* (New York, 1930), p. 237.

2. W. E. B. DuBois, "Returning Soldiers," *The Crisis*, XVIII (May, 1919), 14.

3. W. J. Cash, *The Mind of the South* (New York, 1941), p 345.

4. Benjamin Brawley, *The Negro Genius* (New York, 1944), p. 232.

5. Alain Locke, ed., *The New Negro* (New York, 1925), p. 5.

6. Montgomery Gregory, "The Drama of Negro Life," *ibid.*, pp. 159–60.

7. Loften Mitchell, "Harlem Has Broadway on Its Mind," *Theatre Arts*, XXXVII (June, 1953), 69.

8. Langston Hughes, "Writers: Black and White," in *The American Negro Writer and His Roots* (New York, 1960), p. 42.

9. Garland Anderson, quoted in Vancouver *Sun*, July 4, 1925 (NYPL, Theatre Collection, Garland Anderson Scrapbook, 1925–29).

10. *Ibid.*

11. Garland Anderson, quoted in San Francisco *News*, September 11, 1935 (NYPL, Theatre Collection, Garland Anderson Scrapbook, 1935).

12. Garland Anderson, quoted in *Everyman*, April 10, 1930 (NYPL, Theatre Collection, Garland Anderson Scrapbook, 1935).

13. Metcalfe, *Wall Street Journal*, n.d. (NYPL, Theatre Collection, Garland Anderson Scrapbook, 1925–29).

14. Carl Van Vechten, Note with "Letters to William Jourdan Rapp from Wallace Thurman," n.d. (YUL, James Weldon Johnson Collection, Wallace Thurman Folder).

15. Wallace Thurman, Autobiographical Notes, n.d. (YUL, James Weldon Johnson Collection, Wallace Thurman Folder). Handwritten.

16. Carl Van Vechten, *Nigger Heaven* (New York, 1926), p. 149.

17. Rudolph Fisher, "The City of Refuge," in *The New Negro*, ed. Alain Locke, pp. 57–58.

18. Wallace Thurman, "Cordelia the Crude, a Harlem Sketch," *Fire!!*, 1 (November, 1926), 5.

19. Burns Mantle, *Daily News*, February 21, 1929 (NYPL, Theatre Collection, "Collection of Newspaper Clippings of Dramatic Criticism, 1928–29").

20. *New Yorker*, March 2, 1929 (NYPL, Theatre Collection, "Collection of Newspaper Clippings of Dramatic Criticism, 1928–29").

21. Theophilus Lewis, *Opportunity*, April, 1929 (YUL, James Weldon Johnson Collection, Wallace Thurman Folder).

22. Edith J. R. Isaacs, *The Negro in the American Theatre* (New York, 1947), p. 86.

23. Johnson, *Black Manhattan*, p. 202.

24. Sterling A. Brown, *Negro Poetry and Drama* (Washington, D.C., 1937), p. 28.

25. Aubrey Bowser, *Amsterdam News*, February 13, 1929 (NYPL, Schomburg Collection, Wallace Thurman Folder).

26. Wallace Thurman, "Negro Artists and the Negro," *New Republic*, n.d. (NYPL, Schomburg Collection, Wallace Thurman Folder).

27. George Jean Nathan, *Judge*, n.d. (YUL, James Weldon Johnson Collection, Wallace Thurman Folder).

28. Brooks Atkinson, New York *Times*, March 3, 1929 (NYPL, "Collection of Newspaper Clippings of Dramatic Criticism, 1928–29").

29. R. Dana Skinner, *Commonweal*, March 6, 1929 (NYPL, Schomburg Collection, Wallace Thurman Folder).

30. Letter to William Jourdan Rapp from Wallace Thurman, n.d. (YUL, James Weldon Johnson Collection, Wallace Thurman Folder).

31. Letter to Rapp from Thurman, August 1, 1929 (YUL, James Weldon Johnson Collection, Wallace Thurman Folder).

CHAPTER III. THE THIRTIES

1. A. Philip Randolph, "The Unfinished Revolution," *The Progressive*, XXVI (December, 1962), 22.

2. Richard Wright, *Lawd Today* (New York, 1963), p. 115.

3. For a detailed account of the Federal Theatre, see Hallie Flanagan, *Arena* (New York, 1940); Jane DeHart Mathews, *The Federal Theatre, 1935–1939* (Princeton, N.J., 1967).

4. Edith J. R. Isaacs, *The Negro in the American Theatre* (New York, 1947), p. 106.

5. Letter from Hallie Flanagan, January 20, 1963.

6. Sterling A. Brown, *Negro Poetry and Drama* (Washington, D.C., 1937), p. 140.

7. Morgan Y. Himelstein, *Drama Was a Weapon* (New Brunswick, N.J., 1963).

8. Brown, *Negro Poetry and Drama*, p. 139.

9. George Sklar, "For a Negro Theatre," *The New Theatre*, July, 1935 (U.S. National Archives, Record of the WPA Federal Theatre Project, Record Group 69).

10. Frank Wilson, "The Theatre Past and Present," *Amsterdam News*, June 15, 1932 (NYPL, Schomburg Collection, Frank Wilson Folder).

11. "Report of the Activities and Accomplishments of Negro Dramatists Laboratory," n.d. p. 1 (U.S. National Archives, Record of the WPA Federal Theatre Project, Record Group 69).

12. *Ibid.*, p. 2.

13. Hilda Josephine Lawson, "The Negro in American Drama" (unpublished Ph.D. dissertation, Dept. of English, University of Illinois, 1939), p. 114.

14. U.S. National Service Bureau, "A List of Negro Plays," p. 1, Federal Theatre Project Publication No. 24-L, March, 1938 (NYPL, Schomburg Collection). Mimeographed.

15. Letter from Amy Goodwin, May 29, 1963.

16. Kenneth Burke, "The Negro Pattern of Life," *Saturday Review of Literature*, X (July 27, 1933), 1.

17. Joseph R. Washington, Jr., *Black Religion* (Boston, 1964), p. 33.

18. Personal interview with Hall Johnson, June 7, 1963. Lew Cooper is listed on the library card as co-author of the play. Hall Johnson made it clear in this interview that he alone wrote *Run, Little Chillun*, rewriting all through the rehearsal period.

19. U.S. National Service Bureau, "A List of Negro Plays," p 4.

20. J. Brooks Atkinson, New York *Times*, February 7, 1928, p. 30 (NYPL, Schomburg Collection, Frank Wilson Folder).

21. Fannin S. Belcher, Jr., "The Place of the Negro in the Evolution of the American Theatre, 1767 to 1940" (unpublished Ph.D. dissertation, Graduate School of Yale University, 1945), p. 230.

22. U.S. National Service Bureau, "A List of Negro Plays," p. 12.

23. J. Brooks Atkinson, New York *Times*, February 4, 1936 (NYPL, Schomburg Collection, Frank Wilson Folder).

24. Langston Hughes, *The Big Sea* (New York, 1940), p. 240.

25. Pearl M. Fisher, "Notes," May 9, 1951 (NYPL, Schomburg Collection, Rudolph Fisher Folder).

26. Rudolph Fisher, quoted in Pittsburgh *Courier*, January 21, 1933 (NYPL, Schomburg Collection, Rudolph Fisher Folder).

27. *Time*, August 1, 1932 (NYPL, Schomburg Collection, Rudolph Fisher Folder).

28. Although the only existing script has the working title *The Conjure Man Dies*, the production title, *Conjur Man Dies*, is used here to avoid confusion with the novel.

29. Flanagan, *Arena*, p. 69. According to Mrs. Flanagan, 83,000 persons saw *Conjur Man Dies* in Harlem.

30. *Time*, August 1, 1932.

31. Brooks Atkinson, New York *Times*, March 12, 1936 (NYPL, Schomburg Collection, Rudolph Fisher Folder).

32. Now that Federal Theatre material has been moved to the New York Public Library Theatre Collection at the Lincoln Center Library, scripts of plays and other lost Federal Theatre documents have come to light.

33. Flanagan, *Arena*, p. 75.

34. *Ibid.*, p. 254.

35. Herbert Drake, New York *Herald Tribune*, August 10, 1937 (NYPL, "Collection of Newspaper Clippings of Dramatic Criticism, 1937–38").

36. Himelstein, *Drama Was a Weapon*, p. 90.

37. U.S. Federal Arts Council, Negro Arts Committee, "A Brief," pp. 12–13, New York City Project No. 1 (U.S. National Archives, Record of the WPA, Federal Theatre Project, Record Group 69).

38. *Ibid.*, p. 13.

39. *Ibid.*

40. Undated letter from Emmet Lavery (U.S. National Archives, Record of the WPA, Federal Theatre Project, Record Group 69).

41. Eric Bentley, "Give My Regards to Broadway," in *The Arts at Mid-Century*, ed. Robert Richman (New York, 1954), pp. 292–93.

42. John Gassner, "Social Realism and Imaginative Theatre: Avant-Garde Stage Production in the American Social Theatre of the Nineteen-Thirties," *Theatre Survey*, III (1962), 10–11.

43. Webster Smalley, ed., *Five Plays by Langston Hughes* (Bloomington, Ind., 1963), p. vii.

44. Langston Hughes, "The Negro in American Culture," in *The New Negro*, ed. Mathew H. Ahmann (Notre Dame, Ind., 1961), p. 112.

45. Hughes, *The Big Sea*, p. 15.

46. *Ibid.*, p. 85.

47. Isaacs, *The Negro in the American Theatre*, p. 100.

48. *The Weary Blues* (New York, 1931), p. 52.

49. Langston Hughes, "Ballad of Lenin," in *Proletarian Literature in the United States*, ed. Granville Hicks *et al.* (New York, 1935), pp. 166–67.

50. Hughes, *The Big Sea*, p. 263.

51. Hugh M. Gloster, *Negro Voices in American Fiction* (Chapel Hill, N.C., 1948), p. 12.

52. James Weldon Johnson, *Black Manhattan* (New York, 1930), p. 194.

53. Langston Hughes, "Trouble with the Angels," *New Theatre*, II (July, 1935), 7.

54. Langston Hughes, *Selected Poems of Langston Hughes* (New York, 1959), p. 160.

55. Smalley, ed., *Five Plays* p. xi.

56. Langston Hughes, *I Wonder as I Wander* (New York, 1956), p. 311. The script used for the Broadway production of *Mulatto* is unavailable.

57. John Gassner, "Social Realism and Imaginative Theatre: Avant-Garde Stage Production in the American Social Theatre of the Nineteen-Thirties," *Theatre Survey*, III (1962), 12.

58. Letter from Langston Hughes, May 4, 1963.

59. Hilda Josephine Lawson, "The Negro in American Drama" (unpublished Ph.D. dissertation, Dept. of English, University of Illinois, 1939), p. 160.

60. *Ibid.*, pp. 106–7.

61. Hughes, *Selected Poems of Langston Hughes*, p. 190.

62. Hughes, *I Wonder as I Wander*, p. 311.

63. Charles W. Feinberg, "The Negro in American Drama," n.d., p. 1 (U.S. National Archives, Record of the WPA Federal Theatre Project, Record Group 69).

64. Kenneth Burke, "The Negro Pattern of Life," *Saturday Review of Literature*, X (July 27, 1933), 2.

65. Darwin T. Turner, "The Negro Dramatist's Image of the Universe," *Images of the Negro in America*, ed. Darwin T. Turner and Jean M. Bright (Boston, 1965), p. 95.

66. T. J. Spencer and Clarence J. Rivers, "Langston Hughes: His Style and Optimism," *Drama Critique*, VII (Spring, 1964), 101.

67. Langston Hughes, "Don't You Want to Be Free? A Negro History

Play," Centennial Version, 1963, p. 36. Typescript borrowed from Langston Hughes.

CHAPTER IV. THE FORTIES

1. Langston Hughes, *Selected Poems of Langston Hughes* (New York, 1959), pp. 237 and 255.
2. Franklin D. Roosevelt, *Public Papers*, 1943, pp. 503–4. Quoted by Edgar Eugene Robinson, *The Roosevelt Leadership*, 1933–1945 (New York, 1955), pp. 323–24.
3. Denis W. Brogan, *The Era of Franklin D. Roosevelt* (New Haven, 1951), p. 332.
4. A. Philip Randolph, "The Unfinished Revolution," *The Progressive*, XXVI (December, 1962), 23.
5. W. E. B. DuBois, Introduction to *An Appeal to the World: A Statement on the Denial of Human Rights to Minorities in the Case of Citizens of Negro Descent in the United States of America and an Appeal to the United Nations for Redress* (New York, 1947), p. 2.
6. Though listed in the brochure as an active member, Hughes later stated that he was not one, as he was "in California or someplace most of the time it functioned, did not get sued by the creditors when the breakup came." Letter from Langston Hughes, May 4, 1963.
7. Negro Playwrights Company, "Perspective," *A Professional Theatre with an Idea*, 1940, unpaged (NYPL, Schomburg Collection, George Norford Scrapbook).
8. *Ibid.*
9. Other associate members were Edna Thomas, Max Yergan, Gwendolyn Bennett, Rev. John W. Robinson, and George B. Murphy, Jr. The list of patrons was also impressive: Eleanor Roosevelt, Franz Boas, Countee Cullen, Edna Ferber, George S. Kaufman, Sophie Tucker, and Orson Welles.
10. Negro Playwrights Company, "Deserving of Support," *A Professional Theatre with an Idea*.
11. Abram Hill, quoted in Mary Bragotti, "Stagecraft in Harlem," New York *Post*, December 29, 1943 (NYPL, Schomburg Collection, Abram Hill Folder).
12. Letter from Frederick O'Neal, July 23, 1965.
13. Loften Mitchell, "Harlem Has Broadway on Its Mind," *Theatre Arts*, XXXVII (June, 1953), 68.
14. Arthur H. Quinn, *A History of the American Drama* (New York, 1936), p. 282.
15. Personal interview with Theodore Ward, July 12, 1963.
16. George Jean Nathan, *The Theatre Book of the Year 1947–48* (New York, 1948), p. 48.
17. The play was originally produced by the Rose McClendon Players

from January 3 to 27, 1940. The American Negro Theatre presented it as its first production, September 11, 1940; it lasted until late February, 1941. There was also a revival of the play by ANT in 1946.

18. Carl Van Vechten, *Nigger Heaven* (New York, 1926), pp. 77–78.

19. E. Franklin Frazier, *Black Bourgeoisie* (Glencoe, Ill., 1961), p. 213.

20. One wonders if the reference to New Deal measures of the thirties was cut by the time of the 1946 production.

21. Frazier, *Black Bourgeoisie*, p. 25.

22. Louis Kronenberger, *PM*, March 3, 1946 (NYPL, Schomburg Collection, American Negro Theatre Folder).

23. Frazier, *Black Bourgeoisie*, p. 232.

24. Letter to F. S. Belcher, West Virginia Players, from Irwin A. Rubinstein, Manager of National Service Bureau, 1939 (U.S. National Archives, Subject File N, Negro Theatre 1939 Folder).

25. U.S. National Service Bureau, WPA Federal Theatre Project, *A List of Negro Plays*, p. 9 (Washington, D.C.: The Project, March, 1938). Mimeographed.

26. Frederick O'Neal, "The American Negro Theatre—A Ten Year Effort, Notes for Theatre Arts Seminar at Southern Illinois University," October 27, 1962, pp. 2–3. Typescript in possession of Frederick O'Neal.

27. S. W. Bennett, "Notes" (on slip case), *Tol' My Captain: Chain Gang and Work Songs Sung by Leon Bibb*. Vanguard VRS–9058.

28. Louis Kronenberger, *PM*, May 8, 1941 (NYPL, Schomburg Collection, Theodore Browne Folder).

29. John Mason Brown, New York *Post*, May 8, 1941 (NYPL, Schomburg Collection, Theodore Browne Folder).

30. Ralph Warner, *Daily Worker*, May 12, 1941 (NYPL, Schomburg Collection, Theodore Browne Folder).

31. Brooks Atkinson, New York *Times*, May 8, 1941 (NYPL, Schomburg Collection, Theodore Browne Folder).

32. Information about his background and all quotations are from personal interview with Theodore Ward, July 12, 1963.

33. Marcus Garvey, quoted in Hugh M. Gloster, *Negro Voices in American Fiction* (Chapel Hill, N.C., 1948), p. 103.

34. Wallace Thurman, *The Blacker the Berry* (New York, 1929), p. 165.

35. Richard Lockridge, "The Case of Mr. Odets," New York *Sun*, December 14, 1935 (NYPL, Theatre Collection, "Collection of Newspaper Clippings of Dramatic Criticism 1935–36").

36. Dennis Gobbins, "Story of Theo. Ward, Leading Negro Playwright," *Daily Worker*, March 9, 1950 (NYPL, Schomburg Collection, Theodore Ward Folder). There is no way of checking the validity of these figures, which were probably devised to rationalize the lack of support for *Big White Fog*.

37. *Ibid.*

38. *Ibid.*

39. Isidor Schneider, *New Masses*, October 14, 1947 (NYPL, Schomburg Collection, Theodore Ward Folder).
40. Personal interview with Theodore Ward, July 12, 1963.
41. Gobbins, *Daily Worker*, March 9, 1950.
42. Kenneth Thorpe Rowe, *A Theater in Your Head* (New York, 1960), p. 257.
43. Rowe comments on the dialect: "Like the Irish dialects of the plays of Synge and O'Casey, Negro folk speech is more than local color; it contributes an inherent expressiveness and beauty to drama" (*ibid.*, p. 260).
44. Richard N. Current, ed., *Reconstruction* [1865–1877] (Englewood Cliffs, N.J., 1965), p. 18.
45. Willie Lee Rose, *Rehearsal for Reconstruction: The Port Royal Experiment* (New York, 1964), p 350. Chapter 13, "Plantation Bitters," is largely concerned with General Sherman's Field Order 15 and subsequent events.
46. Theodore Ward, *Our Lan'*, in Rowe, *A Theater in Your Head*, p. 286.
47. Horace Mann Bond, *The Education of the Negro in the American Social Order* (New York, 1934), pp. 22–23. According to Bond, the Freedmen's Bureau, in five years of operation, established more than 4,000 schools, in which 9,000 teachers gave instruction to nearly 250,000 pupils (p. 29).
48. This association of Lincoln with Jesus is borne out by what a Northern teacher claimed an old Negro said to her: "Lincoln died for we, Christ died for we, and me believe him de same mans." Laura Towne, quoted in J. W. Schulte Nordholt, *The People That Walk in Darkness*, trans. M. B. Van Wijngaarden (New York, 1960), p. 160.
49. Elizabeth Botume, quoted in Rose, *Rehearsal for Reconstruction*, p. 371.
50. *Ibid.*, pp. 370–73.
51. General Howard was an actual person, General O. O. Howard, who, along with Rufus Saxton, was caught between the President's orders and his own commitment under the Freedmen's Bureau Act to carry out a resettlement program on the coastal islands.
52. Alfred Kazin, "The Negro in American Culture," in *The New Negro*, ed. Mathew Ahmann (Notre Dame, Ind., 1961), p. 124.
53. Obituary, New York *Times*, November 30, 1960 (NYPL, Schomburg Collection, Richard Wright Folder).
54. *Ibid.*
55. See James Baldwin, *Notes of a Native Son* (Boston, 1962), pp. 13–46; James Baldwin, *Nobody Knows My Name: More Notes of a Native Son* (New York, 1962), pp. 181–200; Ralph Ellison, *Shadow and Act* (New York, 1964), pp. 77–95, 107–44; Irving Howe, "Black Boys and Native Sons," *A World More Attractive* (New York, 1963), pp. 98–122.
56. Nelson Algren, "Remembering Richard Wright," *Nation*, CXCII (January 28, 1961), 85.
57. James Baldwin, "Many Thousands Gone," *Notes of a Native Son*, p. 32.

58. Letter from Paul Green, September 29, 1965.
59. Lajos Egri, *The Art of Dramatic Writing* (New York, 1960), p. 241.
60. Paul Green, *Dramatic Heritage* (New York, 1953), p. 84.
61. Richard Wright, *Native Son* (New York, 1940), p. 9.
62. Nathan Glazer, "Negroes and Jews: The New Challenge to Pluralism," *Commentary*, Vol. XXXVIII (December, 1964).
63. Baldwin, *Notes of a Native Son*, p. 69.
64. Wright, *Native Son*, p. 60.
65. Richard Wright, *Uncle Tom's Children* (New York, 1948), p. 7.
66. James Baldwin, "Alas, Poor Richard," *Nobody Knows My Name*, p. 97.
67. Wright, *Native Son*, p. 97.
68. Baldwin, "Many Thousands Gone," *Notes of a Native Son*, pp. 44–45.
69. Wright, *Native Son*, p. 307.
70. Richard Lockridge, New York *Sun*, March 25, 1941 (NYPL, "Critics' Theatre Reviews," Vol. II, No. 24).
71. John Mason Brown, New York *Post*, March 25, 1941 (NYPL, "Critics' Theatre Reviews," Vol. II, No. 24).
72. Louis Kronenberger, *PM*, March 25, 1941 (NYPL, "Critics' Theatre Reviews," Vol. II, No. 24).
73. Brooks Atkinson, New York *Times*, March 25, 1941 (NYPL, "Critics' Theatre Reviews," Vol. II, No. 24).
74. Personal interview with Langston Hughes, May 16, 1963.
75. Theodore Ward, quoted in "Big White Fog Programme," October 22, 1940 (NYPL, Schomburg Collection, George Norford Scrapbook). This was the printed version of his response to Morris Carnovsky, who extended greetings from the New Theatre League on the occasion of a benefit for the Negro Playwrights Company, September 6, 1940, at the Golden Gate Ballroom.
76. Personal interview with Theodore Ward, July 12, 1963.
77. "Big White Fog Programme."
78. Gail Borden, "Radical Plays Should Be Allowed," Chicago *Sunday Times*, April 10, 1938, p. 14 (NYPL, Schomburg Collection, Theodore Ward Folder).
79. John Mason Brown, New York *Post*, October 23, 1940 (NYPL, Schomburg Collection, George Norford Scrapbook).
80. Brooks Atkinson, New York *Times*, October 23, 1940 (NYPL, Schomburg Collection, George Norford Scrapbook).
81. Ralph Ellison, *New Masses*, November 12, 1940 (NYPL, Schomburg Collection, George Norford Scrapbook).
82. Sterling Brown, quoted in Abram Hill, *On Strivers Row: A Comedy about Sophisticated Harlem*, 1945 (NYPL, Schomburg Collection).
83. Darwin T. Turner, "The Negro Dramatist's Image of the Universe," in Darwin T. Turner and Jean M. Bright, eds., *Images of the Negro in America* (Boston, 1965), p. 93.

84. Richard Wright, *How "Bigger" Was Born* (New York, 1940), p. 10.
85. Baldwin, *Notes of a Native Son*, p. 43.
86. Edith J. R. Isaacs, *The Negro in the American Theatre* (New York, 1947), p. 115.
87. John Randolph, quoted in Robert L. Hilliard, "The Drama and American Negro Life," *Southern Theatre*, X (Winter, 1966), 12–13.
88. Personal interview with Theodore Ward, July 12, 1963.
89. Letter from Theodore Ward, October 6, 1965.

CHAPTER V. THE FIFTIES

1. Langston Hughes, *Selected Poems of Langston Hughes* (New York, 1959), p. 268.
2. William Brink and Louis Harris, *The Negro Revolution in America* (New York, 1963), pp. 19–20.
3. Sterling A. Brown, "Count Us In," in *Primer for White Folks*, ed. Bucklin Moon (New York, 1945), p. 384.
4. Harry Ashmore, "The Desegregation Decision," *Saturday Review* (May 16, 1964), p. 70.
5. Louis E. Lomax, *The Negro Revolt* (New York, 1963), p. 264. Italics added.
6. Loften Mitchell, "The Negro Theatre and the Harlem Community," *Freedomways*, III (Summer, 1963), 392. In answer to an inquiry about his early play *Alice in Wonder* (1952), Ossie Davis wrote, "Must most sorrowfully report—no copies extant" (Letter from Ossie Davis, July 15, 1965).
7. *Organizational Report*, March 16, 1947, p. 1 (NYPL, Schomburg Collection, Committee for the Negro in the Arts Folder). Mimeographed.
8. *CNA Bulletin*, February, 1951, p. 2 (NYPL, Schomburg Collection, Committee for the Negro in the Arts Folder). Mimeographed.
9. *Ibid.*
10. Nathan Glazer, "The Peoples of America," *Nation*, CCI (September 20, 1965), 141.
11. Loften Mitchell, "The Negro Theatre and the Harlem Community," *Freedomways*, III (Summer, 1963), 392.
12. *Ibid.*, p. 393.
13. Letter from William Branch, January 19, 1966.
14. *Ibid.* He has written three plays for the legitimate theatre, has written material for five television programs, an equal number of radio programs, and a documentary film. Among the awards he has won for his writing are the Hannah B. Del Vecchio Award in Playwriting, 1958, and a John Simon Guggenheim Fellowship, 1959–60.
15. Charles L. Anderson, "Question," in *Beyond the Blues*, ed. Rosey E. Pool (London, 1962), p. 39.
16. Louis Lomax tells of a Negro school principal whose white supervisor

ordered him to type an annual report and warned him not to "get any nigger funk on them papers." Lomax, *The Negro Revolt*, p. 65.

17. Ralph Ellison, "The Way It Is," *Shadow and Act* (New York, 1964), pp. 292–93.

18. Letter from William Branch, March 28, 1966.

19. *Ibid.* He may also have had the first three volumes of Philip Foner's four-volume *Life and Writings of Frederick Douglass* (1950–55), which he seems to remember acquiring in the summer of 1952.

20. *Ibid.*

21. In the Greenwich Mews production, Douglass was played by the talented Negro actor William Marshall, who fits well a description of the historical Douglass: "He was a good-looking man, tall, well-made, with olive skin and a halo of hair. . . . His physical presence moved people; so did the rolling thunder of his voice." Lerone Bennett, Jr., *Confrontation: Black and White* (Chicago, 1965), p. 69.

22. There is an account in *Life and Times of Frederick Douglass* of Brown's insisting on paying three dollars a week for this privilege.

23. The play is not in verse, but the arrangement of lines on the page sometimes gives this impression.

24. W. E. B. DuBois, *John Brown* (New York, 1962), p. 219.

25. *Ibid.*, p. 225.

26. Frederick Douglass, *Life and Times of Frederick Douglass* (Boston, 1892), pp. 380–81. He is quoting from a letter that he wrote to the Rochester *Democrat and American*, October 31, 1859.

27. *Ibid.*, p. 390.

28. Lewis Funke, New York *Times*, October 27, 1954 (NYPL, Schomburg Collection, William Branch Folder).

29. Harry Raymond, *Daily Worker*, November 1, 1954 (NYPL, Schomburg Collection, William Branch Folder). The *Times* critic had assumed that John Brown was a fanatic and called him "that benighted champion of abolition." Brown's role in American history is still debated among historians.

30. Letter from William Branch, March 28, 1966.

31. Information about her background and all quotations are from personal interview with Alice Childress, April 1, 1964.

32. Alice Childress, quoted in *The American Negro Writer and His Roots* (New York, 1960), p. 59.

33. This production was directed by Alice Childress and Clarice Taylor, who also played Wiletta. The play was then in two acts but was later changed to three. The script analyzed here is considered definitive by Miss Childress.

34. Alice Childress, quoted in *The American Negro Writer and His Roots*, p. 59.

35. Lorraine Hansberry, quoted in *The New Negro*, ed. Mathew H. Ahmann (Notre Dame, Ind., 1961), p. 126.

36. Mildred, the heroine of *Like One of the Family*, discusses acting in at

least two of her monologues. Alice Childress, *Like One of the Family* (Brooklyn, 1956), pp. 110–13, 123–28.

37. Harry Raymond, *Daily Worker*, November 8, 1955 (NYPL, Schomburg Collection, "Trouble in Mind" Folder).

38. Brooks Atkinson, New York *Times*, November 5, 1955 (NYPL, Schomburg Collections, "Trouble in Mind" Folder).

39. Alice Childress, quoted in *The American Negro Writer and His Roots*, p. 59.

40. Helen Davis, "Laughter and Anger," *Masses and Mainstream*, IX (July, 1956), 51.

41. Loften Mitchell, "Harlem Reconsidered—Memories of My Native Land," *Freedomways*, IV (Fall, 1964), 471.

42. "Notes on the back cover," Loften Mitchell, *A Land Beyond the River* (Cody, Wyo., 1963).

43. "These Are They," *A.M.E. Church Review*, LXXXIII (October-December, 1957), 15.

44. New York *Times*, January 17, 1956 (NYPL, Schomburg Collection, J. A. DeLaine Folder).

45. Letter from Loften Mitchell, August 20, 1965.

46. Joseph A. DeLaine once explained firing on a group of whites who ambushed his parsonage by saying, "I shot in Jesus' name. I wasn't trying to kill anyone. I shot to mark the car." *Jet*, VIII (November 3, 1955), 8.

47. Martin Luther King, Jr., *Stride Toward Freedom: The Montgomery Story* (New York, 1958), p. 179.

48. Langston Hughes, "Migration," *Fields of Wonder* (New York, 1947), p. 100.

49. King, *Stride Toward Freedom* p. 177.

50. In 1954 the Supreme Court ruled that "separate educational facilities are inherently unequal." Document No. 22A, *Brown v. Board of Educ., Briggs v. Elliot, Davis v. County School Board, Gebhart v. Benton, May 17, 1954,* quoted in Rayford W. Logan, *The Negro in the United States* (Princeton, N.J., 1957), p. 177.

51. Kenneth Clark, "The New Negro in the North," quoted in *The New Negro*, ed. Mathew H. Ahmann, p. 37.

52. "Notes on the back cover," Mitchell, *A Land Beyond the River.*

53. Brooks Atkinson, New York *Times*, March 29, 1957 (NYPL, Schomburg Collection, Loften Mitchell Folder).

54. Frances Herridge, New York *Post*, March 29, 1957 (NYPL, Schomburg Collection, Loften Mitchell Folder).

55. Burt Lancaster, Harold Hecht, and James Hill produced a filmed version of *Take a Giant Step* which was released in 1959 by United Artists. Louis Peterson co-authored the screenplay with Julius Epstein. The film is now out of circulation. For pictures from and commentary on it, see *Ebony*, XIV (September, 1959), 48–50.

56. Letter from Louis Peterson, February 16, 1966.

57. *Ibid.*

58. Louis Kronenberger, ed., *The Burns Mantle Yearbook: The Best Plays of 1953–54* (New York, 1954), p. 7.

59. Lillian Smith, "Addressed to White Liberals," in *Primer for White Folks*, ed. Bucklin Moon, p. 486.

60. Kronenberger, ed., *Burns Mantle Yearbook, 1953–54*, p. 6.

61. George Jean Nathan called *Take a Giant Step* "a kind of Negro *Ah, Wilderness!*, deeper in meaning." "The Theatre at Mid-Season," *The Atlantic*, March, 1953, p. 65 (NYPL, Schomburg Collection, Louis Peterson Folder).

62. The original title of the play, according to the 1952 copyright, was *Merry Let Us Part*.

63. Max Lerner, *America as a Civilization* (New York, 1957), p. 582.

64. Wolcott Gibbs, *New Yorker*, October 3, 1953, p. 79.

65. LeRoi Jones, *The System of Dante's Hell* (New York, 1965), p. 154.

66. Langston Hughes, *Fight for Freedom: The Story of the NAACP* (New York, 1962), p. 119.

67. E. B. White, "The Talk of the Town," *New Yorker*, May 9, 1959, p. 34 (NYPL, Schomburg Collection, Lorraine Hansberry Folder).

68. *Ibid.*

69. *Ibid.*, p. 35.

70. Lorraine Hansberry, quoted in Nan Robertson, "Dramatist Against Odds," New York *Times*, March 8, 1959 (NYPL, Schomburg Collection, "A Raisin in the Sun" Folder).

71. *Ibid.*

72. *Ibid.*

73. Harold Clurman, "Theatre," *Nation*, April 4, 1959, p. 301 (NYPL, Schomburg Collection, "A Raisin in the Sun" Folder).

74. See Richard Wright's short story "Man of All Work," in which a Negro male disguises himself as a female in order to get work, with tragicomic, bizarre results.

75. Edward Sheldon, *"The Nigger"* (New York, 1910), p. 24.

76. Lorraine Hansberry, quoted in Nan Robertson, "Dramatist Against Odds," New York *Times*, March 8, 1959.

77. *Ibid.*

78. Abram Kardiner and Lionel Ovesey, "Psychodynamic Inventory of the Negro Personality," in *The Angry Black*, ed. John William (New York, 1962), p. 98.

79. Max Lerner, "A Dream Deferred," New York *Post*, April 5, 1959 (NYPL, Schomburg Collection, "A Raisin in the Sun" Folder).

80. Tom F. Driver, "A Raisin in the Sun," *New Republic*, CL (April 13, 1959), 21.

81. Robert Nemiroff, "Introduction," *The Sign in Sidney Brustein's Window* (New York, 1965), p. xxi.

82. John A. Davis, "Preface," *The American Negro Writer and His Roots*, pp. iii–iv.

83. Henry Hewes, "A Plant Grows in Chicago," *Saturday Review*, April 4, 1959, p. 28.

84. Brooks Atkinson, New York *Times*, March 12, 1959 (NYPL, Theatre Collection, "New York Theatre Critics' Reviews, 1959").

85. Kenneth Tynan, *New Yorker*, March 21, 1959 (NYPL, Schomburg Collection, "A Raisin in the Sun" Folder).

86. Personal interview with Norman Rothstein, August 23, 1966. He was stage manager for *The Sign in Sidney Brustein's Window* when it was produced at the Mineola Theatre, Mineola, Long Island, in 1965.

87. Tom F. Driver, "A Raisin in the Sun," *New Republic*, CL (April 13, 1959), 21.

88. Harold Clurman, "Theatre," *Nation*, April 4, 1959, p. 302.

89. Letter from William Branch, March 28, 1966.

90. Loften Mitchell, "The Negro Theatre and the Harlem Community," *Freedomways*, III (Summer, 1963), 392.

91. The only copy of *John Brown* that is available for reading is at the Library of Congress. Copyright February 23, 1950.

92. Letter from Theodore Ward, January 29, 1964.

93. Personal interview with Theodore Ward, July 12, 1963.

94. Letter from Theodore Ward, January 29, 1964.

95. Letter from William Branch, March 28, 1966.

96. *Ibid.*

97. Alice Childress, quoted in David Llorens, "Writers' Conference at Fisk University," *Negro Digest*, XV (June, 1966), 65.

98. Letter from Alice Childress, November 24, 1965.

99. Lorraine Hansberry, quoted in Nan Robertson, "Dramatist Against Odds," New York *Times*, March 8, 1959.

100. Harold Cruse, *The Crisis of the Negro Intellectual* (New York, 1967), p. 267.

101. Loften Mitchell, "The Negro Writer and His Materials," in *The American Negro Writer and His Roots*, p. 58.

102. George Jean Nathan, "The Theatre at Mid-Season," *The Atlantic*, March, 1953, p. 65.

103. Robert Anderson, "Tea and Sympathy," *Famous American Plays of the 1950's*, ed. Lee Strasberg (New York, 1962), p. 312.

104. Letter from Louis Peterson, February 16, 1966.

105. *Ibid.*

106. Cruse, *The Crisis of the Negro Intellectual*, p. 280.

107. *Ibid.*, pp. 277–78.

108. Gerald Weales, "Thoughts on 'A Raisin in the Sun,'" *Commentary*, June, 1959, p. 528 (NYPL, Schomburg Collection, "A Raisin in the Sun" Folder).

109. Tom F. Driver, "A Raisin in the Sun," *New Republic*, CL (April 13, 1959), 21.

110. Harold Clurman, "Theatre," *Nation*, April 4, 1959, p. 301.

111. *Ibid.*
112. Nemiroff, "Introduction," *The Sign in Sidney Brustein's Window,* p. xxii.
113. Max Lerner, "A Dream Deferred," New York *Post,* April 5, 1959.
114. Henrik Ibsen, quoted in Eric Bentley, *The Playwright as Thinker* (New York, 1955), p. 103.

EPILOGUE

1. Loften Mitchell, "Alligators in the Swamp," *The Crisis,* LXXII (February, 1965), 85.
2. Renata Adler, "The Negro That Movies Overlook," New York *Times,* March 3, 1968, p. 1D.
3. Brooks Atkinson, "No Time for American Drama," *The Critic,* XXV (December, 1966–January, 1967), 17.
4. Arthur P. Davis, "Integration and Race Literature," in *The American Negro Writer and His Roots* (New York, 1960), p. 37.
5. Claude Brown, *Manchild in the Promised Land* (New York, 1966), p. 288.
6. For a detailed account of Jones's revolutionary theatre, see Harold Cruse, *The Crisis of the Negro Intellectual* (New York, 1967), pp. 440, 530–31, 537–39.
7. LeRoi Jones, "Philistinism and the Negro Writer," in *Anger, and Beyond,* ed. Herbert Hill (New York, 1966), pp. 54–55.
8. Cruse, *The Crisis of the Negro Intellectual,* p. 111.
9. *Ibid.,* p. 412.
10. Marya Mannes, *The Reporter,* October 26, 1961, p. 52.
11. Howard Taubman, New York *Times,* September 29, 1961, p. 1D.
12. Philip Rose, quoted in Milton Esterow, "New Role of Negroes in Theater Reflects Ferment of Integration," New York *Times,* June 15, 1964, p. 35.
13. James Baldwin, *Blues for Mister Charlie* (New York, 1964), p. xv.
14. Tom Driver, "Barking Off Cue, or Mr. Charlie's Dilemma," *The Village Voice,* IX (June 4, 1964), 17.
15. Philip Roth, "Channel X: Two Plays on the Race Conflict," *The New York Review,* II (May 28, 1964), 11.
16. Susan Sontag, *Against Interpretation* (New York, 1966), p. 153.
17. *Ibid.,* p. 156.
18. Philip Roth, "Channel X: Two Plays on the Race Conflict," *The New York Review,* II (May 28, 1964), 13.
19. Saunders Redding, "The Problems of the Negro Writer," *Massachusetts Review,* VI (Autumn–Winter, 1964–65), 64.
20. LeRoi Jones, "LeRoi Jones Speaking," New York *Herald Tribune,* July 26, 1964, p. 8.

21. Langston Hughes, "That Boy LeRoi," an early draft of an article for the New York *Post*; typescript enclosed in letter, January 4, 1965. In this article Hughes suggested alternative casting for LeRoi Jones's plays: "I would like to see white school boys in 'The Toilet' beating up a colored boy and sticking his head in a urinal. In 'The Slave' let a bullying white man kick, curse, browbeat and shoot a nice liberal black professor and his wife in their suburban living room."

22. LeRoi Jones, quoted in Sidney Bernard, "An Interview with LeRoi Jones," Chicago *Literary Times*, May–June, 1967 (NYPL, Schomburg Collection, LeRoi Jones Folder).

23. Thomas A. Johnson, "Black Nationalists Gain More Attention in Harlem," New York *Times*, July 3, 1966, p. 29.

24. Cruse, *The Crisis of the Negro Intellectual*, p. 541.

25. LeRoi Jones, "LeRoi Jones Speaking," New York *Herald Tribune*, July 26, 1964, p. 7.

26. Walter Kerr, New York *Times*, October 12, 1966 (NYPL, Schomburg Collection, Ronald Milner Folder).

27. Langston Hughes, "Tambourines to Glory," *Five Plays*, ed. Webster Smalley (Bloomington, Ind., 1963), p. xv.

28. Martin Esslin, *The Theatre of the Absurd* (New York, 1961), p. 307. Jean Genet, rather than a black playwright, may well have been an influence on Adrienne Kennedy.

29. Howard Taubman, quoted in *Black Magic*, ed. Langston Hughes and Milton Meltzer (New York, 1967), p. 250.

30. Loften Mitchell, *Black Drama* (New York, 1967), pp. 198–99. Cynthia Belgrave, an actress who was featured in *The Funnyhouse of a Negro*, calls the play "an important fragment" and the production "totally theatrical, a strong experience for both actors and audience."

31. Archie Shepp, "Black Power and Black Jazz," New York *Times*, November 26, 1967, p. 13:1.

32. Dan Sullivan, New York *Times*, February 21, 1967 (NYPL, Schomburg Collection, Archie Shepp Folder).

33. *Ibid.*

34. Archie Shepp, quoted in Howard Smith, "Young Man with a Pen," New York *Times*, February 19, 1967, p. 2:3.

35. Cruse, *The Crisis of the Negro Intellectual*, p. 505.

36. Alice Childress, quoted in *Negro Digest*, XVII (January, 1968), 36.

37. William Branch, quoted in *Negro Digest*, XVII (January, 1968), 30.

38. Letter from Theodore Ward, December 6, 1967.

39. Loften Mitchell, quoted in David Llorens, "Writers Conference at Fisk University," *Negro Digest*, XV (June, 1966), 64.

40. Announcement in *Negro Digest*, XVII (March, 1968), 53.

41. Robert Brustein, "Why American Plays Are Not Literature," in *American Drama and Its Critics*, ed. Alan S. Downer (Chicago, 1965), p. 255.

42. Irving Howe, "Black Boys and Native Sons," A *World More Attractive* (New York, 1963), p. 113.

43. Hoyt W. Fuller, "Toward a Black Aesthetic," *The Critic*, XXVl April–May, 1968), 73.

44. Cruse, *The Crisis of the Negro Intellectual*, p. 520.

45. James Baldwin, quoted in Fern Marja Eckman, *The Furious Passage of James Baldwin* (New York, 1967), p. 240.

46. Mitchell, *Black Drama*, p. 217.

47. Walter Kerr, "Skin Deep Is Not Good Enough," New York *Times*, April 14, 1968, p. 1D.

48. Richard Gilman, "White Standards and Negro Writing," *New Republic*, CLXVIII (March 9, 1968), 25.

BIBLIOGRAPHY

PLAYS BY NEGRO PLAYWRIGHTS

Anderson, Garland. "Appearances." 1925. New York Public Library, Theatre Collection. (Film Reproduction *2–17.)

Baldwin, James. *Blues for Mister Charlie*. New York: Dial Press, 1964.

Branch, William. "In Splendid Error." 1955. New York Public Library, Schomburg Collection. (Mimeographed.)

—— "A Medal for Willie." n.d. New York Public Library, Schomburg Collection. (Mimeographed.)

Brown, William Wells. *The Escape; or, A Leap for Freedom: A Drama, in Five Acts*. Boston: R. F. Wallcut, 1858.

Browne, Theodore. "The Natural Man (Based on the Legend of John Henry): A Play in Eight Episodes." 1936. New York Public Library, Schomburg Collection. (Mimeographed.) Production title was "Natural Man."

Childress, Alice. "Florence: A One-Act Drama," *Masses and Mainstream*, III (October, 1950), 34–47.

—— "Trouble in Mind." 1955. (Mimeographed copy in possession of Alice Childress.)

Cotter, Joseph S. *Caleb, The Degenerate: A Study of the Types, Customs, and Needs of the American Negro*. Louisville, Ky.: The Bradley & Gilbert Co., 1903.

Davis, Ossie. *Purlie Victorious*. New York: Samuel French, 1961.

Fisher, Rudolph. "The Conjure Man Dies." 1931? New York Public Library, Schomburg Collection. (Mimeographed.)

Hansberry, Lorraine. *A Raisin in the Sun.* New York: The New American Library, 1961.

—— *The Sign in Sidney Brustein's Window.* New York: Random House, 1965. Introduction by Robert Nemiroff. Foreword by John Braine.

Hill, Abram. "On Strivers Row: A Comedy about Sophisticated Harlem." 1945. New York Public Library, Schomburg Collection. (Mimeographed.)

Hughes, Langston. "Don't You Want to Be Free?: A Negro History Play." Centennial Version, 1963. (Typescript in the possession of Langston Hughes.)

—— "Don't You Want to Be Free? (A Poetry Play)," *One-Act Play Magazine,* II (October, 1938), 359–93.

—— "Mulatto," in *Five Plays by Langston Hughes.* Ed. Webster Smalley. Bloomington: Indiana University Press, 1963. Pp. 1–35.

Johnson, Hall. "Run, Little Chillun." n.d. New York Public Library, Schomburg Collection. (Typewritten.)

Jones, LeRoi. *The Baptism & The Toilet.* New York: Grove Press, 1967.

—— "Dutchman," in *New Theatre in America.* Ed. Edward Parone. New York: Dell Publishing Co., 1965.

Mitchell, Loften. *A Land Beyond the River.* Cody, Wyo.: Pioneer Drama Service, 1963.

Peterson, Louis. *Take a Giant Step.* New York: Samuel French, 1954.

Thurman, Wallace, and William Jourdan Rapp. "Harlem." 1929. Yale University Library, James Weldon Johnson Collection. (Typewritten.)

Ward, Douglas Turner. *Happy Ending and Day of Absence.* New York: Dramatists Play Service, 1966.

Ward, Theodore. "Big White Fog: A Negro Tragedy." 1937. New York Public Library, Schomburg Collection. (Mimeographed.)

—— "Our Lan'," in Kenneth Thorpe Rowe, *A Theater in Your Head.* New York: Funk & Wagnalls Co., 1960. Pp. 261–425.

Wilson, Frank. "Brother Mose: A Comedy of Negro Life with Music and Spirituals." 1937. U.S. National Archives, National Service Bureau Publication No. 7. (Mimeographed.)

Wright, Richard, and Paul Green. *Native Son, a Biography of a Young American.* New York: Harper & Bros., 1941.

UNPUBLISHED MATERIALS

Collections

Harvard College Library, Theatre Collection.

New York Public Library, Schomburg Collection of Negro Literature and History.

New York Public Library, Theatre Collection.

U.S. National Archives.

Yale University Library, James Weldon Johnson Collection.

Letters
Branch, William. New Rochelle, New York, January 19, 1966; March 28, 1966.
Childress, Alice. New York City. November 24, 1965.
Davis, Ossie. New Rochelle, New York. July 15, 1965.
Flanagan, Hallie. Poughkeepsie, New York. January 20, 1963.
Goodwin, Amy. Amherst, Massachusetts. May 29, 1963.
Green, Paul. Chapel Hill, North Carolina. September 29, 1965.
Hughes, Langston. New York City. May 4, 1963; January 4, 1965.
Mitchell, Loften. St. Albans, Long Island, New York. August 20, 1965.
O'Neal, Frederick. New York City. July 23, 1965.
Peterson, Louis. New York City. February 16, 1966.
Ward, Theodore. Chicago, Illinois. January 29, 1964; October 6, 1965; December 6, 1967.

Personal Interviews
Childress, Alice. New York City. April 1, 1964.
Hughes, Langston. New York City. May 16, 1963.
Johnson, Hall. New York City. June 7, 1963.
Rothstein, Norman. New York City. August 23, 1966.
Ward, Theodore. Brooklyn, New York. July 12, 1963.

BOOKS AND ARTICLES

Adler, Renata. "The Negro That Movies Overlook," New York *Times*, March 3, 1968, p. 1D.
Ahmann, Mathew H., ed. *The New Negro*. Notre Dame, Ind.: Fides Publishers, 1961.
Algren, Nelson. "Remembering Richard Wright," *Nation*, CXCII (January 28, 1961), 85.
The American Negro Writer and His Roots. Selected Papers from the First Conference of Negro Writers. March, 1959. New York: American Society of African Culture, 1960.
Aptheker, Herbert. "Some Unpublished Writings of W. E. B. DuBois," *Freedomways*, V (Winter, 1965), 103–28.
Ashmore, Harry. "The Desegregation Decision," *Saturday Review*, May 16, 1964, p. 70.
Atkinson, Brooks. "No Time for American Drama," *The Critic*, XXV (December, 1966–January, 1967), 16–23.
Baldwin, James. *Nobody Knows My Name: More Notes of a Native Son*. New York: A Delta Book, 1962.
—— *Notes of a Native Son*. Boston: Beacon Press, 1962.
Bardolph, Richard. *The Negro Vanguard*. New York: Random House, 1959.
Belcher, Fannin S., Jr. "The Place of the Negro in the Evolution of the

American Theatre, 1767 to 1940." Unpublished Ph.D. dissertation, Graduate School of Yale University, 1945. The study is concerned with what the Negro has contributed generally to the American theatre during this period.

Bennett, Lerone, Jr. *Confrontation: Black and White.* Chicago: Johnson Publishing Co., 1965.

Bentley, Eric. *The Playwright as Thinker: A Study of Drama in Modern Times.* New York: The Noonday Press, 1955.

Bond, Frederick W. *The Negro and the Drama: The Direct and Indirect Contribution Which the American Negro Has Made to Drama and the Legitimate Stage, with the Underlying Conditions Responsible.* Washington, D.C.: The Associated Publishers, 1940.

Bond, Horace Mann. *The Education of the Negro in the American Social Order.* New York: Prentice-Hall, 1934.

Bone, Robert. *The Negro Novel in America.* New Haven: Yale University Press, 1958.

Bradley, Gerald. "Goodbye, Mister Bones: The Emergence of Negro Themes & Characters in American Drama," *Drama Critique,* VII (Spring, 1964), 79–85.

Brawley, Benjamin. *The Negro Genius: A New Appraisal of the Achievement of the American Negro in Literature and the Fine Arts.* New York: Dodd, Mead & Co., 1944.

—— *A Short History of the American Negro.* New York: The Macmillan Co., 1931.

Brink, William, and Louis Harris. *The Negro Revolution in America.* New York: Simon and Schuster, 1963.

Broderick, Francis L., and August Meier, eds. *Negro Protest Thought in the Twentieth Century.* New York: Bobbs-Merrill, 1965.

Brogan, Denis W. *The Era of Franklin D. Roosevelt: A Chronicle of the New Deal and Global War.* New Haven: Yale University Press, 1951.

Brown, Claude. *Manchild in the Promised Land.* New York: The Macmillan Co., 1966.

Brown, Sterling A. "The American Race Problem as Reflected in American Literature," *Journal of Negro Education,* VIII (July, 1939), 275–90.

—— "The Negro in Fiction and Drama," *Christian Register,* CXIV (Feb. 14, 1935), 111.

—— *Negro Poetry and Drama.* Washington, D.C.: The Associates in Negro Folk Education, 1937.

—— Review of *Native Son, Opportunity,* XVIII (June, 1940), 185–86.

—— Review of *Not Without Laughter, Opportunity,* VIII (September, 1930), 279–80.

Burke, Kenneth. "The Negro Pattern of Life," *Saturday Review of Literature,* X (July 27, 1933), 1–3.

Butcher, Margaret Just. *The Negro in American Culture.* New York: New American Library, 1957. Based on materials left by Alain Locke.

Carmichael, Stokely. "Toward Black Liberation," *Massachusetts Review*, VII (Autumn, 1966), 639–51.

Cash, W. J. *The Mind of the South*. New York: Vintage Books, 1941.

Childress, Alice. *Like One of the Family*. Brooklyn, N.Y.: Independence Publishers, 1956.

Clurman, Harold. *The Fervent Years*. New York: Alfred A. Knopf, 1945.

—— "The Theatre of the Thirties," *Tulane Drama Review*, IV (Winter, 1959), 3–11.

Cronon, Edmund David. *Black Moses: The Story of Marcus Garvey and the United Negro Improvement Association*. Madison: University of Wisconsin Press, 1964.

Crumpler, Gloria Thomas. "The Negro in the American Theatre and Drama from 1950 to 1956." Unpublished M.A. Thesis, Tennessee Agricultural and Industrial State University, May, 1957.

Cruse, Harold. *The Crisis of the Negro Intellectual*. New York: William Morrow & Co., 1967.

Current, Richard, ed. *Reconstruction* [1865–1877]. Englewood Cliffs, N.J.: Prentice-Hall, 1965.

Davis, Helen. "Laughter and Anger," *Masses and Mainstream*, IX (July, 1956), 50–51.

Douglass, Frederick. *Life and Times of Frederick Douglass, Written by Himself—His Early Life as a Slave, His Escape from Bondage and His Complete History to the Present Time*. Boston: DeWofe, Fiske & Co., 1892.

Dover, Cedric. *American Negro Art*. Greenwich, Conn.: Graphic Society, 1960.

Downer, Alan S., ed. *American Drama and Its Critics: A Collection of Critical Essays*. Chicago: University of Chicago Press, 1965.

Drake, St. Clair, and Horace R. Cayton. *Black Metropolis: A Study of Negro Life in a Northern City*. New York: Harcourt, Brace and Co., 1945. Introduction by Richard Wright.

Drew, Elizabeth. *Discovering Drama*. London: Jonathan Cape, 1937.

Driver, Tom F. "Barking Off Cue, or Mister Charlie's Dilemma," *The Village Voice*, IX (June 4, 1964), 16–17.

—— "A Raisin in the Sun," *New Republic*, CL (April 13, 1959), 21–22.

DuBois, W. E. Burghardt. *Black Reconstruction in America*. New York: Harcourt, Brace and Co., 1935.

—— "Close Ranks," *The Crisis: A Record of the Darker Races*, XVI (July, 1918), 111.

—— *Darkwater*. New York: Harcourt, Brace and Co., 1920.

—— *Dusk of Dawn: An Essay Toward the Autobiography of a Race Concept*. New York: Harcourt, Brace and Co., 1940.

—— "The Immediate Program of the American Negro," *The Crisis: A Record of the Darker Races*, IX (April, 1915), 312.

—— "Introduction," *An Appeal to the World: A Statement on the Denial of Human Rights to Minorities in the Case of Citizens of Negro Descent in the United States of America and an Appeal to the United Nations for Redress.* New York: NAACP, 1947.

—— *John Brown.* New York: International Publishers, 1962.

—— "Returning Soldiers," *The Crisis: A Record of the Darker Races,* XVIII (May, 1919), 13–14.

—— *The Souls of Black Folk.* Chicago: A. C. McClurg & Co., 1902.

Eckman, Fern Marja. *The Furious Passage of James Baldwin.* New York: Evans & Co., 1967.

Egri, Lajos, *The Art of Dramatic Writing: Its Basis in the Creative Interpretation of Human Motives.* New York: Simon and Schuster, 1960.

Ellison, Ralph. "Juneteenth," *Quarterly Review of Literature,* XIII (1965), 262–76.

—— *Shadow and Act.* New York: Random House, 1964.

Esslin, Martin. *The Theatre of the Absurd.* New York: Doubleday & Co., 1961.

Esterow, Milton. "New Role of Negroes in Theater Reflects Ferment of Integration," *New York Times,* June 15, 1964, pp. 1, 35.

Federal Theatre Plays. New York: Random House, 1938. Introduction by Hallie Flanagan.

Fisher, Rudolph. *The Conjure-Man Dies: A Mystery Tale of Dark Harlem.* New York: Covici-Friede, 1932.

Flanagan, Hallie. *Arena.* New York: Duell, Sloan, and Pearce, 1940.

Franklin, John Hope. "Civil Rights in American History," *The Progressive,* XXVI (December, 1962), 6–8.

—— *From Slavery to Freedom: A History of American Negroes.* New York: Alfred A. Knopf, 1947.

Frazier, E. Franklin. *Black Bourgeoisie.* Glencoe, Ill.: The Free Press, 1961.

Fuller, Hoyt W., ed. "Black Writers' Views on Literary Lions and Values," *Negro Digest,* XVII (January, 1968), 10–47.

—— "Toward a Black Aesthetic," *The Critic,* XXVI (April–May, 1968), 70–73.

Gassner, John. "Social Realism and Imaginative Theatre: Avant-Garde Stage Production in the American Social Theatre of the Nineteen-Thirties," *Theatre Survey,* III (1962), 3–18.

Gilman, Richard. "White Standards and Negro Writing," *New Republic,* CLXVIII (March 9, 1968), 25–30.

Glazer, Nathan. "Negroes and Jews: The New Challenge to Pluralism," *Commentary,* Vol. XXXVIII (December, 1964), in *Commentary Reprints.* New York: The American Jewish Committee, 1965.

—— "The Peoples of America," *Nation,* CCI (September 20, 1965), 140–43.

Gloster, Hugh M. *Negro Voices in American Fiction.* Chapel Hill: University of North Carolina Press, 1948.

Green, Paul. *Dramatic Heritage.* New York: Samuel French, 1953.

Gross, Seymour L., and John Hardy, eds. *Images of the Negro in American Literature*. Chicago: University of Chicago Press, 1967.

Handlin, Oscar. *Race and Nationality in American Life*. New York: Doubleday & Co., 1957.

Hawkins, Hugh, ed. *Booker T. Washington and His Critics*. Boston: D. C. Heath & Co., 1962.

Hewes, Henry. "A Plant Grows in Chicago," *Saturday Review*, April 4, 1959, p. 28.

Hicks, Granville, et al., eds. *Proletarian Literature in the United States*. New York: International Publishers, 1935.

Hill, Herbert, ed. *Anger and Beyond: The Negro Writer in the United States*. New York: Harper & Row, 1966.

—— *Soon One Morning: New Writing by American Negroes, 1940–1962*. New York: Alfred A. Knopf, 1963.

Hilliard, Robert L. "The Drama and American Negro Life," *Southern Theatre*, X (Winter, 1966), 9–14.

Himelstein, Morgan Y. *Drama Was a Weapon: The Left-Wing Theatre in New York, 1929–1941*. New Brunswick, N.J.: Rutgers University Press, 1963.

Howe, Irving. "Black Boys and Native Sons," *A World More Attractive*. New York: Horizon Press, 1963. Pp. 98–122.

Hughes, Langston. *The Big Sea: An Autobiography*. New York & London: Alfred A. Knopf, 1940.

—— *The Dream Keeper and Other Poems*. New York: Alfred A. Knopf, 1932.

—— *Fields of Wonder*. New York: Alfred A. Knopf, 1944.

—— *Fight for Freedom: The Story of the NAACP*. New York: W. W. Norton & Co., 1962.

—— "Harlem Literati of the Twenties," *Saturday Review of Literature*, XXII (1940), 14.

—— *I Wonder as I Wander: An Autobiographical Journey*. New York: Rinehart & Co., Inc., 1956.

—— *The Langston Hughes Reader*. New York: George Braziller, 1958.

—— "The Negro Artist and the Racial Mountain," *Nation*, CXXII (1926), 694.

—— *Selected Poems of Langston Hughes*. New York: Alfred A. Knopf, 1959.

—— *Simple Speaks His Mind*. New York: Simon and Schuster, 1950.

—— *The Weary Blues*. New York: Alfred A. Knopf, 1931.

Hughes, Langston, and Milton Meltzer. *Black Magic: A Pictorial History of the Negro in American Entertainment*. Englewood Cliffs, N.J.: Prentice-Hall, 1967.

Hutton, Laurence. *Curiosities of the American Stage*. New York: Harper & Brothers, 1891. Chapter II entitled "The American Stage Negro," pp. 89–144.

Isaacs, Edith J. R. *The Negro in the American Theatre*. New York: Theatre Arts, 1947.

Isaacs, Harold R. "Blackness and Whiteness," *Encounter*, XXI (August, 1963), 8–21.

Jackson, Esther Merle. "The American Negro and the Image of the Absurd," *Phylon: The Atlantic University Review of Race and Culture*, XXIII (Winter, 1962), 359–71.

Jefferson, Miles M. "The Negro on Broadway—1944," *Phylon: The Atlantic University Review of Race and Culture*, VI (First Quarter, 1945), 42–52.

Johnson, James Weldon. *Along This Way*. New York: The Viking Press, 1933.

—— *Black Manhattan*. New York: Alfred A. Knopf, 1930.

—— "The Dilemma of the Negro Author," *American Mercury*, XV (December, 1928), 477–81.

—— "Race Prejudice and the Negro Artist," *Harper's Magazine*, CLVII (November, 1928), 769–76.

—— "Romance and Tragedy in Harlem," *Opportunity*, IV (October, 1926), 316–17, 330.

Johnson, Thomas A. "Black Nationalists Gain More Attention in Harlem," New York *Times*, July 3, 1966, pp. 1, 29.

Jones, LeRoi. "LeRoi Jones Speaking," New York *Herald Tribune Magazine*, July 26, 1964, pp. 7–8.

—— *The System of Dante's Hell*. New York: Grove Press, 1965.

Kaplan, Sidney. "Notes on the Exhibition," *The Portrayal of the Negro in American Painting*. Brunswick, Me.: Bowdoin College, 1964.

Kardiner, Abram, and Lionel Ovesey. *The Mark of Oppression: A Psychosocial Study of the American Negro*. New York. W. W. Norton & Co., 1951.

Kazin, Alfred. "Does Anyone Remember the Thirties?" *Saturday Review*, October 13, 1962, pp. 17–19.

Kerr, Walter. "Skin Deep Is Not Good Enough," New York *Times*, April 14, 1968, pp. 1, 3D.

King, Martin Luther, Jr. *Stride Toward Freedom: The Montgomery Story*. New York: Ballantine Books, 1953.

Kronenberger, Louis, ed. *The Burns Mantle Yearbook: The Best Plays of 1953–54*. New York: Dodd, Mead and Co., 1954.

Lawson, Hilda Josephine. "The Negro in American Drama." Unpublished Ph.D. dissertation, Dept. of English, University of Illinois, 1939.

Lerner, Max. *America as a Civilization: Life and Thought in the United States Today*. New York: Simon and Schuster, 1957.

Link, Arthur S. *American Epoch: A History of the United States Since the 1890's*. New York: Alfred A. Knopf, 1955.

Llorens, David. "Writers' Conference at Fisk University," *Negro Digest*, XV (June, 1966), 54–68.

Locke, Alain, ed. *The New Negro: An Interpretation*. New York: Albert and Charles Boni, 1925.

Logan, Rayford W. *The Negro in the United States: A Brief History.* Princeton, N.J.: D. Van Nostrand Co., 1957.

Loggins, Vernon. *The Negro Author: His Development in America to 1900.* New York: Columbia University Press, 1959.

Lomax, Louis E. *The Negro Revolt.* New York: The New American Library, 1963.

MacInnes, Colin. "Dark Angel: The Writings of James Baldwin," *Encounter,* XXI (August, 1963), 22–33.

Mantle, Burns, ed. *The Best Plays of 1932–33 and The Year Book of the Drama in America.* New York: Dodd, Mead and Co., 1933.

—— *The Best Plays of 1940–41 and The Year Book of the Drama in America.* New York: Dodd, Mead and Co., 1941.

Mathews, Jane DeHart. *The Federal Theatre, 1935–1939.* Princeton, N.J.: Princeton University Press, 1967.

Meier, August. *Negro Thought in America, 1880–1915: Racial Ideologies in the Age of Booker T. Washington.* Ann Arbor: University of Michigan Press, 1964.

Miller, Althea Ann. "The Negro in American Drama." Unpublished M.F.A. Thesis, University of Oklahoma, 1958.

Mitchell, Loften. "Alligators in the Swamp," *The Crisis: A Record of the Darker Races,* LXXII (February, 1965), 84–87.

—— *Black Drama: The Story of the American Negro in the Theatre.* New York: Hawthorn Books, 1967.

—— "Harlem Has Broadway on Its Mind," *Theatre Arts,* XXXVII (June, 1953), 68–70.

—— Harlem Reconsidered—Memories of My Native Land," *Freedomways,* IV (Fall, 1964), 465–78.

—— "The Negro Theatre and the Harlem Community," *Freedomways,* III (Summer, 1963), 384–94.

Moon, Bucklin, ed. *Primer for White Folks.* Garden City, N.Y.: Doubleday, Doran, 1945.

Murdock, John. *The Triumph of Love; or, Happy Reconciliation.* Philadelphia: R. Folwell Publishers, 1795.

Nathan, George Jean. *Passing Judgment.* New York: Alfred A. Knopf, 1933.

—— *Testament of a Critic.* New York: Alfred A. Knopf, 1931.

—— *The Theatre Book of the Year 1947–48: A Record and an Interpretation.* New York: Alfred A. Knopf, 1948.

The Negro Problem. A Series of Articles By Representative American Negroes of Today. Contributions by Booker T. Washington, Principal of Tuskegee Institute, W. E. Burghardt DuBois, Paul Laurence Dunbar, Charles W. Chesnutt, and Others. New York: James Pott & Co., 1903.

Odum, Howard W. *Race and Rumors of Race: Challenge to American Crisis.* Chapel Hill: University of North Carolina Press, 1943.

O'Neal, Frederick. "The American Negro Theatre—a Ten-Year Effort, Notes for Theatre Arts Seminar at Southern Illinois University," October 27, 1962. (Typescript in possession of the author.)

Persons, Stow. *American Minds: A History of Ideas*. New York: Henry Holt & Co., 1959.

Pool, Rosey E., ed. *Beyond the Blues*. London: Hand and Flower Press, 1962.

Pratt, Julius W. *A History of United States Foreign Policy*. New York: Prentice-Hall, 1955.

Quinn, Arthur H. *A History of the American Drama*. New York: F. S. Crofts & Co., 1936.

Quinn, Edward, and Paul J. Dolan, eds. *The Sense of the Sixties*. New York: The Free Press, 1968.

Randolph, A. Philip. "The Unfinished Revolution," *The Progressive*, XXVI (December, 1962), 22–24.

Redding, Saunders. "The Problems of the Negro Writer," *Massachusetts Review*, VI (Autumn–Winter, 1964–65), 57–70.

Richman, Robert, ed. *The Arts at Mid-Century*. New York: Horizon Press, 1954.

Robinson, Edgar Eugene. *The Roosevelt Leadership, 1933–45*. Philadelphia: J. B. Lippincott Co., 1955.

Rose, Arnold. *The Negro in America*. Boston: Beacon Press, 1962. The classic condensation of Gunnar Myrdal's *The American Dilemma*. Foreword by Gunnar Myrdal.

Rose, Willie Lee. *Rehearsal for Reconstruction: The Port Royal Experiment*. Indianapolis: The Bobbs-Merrill Co., 1964. Introduction by C. Vann Woodward.

Roth, Philip. "Channel X: Two Plays on the Race Conflict," *The New York Review*, II (May 28, 1964), 10–13.

Rowe, Kenneth Thorpe. *A Theatre in Your Head*. New York: Funk & Wagnalls Co., 1960.

Schulte Nordholt, J. W. *The People That Walk in Darkness*. Tr. by M. B. Van Wijngaarden. London: Burke Publishing Co., 1960.

Shannon, David A. *The Great Depression*. Englewood Cliffs, N.J.: Prentice-Hall, 1960.

Shepp, Archie. "Black Power and Black Jazz," New York *Times*, November 26, 1967, p. 13:1,4.

Skinner, R. Dana. *Our Changing Theatre*. New York: The Dial Press, 1931.

Smalley, Webster, ed. *Five Plays by Langston Hughes*. Bloomington: Indiana University Press, 1963.

Smith, Howard. "Young Man with a Pen," New York *Times*, February 19, 1967, p. 2:3.

Sontag, Susan. *Against Interpretation*. New York: Dell Publishing Co., 1966.

Spencer, T. J., and Clarence J. Rivers. "Langston Hughes: His Style and Optimism," *Drama Critique*, VII (Spring, 1964), 99–102.

Thurman, Wallace, *The Blacker the Berry*. New York: The Macaulay Co., 1929.

—— "Cordelia the Crude, a Harlem Sketch," *Fire!!*, I (November, 1926), 5–6.

Tol' My Captain: Chain Gang and Work Songs Sung by Leon Bibb. Vanguard, VRS–9058. Notes by S. W. Bennett.

Trowbridge, John T. The South: A Tour of Its Battlefields and Ruined Cities, a Journey Through the Desolated States, and Talks with the People. Hartford, Conn., 1866.

Turner, Darwin T., and Jean M. Bright, eds. Images of the Negro in America. Boston: D. C. Heath and Co., 1965.

U.S. National Service Bureau, WPA Federal Theatre Project. A List of Negro Plays. Washington, D.C.: The Project, March, 1938. (Mimeographed.)

Van Vechten, Carl. "The Negro in Art: How Shall He Be Portrayed?" The Crisis: A Record of the Darker Races, XXXI (1926), 219.

—— Nigger Heaven. New York: Alfred A. Knopf, 1926.

Washington, Booker T. The Future of the American Negro. Boston: Small, Maynard & Co., 1899.

—— My Larger Education. New York: Doubleday, Page & Co., 1911.

—— Selected Speeches. Ed. E. Davidson Washington. New York: Doubleday, Doran & Co., 1932.

—— Up from Slavery. New York: Doubleday, Doran & Co., 1901.

Wecter, Dixon. The Age of the Great Depression. New York: The Macmillan Co., 1948.

Williams, John A., ed. The Angry Black. New York: Lancer Books, 1962.

Woodson, Carter G. Negro Orators and Their Orations. Washington, D.C.: The Associated Publishers, 1925.

Wright, Richard. How "Bigger" Was Born: The Story of "Native Son," One of the Most Important Novels of Our Time, and How it Came to Be Written. New York: Harper & Brothers, 1940.

—— Lawd Today. New York: Walker & Co., 1963.

—— Native Son. New York: Harper & Brothers, 1940.

—— Uncle Tom's Children. New York: The New American Library, 1948.

—— White Man, Listen! Garden City, N.Y.: Doubleday & Co., 1957.

INDEX

American Revolution, 5, 126
American Society of African Culture,
    252
American Theatre, St. Louis, 162
Amsterdam News (newspaper), 65
Anderson, Garland, vii, 27–32, 164,
    268; Thurman and, 27, 32, 39–40,
    41, 269; Wilson and, 55, 86; Ossie
    Davis and, 274
Anderson, Maxwell, 268, 269
Anderson, Robert, 261–62
Anna Lucasta (Yordan), 94, 189
ANTA Theatre, N.Y.C., 275
Anti-Semitism, 56–57, 115, 142, 236
Apollo Theatre, N.Y.C., 169–70
Appearances (Anderson), vii, 27–32,
    39–40, 63, 164; Wilson and, 55,
    86
Ardrey, Robert, 255
Ashmore, Harry, quoted, 166
Atkinson, Brooks, 109, 286; quoted,
    41, 58, 59, 63, 155, 158, 204,
    220, 253–54, 269
Atlanta, Ga., 15, 16, 96, 221
Atlantic Monthly (periodical), 60
Attucks, Crispus, 126
Audiences, 2, 3, 13, 21; Harlem, x,
    59, 63, 80, 116, 157, 159, 168,
    169–70, 271, 283–84, 286; mis-
    cegenation theme and, 70, 71;
    middle class, 99, 158, 159, 271,
    272; *Native Son* and, 161–63;
    Trouble in Mind and, 203–4; *A
    Raisin in the Sun* and, 240, 241;
    for Jones, 271, 272, 276–77; for
    Baldwin, 275
Awake and Sing! (Odets), 157, 270

Back-to-Africa Movement, 24; Ward
    and, 111–15, 116, 158
Baldwin, James, 272, 273, 274–75,
    278, 279, 285; on playwrights, 2,
    259; Wright and, 137, 142, 146–
    47, 152, 161, 162; on integration,
    286
Ballad for Bimshire (Mitchell and

    Burgie), 205
Ballad of a Blackbird (Mitchell),
    205
Bancroft Dynasty (Mitchell), 205
Barnard, Henry, 127
Barry, Philip, 269
Behrman, S. N., 269
Belcher, Fannin S., Jr., viii; quoted,
    59
Belgrave, Cynthia, quoted, 305*n*30
Bennett, Gwendolyn, 296*n*7
Bentley, Eric, quoted, 66
Beyond the Horizon (O'Neill), 79
Bible, the, 188. *See also* Christianity;
    Jews
Bickerstaffe, Isaac, 5
Big Sea, The (Hughes), 68
Big White Fog (Ward), 4, 92–93,
    96, 109–17, 257, 261, 269–70,
    298*n*75; failure of, 95, 157–59,
    163
Black Arts Repertory Theatre **and**
    School, Harlem, 271, 277, 282
Black Boy (Wright), 136
Black Drama (Mitchell), ix, 205
Blacker the Berry, The (Thurman),
    33, 40
Blackface, 5, 6, 7, 30
Black Magic (Hughes and Meltzer),
    ix
Black Manhattan (Johnson), ix
Black Muslim movement, 166, 282,
    283
Black Power movement, 281–82
Black Star steamship line, 24, 111,
    113
Bloodstream (Schlick), 55
Blue Holiday (variety show), 95
Blues, 26, 39, 44, 169, 190
Blues for Mister Charlie (Baldwin),
    272, 273, 274–75
Boas, Franz, 295*n*9
Bond, Frederick W., viii–ix
Bond, Horace Mann, quoted, 127,
    297*n*47
Bone, Robert, quoted, **2–3**